Major Trends in Land Development Banking

Major Trends in Land Development Banking

Anshu Rohtagi

CYBER TECH PUBLICATIONS
4264/3, Ansari Road, Daryaganj, New Delhi-110002 (India)
Ph.: 011-23244078. Fax: 011-23280028
E-Mail: cyberpublicationsdelhi@yahoo.com

MAJOR TRENDS IN LAND DEVELOPMENT BANKING

Anshu Rohtagi

First Edition 2009

Published by :

G.S. Rawat for **Cyber Tech Publications**
4264/3, Ansari Road, Daryaganj, New Delhi-110002 (India)
Ph.: 011-23244078. Fax: 011-23280028
E-Mail: cyberpublicationsdelhi@yahoo.com

Printed at : **Amit Enterprises**, Maujpur, Delhi, (9810878184)

Preface

This book attempts to measure the growth of physical farm capital in five major categories from 1870 to 2005, and that of all financial assets used in farming after 1900; to relate this growth of capital to that of the farm labor force and to output; and to discover the principal determinants of investment in the various types of agricultural capital and the sources of financing that made the investments possible.

Where possible the data were developed and analyzed by type-of-farming regions. Such treatment not only permitted a closer identification of capital formation with historical and geographical influences in general, but it revealed also the particular influence of the type of farming that was dominant in each region. Here, to be sure, the picture may be somewhat blurred by reason of the lack of complete homogeneity of farm operations even in regions differentiated according to type of farming. But there was no really satisfactory alternative.

Complete homogeneity of farm operation cannot be found even in single counties, and basic agricultural data are not widely available by type of farm product. Thus procedures by which the influence could perhaps be more clearly revealed were not feasible, and we rely on regional comparisons to reflect the influence of type of farming on capital formation even though the image may not always, do full justice to this factor. The Banks also provide loans for the development of the land.

—Author

CONTENTS

1

Land Development Banking: A Decade of Collaboration

Collaboration between government and non government organisations (NGOs) has been one outcome of the greater emphasis placed on participation, sustainability and democratic processes in India. This paper outlines how the role and space for elected government in development is being redefined. It begins by outlining the diversity among NGOs and the roles they seek to play. It then examines the mutual practical needs which draw NGOs and government towards each other. For NGOs, these include the need to access technical or managerial resources, to gain legitimacy or recognition, to promote greater accountability and transparency and to promote reform in public systems. Government agencies on the other hand work with NGOs to enhance people's participation in their programmes, to extend coverage of programmes to areas and groups that are poorly served by government staff, to test and replicate innovative approaches and to achieve greater cost effectiveness.

This paper explores how government and NGOs converge on a number of development objectives that have become social and political imperatives, divide roles along expected lines and prevailing notions of each other's capacities, but still end up with problems in certain areas. It outlines the reasons for this, including overlapping of professional domains, issues relating to NGO capacity, the role of individuals and personalities, inadequate consultation mechanisms, the lack of inclusive networking and weak management structures. It stresses the importance of achieving reform through indirect means, through cross learning by gradual exposure to alternative models and by providing space so that the two systems can be brought together in creative competition. Donor agencies occupy an influential niche in the affairs of governments and NGOs. The final section of the paper analyses the aspects of GO–NGO collaboration that merit the attention of donor agencies and are likely to be positively influenced by a more proactive and considered donor response.

INTRODUCTION

Approaches to development in India have undergone a dramatic change. Collaboration between government and NGOs has been one outcome of the greater emphasis placed on participation, sustainability, and democratic processes. New roles are therefore required of the government, and new organisations outside government play an increasingly significant role.

New Approaches

Although many examples of old style top-down delivery of services still remain, new style bottom-up planning programmes are here to stay. The development bureaucracy, whose size is difficult for the exchequer to sustain, suffers from a lack of motivation to eradicate poverty. Centralised decision-making, which remains a norm in government, is proving less effective than what seems possible with users' groups, though process work in the latter is intensive and is often expensive. The challenge of reaching out to large numbers of the poor has compelled governments to work with NGOs who are, it is hoped, more cost effective and better at targeting beneficiary populations. Local human resources, appropriate technology, and traditional systems of resource management or health care are being given space in designing more sustainable programme interventions.

New Roles and Actors

The role and space for elected government in development in India is being redefined. The private for-profit sector and voluntary agencies are playing roles earlier reserved for the government.

Many NGOs, who previously depended entirely on external funds, are beginning to work with government agencies and are discovering new roles for themselves in substituting for or influencing them. *Panchayati Raj* institutions armed with their new Constitutional mandate, are carving a new space in grassroots development, particularly in programme implementation which was once dominated by State government and NGOs.

Increasing institutional plurality has opened the door for new ways of role and space sharing.

Recognition of inherent complementarity has replaced the perception that the roles of these institutions are essentially conflicting and adversarial. There is an increasing interest among international donors, bilateral and multi-lateral, to support closer relationships within the projects they sponsor.

The Government of Rajasthan (GoR) has, over the past few years, devised many creative ways of working with NGOs. It has drawn up strategies, which with the help of NGOs, increase outreach and enhance the effectiveness of its programmes. It has also made a number of institutional changes to shape a new and more effective relationship with the NGOs.

Despite these efforts, some of which have been operative for almost a decade, the two still remain 'uneasy bedfellows' and a huge potential remains untapped. Critics of collaboration, continue to equate it to 'co-option' and 'sub-contracting'. This paper describes how NGOs and the government converge on a number of development objectives that have become social and political imperatives.

Roles have been divided along expected lines and notions of each institutions' capabilities. Problems still however occur in some programmes, while succeeding in others. The paper draws lessons from ten years of collaboration across sectors in Rajasthan.

Typology of NGOs

NGOs are, at one level, an expression of voluntarism by the citizenry. They do not work in the same legal and institutional framework as government agencies; government does not sponsor them. Distinguishing them from government is however not enough, as considerable variation exists among NGOs. It is reflected in their voluntarily chosen ideologies, modalities of catalysing change, their scale of operations and their connectedness or remoteness from grassroots action. This paper focuses particularly on the relationship between government and grassroots development organisations, hereafter referred to as NGOs.

Typology of NGOs in Rajasthan, India

- *Private philanthropy/charitable trusts: their basic motivation is relief and welfare.*
- *Intermediary organisations: their main agenda is to conduct research, support and training or to bring grassroots NGOs together on a common platform with a common agenda.*
- *Grassroots development support organisations: these are involved in implementing grassroots development projects and promoting groups; leadership may or may not be local.*
- *Membership organisations: including local people's groups and organisations with local leaders such as artisan groups, women's self-help groups or users' groups.*
- *State sponsored or dependent NGOs (GONGOs): a new breed of NGO promoted outside the rigid framework of government to gain flexibility (particularly from accounting and financial procedures) and sometimes to reduce interference from political processes.*
- *Social Action Groups: work to change governance processes and structures; adopt mobilisation and confrontation as methods to challenge existing structures and mindsets; are not interested in implementing projects.*

OBJECTIVES OF NGO–GOVERNMENT COLLABORATION

Practical needs draw NGOs and government towards each other. NGOs seek collaboration with government for many reasons:

(i) to access technical or managerial resources;

(ii) to gain legitimacy or recognition;

(iii) to adapt a programme to their area;

(iv) to obtain appropriate solutions to development problems;

(v) to enhance people's participation in government programmes; and

(vi) to promote greater accountability and transparency, and promote reforms in public systems.

Broadly speaking, specific needs at any point in time are a function of the direction and pace of an NGO's organisational growth or leadership orientation, i.e. the needs of an NGO change as it grows in size and scale. In the initial stages, the need to survive is crucial. Government resources and linkages may be sought for that purpose. In the later stages, when there is relative stability of funds and a sufficient pool of experience to draw upon, the NGO's priorities may change: it may be motivated to make larger scale impacts or inform public policy through its work. Secondly, the ideology and the quality of leadership strongly influences the motivation of the agency in working with the government. Most NGOs are led by strong dynamic personalities, who have set up these organisations to carry out a defined agenda. The personal motivations and beliefs of the leader have a strong bearing on the organisation's strategy.

Government agencies on the other hand work with NGOs to:

(i) enhance people's participation in their programmes;

(ii) to extend coverage of programmes to areas and groups that are poorly served by government staff;

(iii) to test and replicate innovative approaches; and

(iv) to achieve greater cost effectiveness.

Therefore, behind a NGOs' interest in working with the government, or conversely, the government extending an invitation to NGOs, lies a certain degree of convergence in their development objectives and certain needs.

NGOs and Government Converge on Development Objectives

The following list contains the basic premises that motivate governments and NGOs to collaborate with each other. These represent the broad rationale that underlies collaborative behaviour.

- Collaboration facilitates the generation and replication of innovations and alternative approaches to development.
- Collaboration is an efficient means of improving the delivery of development programmes and services to rural communities.
- Collaboration has the potential of inducing system/ institutional reforms such as reorienting departments towards bottom-up planning and implementation.
- Collaboration is an effective means of improving people's ability to place demands on public systems and services.

ROLES SHARED IN PROMOTING DEVELOPMENT OBJECTIVES

The roles and space that NGOs acquire, or are assigned, depend on the programme's development objectives and the perceived capacity of NGOs to meet these (and conversely the perceived lack of government capacity). The following section describes the roles that government and NGOs share in working towards the development objectives outlined in the previous section, using examples from Rajasthan.

The *generation and replication of innovations* to solve development problems is a common objective of government and NGOs. In the process of developing appropriate solutions to problems in a specific area, some NGOs – if not all – develop new approaches that have the potential to be adopted elsewhere.

For instance, to address the problem of teacher absenteeism in remotely located villages in a backward region, an NGO experimented with the idea of recruiting and training local youths for the job. This became the basis for the government to promote the *Shikshakarmi* programme in a number of districts. The generation and demonstration of innovative approaches is a role which the State readily agrees NGOs can perform, and it is often prepared to support them in this regard.

This role requires NGO capacity to develop bold, unconventional ideas and to undertake action research. The government role is often limited to funding innovation and research, though it can also allow the NGO to work with a small part of the government system as well. The complexity of this relationship is determined by the scope of innovation. Field-testing and refinement of innovation requires flexibility, imagination and an accurate understanding of the local situation – traits that some NGOs possess.

However, they may not have the resources or structures to work on a large scale, hence collaboration with governments can greatly improve the chances of successfully replicating proven approaches. There are two variants of replication: the diffusion of innovation can be undertaken by government, or the NGO itself may assume responsibility for 'scaling up' with government financial support. The case of an NGO taking up artificial insemination (AI) in 13 districts is a classic example of the second strategy. It is worth pointing out however, that not all NGO innovations are automatically replicable by the government system – choice of actors, technology, local demand, and capacity to manage a larger system without losing quality, are some important considerations when preparing to 'scale up'.

A second area where government and NGO objectives converge is in efforts to *improve the delivery of services*. This can be done either by filling functional gaps or reaching remote geographical areas where government staff find it unattractive to go. The growing acceptance of NGO participation in government programmes reflects recognition that firstly, GO programmes and services are not performing adequately and secondly, NGOs have skills and comparative advantages that can improve the quality of many programmes. NGOs are recognised as local institutions, which work closely with communities, have a limited geographical area to work in and respond flexibly and reasonably quickly to a community's demands. Better outreach and more effective targeting of benefits is expected, often at reasonable cost.

NGOs' participation in government schemes is the most effective form of collaboration. Pure examples of this type in Rajasthan include the Union Government's recently introduced watershed programme. The major requirement for providing services is that a local institution is available to reach the target population or carry out a specific function (such as training, AI) better than the government. Capacity to innovate may be desirable, but not necessary.

'Commitment' to serve the poor (or target population) is often cited as a critical requirement. 'NGO implements–GO funds' is the basic formula. This is the most common division of GO/NGO role in Rajasthan. A third area of convergence is *inducing system or institutional reforms.* System reform can imply structural change as well as changes in values, attitudes and work cultures.

The need for such change arises from the desirability of improving transparency, accountability and efficiency. While system reforms in government agencies are often initiated externally by political mandate or donors, the objectives of senior government officials may sometimes converge with those of NGOs. Where such a convergence exists, NGOs with the requisite skills and experience can productively collaborate with government in the introduction and refinement of new approaches.

For instance, a joint team from the NGO Professional Assistance for Development Action (PRADAN), and the Block Development administration was set up in Alwar district, to improve the implementation effectiveness of the government's poverty alleviation programmes. Another example is *Lok Jumbish*, a programme aimed at achieving universal primary education in the state. The government has promoted a GONGO – *Lok Jumbish Parishad* – to develop new methods and systems which can be taken up by the Education Department.

The objective of pursuing system or institutional reform in government is a complex process. It can rarely be achieved by a single actor, let alone by a single NGO. Actors/NGOs with a strong participation/ empowerment orientation (like the mobilisation agencies of the *Lok Jumbish* Programme) are essential, but they must be accompanied by others – with a systemic understanding – to pull through the changes in government departments (the role that *Lok Jumbish Parishad* plays *vis à vis* the education department).

Institutional reform can also take the shape of introducing a new methodology in a department or substituting public service with NGOs. Finally, collaboration provides a means of addressing *participation and empowerment* objectives in government programmes. While the desirability of people's participation is generally accepted by the state, NGOs – who lobby for this cause – are not always seen as legitimate intermediaries between government programmes and rural communities. NGO philosophies can also carry the concept of empowerment considerably further than governments are comfortable with. NGOs view their own involvement with government as a means of improving the ability of communities to work directly with government. There are many instances where NGOs have succeeded in intervening on behalf of the community. Box 3 illustrates one such example. Another is the collaboration between NGOs and the National Bank for Agriculture and Rural Development (NABARD), which aims to link small, informal savings and credit groups with the commercial banks.

Empowerment and widespread participation in government projects requires that NGOs act as pressure groups and people's organisers and possess understanding and skills to influence the system. NGOs need a deep commitment to this, as the process may be long-drawn and results intangible and unpredictable.

An Attempt to Create a New Institutional Culture and Graft it on to an Old Department: The Case of Lok Jumbish Parishad

Lok Jumbish was initiated in December, 1992, with the objective of realising universal primary education in Rajasthan through both the formal and informal systems. By the end of 1996, the project was operating in 2,826 villages in 58 blocks and is projected to cover the entire state by 2007.

The project is managed through a society – Lok Jumbish Parishad – registered for this specific purpose. The design ensures a high level of involvement and backing by senior government officials.

The Chief Minister is the ex-officio chairman of the governing council and the Education Secretary is the ex-officio vice chairman of the executive committee.

At the block level, Lok Jumbish establishes offices and a committee known as the Khand Stariya Prabandchan Samiti.

Members of this include government and NGO staff, representatives of the teaching community and educationalists.

One-third of the members are drawn from Panchayat Samitis (unit of local governance for between three to five villages). This committee oversees clusters comprising 25–30 villages. Such clusters are controlled operationally either by NGOs or by Lok Jumbish staff. Where such staff are working, they are controlled by a Block Steering Group. There is clear geographic demarcation between NGO and Block Steering Group areas of activity, and there is no day-to-day interaction between the two – interaction occurs only during review and planning meetings.

Lok Jumbish has two clients, the children and the parents who are the decision-makers. To create demand for education, the project works with parents through an environment building exercise and school mapping.

The latter is a key process. It is done by selected male and female members of the village community who form a group known as the Prerak Dal. The map records the social and educational resource base of each village and indicates the number of male and female children of school age and whether or not they attend school. The map forms the base for a community educational plan. A village education committee, a Mahila Samooh (to encourage participation of girls) and a Bhavan Nirman Samiti (for decisions regarding and supervision of building construction) are elected from the Prerak Dal.

FORM AND DYNAMICS OF RELATIONSHIPS THAT EVOLVE AND MANAGEMENT OF THE RELATIONSHIP

What forms do GO–NGO relationships take and what are their dynamics? Once programme implementation begins, what management processes and structures are designed by stakeholders to oversee this role division and relationship?

Four major forms of relationship are evident: *schematic, dyadic, catalytic/confrontational and institutional*. The nature of these linkages are decided by the type and perceived capacity of the participating NGOs and their positioning in the decision-making structure; the scope and coverage of the programme or scheme; the degree of pre-determined designing of components; the target or goal orientation; and the way the roles of the two sides are conceived and divided. Consequently, the relationship can be mutually supportive or confrontational, can enjoy parity or be patently unequal, may or may not have elements of innovation and flexibility, and can be static or evolve dynamically.

The most common relationship is that which we term as *schematic*. For each development scheme, the government proposes standardised criteria for NGO selection, technical and cost norms, preferred approach and mode of implementation. The schemes are designed to accommodate a large number of NGOs. The relationship between the government and NGOs in the schematic relationship may evolve to be one of benefactor and beneficiary. NGOs participating in such schemes often do not feel happy with being treated as little more than sub-contractors.

Dyadic (or bilateral) relations can develop between government and NGOs, in order to execute a mutually agreed project. Projects test an innovation, or the government may provide financial support to an NGO to upscale the latter's successful project. In some senses, this could be considered a special case of a schematic relationship, but the NGO is in a more prominent position. The government strikes a relationship with a single NGO because of confidence in its capability.

Examples include that of the Bharatia Agro-Industries Foundation (BAIF), with strong technical expertise in the livestock sector. They were invited to scale up the AI services provided by the government.

Catalytic roles and relationships exist where the government and NGOs work with each other to enhance the benefits to the third stakeholder – the disadvantaged community. The initiative may often lie with the NGO, which raises issues pertaining to the community it seeks to serve and pressures the government to fulfil its role as welfare provider, or protector of the weak. This relationship is open-ended and can witness certain 'flip flop' behaviour – at times cordial, at times adversarial.

Many new frontiers are won, or at least new doors opened, following this strategy which can result in a programme where the role of NGOs is more clearly legitimised. Joint Forest Management (JFM) provides a well-known example. A variant of this is when an official agency undertakes to reform another official agency – NABARD's attempt to push commercial banks and Regional Rural Banks to lend to the poor with help from NGOs, and to link self-help groups (SHGs) with banks is a good example.

Institutional relationships are attempted where a programme adopts a radically different approach, such as those emphasising process rather than targets. In some so-called 'process projects', where the attempt is to move away from blueprint approaches, NGOs are considered to be important vectors of change. Often there is a role division between the government and NGOs. Based on perceptions of their strengths, NGOs are generally assigned process intensive or software roles, while the government adopts physical implementation or hardware roles.

Such role division and complementarity implies that government and NGOs coordinate their action during field implementation, adjust to contrasting working styles, and are sensitive to mutual needs and compulsions. If the task of managing innovative GO– NGO arrangements cannot be managed within a department, project designers may opt for 'de-linked structures'. Systems are put in place for periodic experience sharing, co-learning and conflict resolution.

In some cases, there is even a package deal for a specified role and output, as opposed to narrow line item controls on salaries and overheads. Such flexibility, and a learning-sensitive approach, is backed by allowing an operating structure de-linked from the usual government bureaucracy.

Processes and structures devised to manage relationships. Sharing roles and spaces of innovation and implementation requires a sensitive and alert management approach from the 'owners' of these projects. In a dyadic relationship, where a single NGO works with a government agency to either promote innovation or provide services on a large scale, committees are set up for reviewing periodic progress. In facilitative relationships, where a mainstream institution together with an NGO is promoting the participation of people in governance or access to formal institutions (such as banks) without any formal agreement, the coordination mechanisms do not take any definite shape. Negotiations can be long and drawn out or may be quickly concluded. In some cases, a situation of confrontation arises when these negotiations break down.

It is in the other two types of relationships – schematic and institutional – where the scale of operations is large, the process of change is complex and a number of NGOs are implementing projects, that coordination or management mechanisms and structures have to be designed.

Beyond Negotiation: Minor Forest Produce

In 1990, following a study by one NGO – Astha – of tendu patta (leaf) collection, representation was made to the government to increase the purchase price from 13.5 to 50 rupees per bundle.

The rate went up to 20 rupees, but a strike was still called. At the suggestion of Rajsangh, a government organisation under the Ministry of Tribal Development responsible for marketing and trading commodities, the Adivasi Tendu Patta Collection and Marketing Cooperative was registered with the help of the NGO.

It was to provide services in direct competition with private contractors who operated collection centres. Operations began in 1991, with financial support provided by Rajsangh at six per cent interest. Threatened by both strike action and the diversion of leaf supplies to the Cooperative, private traders increased their rates to 26 rupees per bundle. In 1991, the Cooperative netted a profit of 600,000 rupees ($15,000).

This success encouraged other NGOs to undertake similar activities and a coalition, the Tendu Patta Samanvaya Samiti, was formed to link their efforts. Rajsangh simultaneously expanded its activities, and with NGOs, successfully lobbied government to set aside collection units in Rajsangh's name for the cooperatives it was supporting. However, because of poor leaf quality, low prices and delays (due to Rajsangh's requirement that sales be made on a tender basis) all cooperatives made a loss in 1992; in 1993 only one made a profit.

By 1992, a new Managing Director took over Rajsangh and relations between Rajsangh and the NGOs soured, initially because of a disagreement over profit sharing. The situation became worse when changes were made to the contract between cooperatives and Rajsangh. Two cooperatives refused to sign the new contract, and a signature was fraudulently obtained from another. After public exposure, an apology was made by Rajsangh and the old terms reinstated. In 1993, another new Managing Director sanctioned support for seven collection units for cooperatives, but in 1994 the brother of a State Minister began negotiating for units for his own cooperative. Rajsangh initially refused and an aggressive campaign was launched against it and the NGOs. As a result, Rajsangh did not finance any cooperatives in 1994 and took over buying operations in the reserved units itself. It also instituted an enquiry into the accounts of the cooperatives and issued an order to seize all the old stocks and property of the cooperatives.

The NGOs and cooperatives felt that Rajsangh was victimising them in response to political pressures and resorted to using the press to pursue their cause. The events attracted considerable coverage in local newspapers. Rajsangh maintained it had evidence of financial irregularities in the cooperatives, but accounts indicated that the Minister had directly threatened the Managing Director with dire consequences if Rajsangh continued to support cooperatives promoted by NGOs. This effectively ended relations between Rajsangh and NGOs.

Management of Schemes

Schemes are managed by Union Ministries, state government departments or special organisations created for NGO funding such as CAPART. NGOs submit their project proposals for approval to these agencies, which are then screened by committees including technical experts. Lately, at least at the centre, NGOs are also represented on the committees. Disbursements are made in instalments to ensure satisfactory performance and are often based on reports of target-achievement and accounts submitted by the implementing agency.

Schemes are not often known to provide flexibility, easy channels of feedback, grievance procedures, or cross learning between relevant departments and NGOs. The more distant the location of the sanctioning authority, the more adversely affected NGOs are by poor communication and inflexibility.

Management of Institutional Relationships

Management processes and structures have to respond to innovation in programme approaches and collaboration with other institutions. Adequate space has to be provided for the decentralisation of decision-making, the flexibility and diversity of approaches, the evolution of models and innovation as opposed to prescribed blueprints, etc. Any management system informed by this new set of conditions cannot, by design, flourish in the existing bureaucratic environment. A new management structure needs to be found – one that is sufficiently *de-linked* from normal government functioning – to meet the demands of the new charter.

This new entity is government sponsored (and controlled) but registered as a 'society' – under the same law as NGOs; thus they are sometimes referred to as GONGOs. The governance structure of such 'de-linked structures' or GONGOs is controlled by politicians and officials, perhaps more by the latter. This is guided in part by the desire to protect the projects from rigid bureaucracy and systems. The underlying assumption is that there are people in the government who, given sufficient operational space, financial powers and flexibility, will produce results not possible in a purely government setting. Once in GONGOs, they engender innovation and cocoon it until it is ready for replication. Many donor agencies also prefer this arrangement. Besides seeding innovation, they are also motivated by the possibility of having a direct link with the project and a more transparent flow of funds. Creating de-linked structures is also considered better for improving the quality of collaborative actions and arrangements. The government is aware that NGOs, particularly those that have adequate resources of their own, do not react favourably to delays and rigidities and would rather not participate in a programme unless assured that their operations and autonomy will not be hampered. Institutional collaboration is a major opportunity for mutual exposure and cross learning between governments and NGOs. The quality of this exposure and learning varies between individuals on both sides. For NGOs, while such an arrangement affords a more substantial partnership with the government, it also implies greater accountability of actions and performance. Their actions are subject to periodic external review, which remains a rare phenomenon in the NGO sector.

CONSTRAINTS TO GO–NGO COLLABORATION AND LESSONS FROM EXPERIENCE

Why does collaboration run into difficulties, despite government and NGOs converging on objectives and dividing roles along the expected lines? Under what circumstances is the collaboration long-lasting? On the other hand, should we see collaboration only as a means to initiate change in government, and once that happens, does the NGO role loses its significance and is withdrawal desirable? Are conflicts a temporary phenomenon or a part of the evolutionary process of mutual coming to terms? How could conflicts be anticipated and processes designed to manage them? This section highlights those factors and constraints that hinder healthy collaboration between government and NGOs. These factors may apply to all manner of GO–NGO collaboration:

- NGOs challenging a department's domain;
- NGOs seeking autonomy and budget parity;
- issues relating to NGO capacity;
- weak management structures to effect change;
- role of individuals, personalities and inter-personal equations;
- inadequacies in consultation with NGOs;
- lack of NGO networking;
- design and administration of schemes for NGOs (specific to schematic relationship);
- role division (specific to institutional relationships).

Potential Overlap

Resistance to NGOs may arise when the government engages them in tasks that also constitute the core activity of a department; any overlap or infringement of the domain of a department can create conflict. Three aspects of conflict are evident: administrative – when a department regulates the ownership and use of natural resources such as forests (for instance, in JFM); technical – when professionals such as engineers and medical doctors have little or no confidence in an NGOs' capability (for instance, AI); or financial – when department employees feel their legitimate or illegitimate pecuniary benefits are threatened (commonly supposed but difficult to prove). For one or all of these reasons, lower department levels may not share the views of their superiors in granting space to NGOs.

De-linked Structures

Projects that depart radically from conventional approaches and that aim for a large scale change need new institutional arrangements. These range from creating a new unit or cell within an existing structure to setting up an external unit or organisation.

In a natural resource management project (PAHAL), a separate office of project director was created to allow for innovative approaches to managing degraded lands in tribal areas. Project staff were brought from other departments on deputation, to work with NGOs.

They tried a number of new technical ideas within self defined targets, and came up with new processes of beneficiary participation. This arrangement of having a separate project director gave way to PAHAL being registered as a 'society' – a structure delinked from government. This gave far more autonomy to the project leadership, particularly to decentralise some of the financial powers to subordinates.

Many of these structures are legally NGOs, but their governance structures are controlled by government. Hence they are nicknamed GONGOs.

NGOs are generally perceived to be low on technical skills and technical experts view their entry into such areas with scepticism. This is well illustrated in the case of the Uttar Rajasthan Milk Union Limited (URMUL) collaboration with the Command Area Development Agency (CADA), where URMUL undertook to demonstrate new techniques of covering water courses and new designs of school buildings. Further, it sought to do this at a cost lower than CADA's rates, thereby suggesting unwittingly that CADA had 'commissions' built into costs. URMUL's efforts ran into problems, since the lobby of engineers in CADA felt that URMUL was encroaching on their professional turf and trying to discredit them. Even in cases where the NGO is professionally competent, there can be resistance.

BAIF, which expanded its AI services with financial support from the Department of Rural Development, has faced opposition in some districts from the Department of Animal Husbandry (DoAH). To eliminate competition, BAIF had to leave areas where the DoAH had subsequently developed insemination facilities. A relatively recent cause of resistance from lower cadres is their perception that NGOs are eroding employment security in the government by offering cheaper contractual services. Employees' trade unions for instance, protested when agriculture extension and the Integrated Child Development Services (ICDS) work was sought to be given to NGOs.

The phenomenon of encroaching on the technical and administrative domains is less likely to occur when NGOs work with departments focusing on specific segments of the population such as the rural poor, tribal groups, women and children.

NGOs exhibit a general inability or indifference to manage lower ranks in the government. Most NGOs prefer to enter into agreements at senior levels, while dynamics at lower levels are left to sort themselves out.

This neglect rarely works in favour of collaboration. There are exceptions, such as BAIF's ability to smooth out contentious issues at district levels, and PRADAN's ability to work with district and regional officials. In both of these cases, agreements between government and NGOs served as a stabilising factor in the environment of turbulence created by frequent transfers.

The promoters of collaboration on both sides need to be prepared for potential opposition from government staff and need to manage this competition creatively. The following strategies can be used to manage this competition:

- Anchor collaboration outside the technical department whenever possible. For instance BAIF has been able to sustain a long term arrangement with the government in the field of AI, in spite of active opposition from the DoAH. One of the reasons has been that it does not get funds from the DoAH.
- Proven ability of the NGO in the area – this permits it to deal effectively with resistance from government, as well as manage a separate geographical domain with competence. BAIF and PRADAN have been able to sustain long term relations with the government because they have high proficiency in the field of AI and lift irrigation respectively. While this competence does not remove all tension, it certainly removes one of the main grounds of complaint by government functionaries.
- Avoid geographical/functional overlaps with the government department. An important corollary of this lesson is that, at least in the beginning, it is much easier for NGOs to move into gaps left by the government development agencies. PRADAN has been successful in mobilising government funds in South Bihar earmarked for Lift Irrigation Schemes because the government department was prevented from participating in the programme.

The above lessons read together should not be interpreted to mean that avoiding collaboration is the best strategy. If service delivery, and not departmental reform, is the agenda of the programme – as in the case of BAIF/PRADAN – then it does not matter which department funds come from. In such cases, it may be preferable not to seek funds from a department which has that service as its core agenda. But if the agenda of the NGO is to reform public policy or programmes, a closer interaction between the governments and NGOs will be necessary.

Enlisting Cooperation from Lower Ranks in the Government

> *PRADAN began setting up small scale lift irrigation schemes (serving about 30 to 40 farmers, with an average command area of 40 acres) in south Bihar. When district authorities offered to provide funds for such schemes, PRADAN's proposal included a service charge (five per cent), and the two parties signed a Memorandum of Understanding (MoU), indicating a shift in the relationship. Similar MoUs were signed in a number of districts. Later when an externally aided project promoted lift irrigation in collaboration with NGOs, the MoU between PRADAN and the project authority was signed on a regional basis. This MoU specified government responsibility, such as sanctioning the schemes that PRADAN would propose, releasing the funds on time and giving completion certificates.*
>
> *BAIF entered into a contract with the state level department for rural development for providing AI services in various districts. Payments for services are based on verification by district level authorities. These included officials from DoAH, who perceived BAIF as their competitor. There were delays in verification and questions on whether BAIF had achieved its targets. In one instance, one of the insemination centres did not achieve the target, while all others had and the aggregate target was also met. In another, the district authorities wanted to measure the number of conceptions rather than the number of the insemination treatments. In both cases, BAIF officers requested a change at the district level, but when it did not happen they waited patiently for the occasion when the MoU at the state level was to be revised and had the amendments made.*

However our analysis of collaboration experience suggests that, even in such cases, reform through indirect means; through demonstration of alternatives in another, less hostile, setting; and/or through cross learning by gradual exposure to alternative models, may be best. By separating geographical domains, the two systems may be brought together in creative competition, where the two learn from each other. Organisational learning may occur better from a distance.

Autonomy and Budget Parity

Most NGOs attach great value to their independence from government. They see themselves as voluntary organisations: their very *raison d'être* arises from a critique of the government. Affiliation with the government dilutes their identity in the eyes of society and their target community, so that in instances of collaboration, they may guard their identity even more zealously. This is reflected in their demand for treatment on par with the governments, for instance in decision-making.

They also resent excessive interference in internal matters by the government. There are examples of NGOs' withdrawal from government programmes because they felt that government procedures were an undue interference. Take, for instance, the government's attempts in collaboration cases, to insist upon the salary and staff pattern for NGOs prescribed in project design. Most well-established NGOs have their own salary structure which has evolved over a period of time, and is rooted in its own history and development ideology. Typically in NGOs people perform multiple tasks.

NGOs are most comfortable in a system where they have consolidated provisions for salaries for performance of certain tasks. NGOs normally resent externally-or funding-induced changes in their salary structure. Their logic is that they cannot have a separate salary structure for the separate projects undertaken. In case of departmental schemes, the phenomenon of depressed budgets for NGOs is even more marked. In numerous schemes, there is no provision for covering staff time or even overheads that the NGO may incur. This poses unrealistic constraints on the agency that is expected to perform the required task. Therefore:

- NGOs must be treated on par with government functionaries. In institutional collaboration, where NGOs work with the government, this parity must be built into the design of the project proposal.

- While allocating salaries for the NGO personnel, the best policy is to allocate a consolidated amount for performance of defined tasks. Its further break up should be left to the discretion of the NGO.

Differing Expectations

Differing expectations continue to undermine constructive collaboration. For instance, many programmes are based on eliciting community participation, and NGOs are expected to devise methods along the lines of micro level planning or participatory rural appraisal (PRA). Since control of resources is still with government agencies, NGOs' roles are reduced to raising awareness or gathering people for meetings, with little control over the subsequent decision-making.

Further problems relate to the uncontrolled growth of NGOs in India since the introduction of new schemes for NGOs and the large sums allocated. Proposals are often sought through newspaper advertisements – although some claim that a genuine NGO would not normally pick up a newspaper to look for 'business', unlike, say, Public Works Department (PWD) contractors. Not unexpectedly, a large number of well written and sometimes identical-looking proposals land on the desk of the issuing agency. This makes NGO screening a difficult task. Some funding agencies such as the Aga Khan Foundation, have adopted word of mouth and workshops as methods of letting prospective NGOs know of different schemes.

ActionAid and Ford Foundation programme officers make personal visits to learn more about the ground capacity of applicants. Finally, misunderstandings occur when NGOs are expected to take on new roles and responsibilities. When a 'process project', designed to carry out institutional reform, inducts a good and reputed NGO into a collaborative relationship with the government, it often finds it difficult to live up to its reputation.

NGOs may have built up their reputation primarily on good service delivery or protest against the government (championing people's causes), but the role required in process projects may be different. Therefore:

- Any programme that is planning a large scale induction of NGOs should develop better screening procedures, such as workshops and personal visits, and it should prepare a capacity-building module to encourage the gradual growth of fledgling NGOs (especially when they are working in a new sector).
- In process projects aiming at institutional change in the government, NGOs should be specifically prepared for this role.

Management Structure

A new project aims for a change and thus causes a flutter in an existing bureaucracy. This is likely to be most felt in lower cadres. Resistance to the entry of an NGO therefore needs to be creatively managed. In *Swasthyakarmi Yojana*, the NGOs were assigned the task of family welfare and their work was to be supervised by the people whose domain was being challenged. When NGOs faced difficulties the managing body – the Standing Committee on Voluntary Agencies (SCOVA) – was not able to help them. Therefore:

- Resistance to change in the system needs to be countered by strong, committed, and sustained leadership to the programme.

Role of Interpersonal Relations

There is unanimous agreement between governments and NGOs that individuals, personalities and interpersonal relations can make or break collaborative efforts. This is perhaps the most subjective and unpredictable issue in GO–NGO relations. It is rare for collaborative initiatives to be institutionalised or made formal and hence they last only as long as the individual government officer remains in post. An enormous amount of energy may be spent or wasted if the NGO has to convince a new incumbent to fulfil commitments made by his/her predecessor.

Personal relations between the leaders of NGOs and senior government officers have their own dynamics, and in a number of cases this has led to more creative institutional partnership between government and NGOs. Any perceived links between NGOs and senior bureaucrats may also result in increased alienation from the NGOs of the junior levels in government. Since transfers within the system are routine, and the number of 'pro-NGO' or 'pro-people' officers may decline, programme designers and NGOs have to develop broader coalitions, and must build up political support.

In the *tendu patta* case (Box 3), part of the reason for the successful experiment with tribal collectors gaining marketing licenses and finance was political opposition. In the *Lok Jumbish* programme, support from the Chief Minister has ensured longevity to the programme, despite resistance from bureaucracy. Therefore:

- Build broader coalitions to support the programme, and involve political leaders to make programmes 'transfer proof.'

Consultation Inadequacies

The level of consultation between governments and NGOs is increasing but there are still several problems. Consultations are often hastily convened, one-off events. There is frequently a preponderance of high profile NGOs present and thus the diversity of views is not captured. Consultations are one sided in that 'the government invites and the NGO attends', while the reverse is difficult to achieve. There is a tendency to 'tokenise', which is apparent in rushing through issues and discouraging discussion on substantive matters. Consultations on controversial or contentious issues are generally avoided.

A fundamental problem is the near complete lack of effective forums or mechanisms by which governments and NGOs can interact with each other on a continuous basis. They are generally absent in line departments at the district and state level, and are weak or erratic at other levels of development administration. Nor is there any state level mechanism by which NGOs can regularly interface with the government on development issues, or those that affect their capacity to work with each other.

An underdeveloped link in Rajasthan is the lack of involvement of NGO networks with the government. Though networking among NGOs is increasing, there is no broad-based coalition of NGOs for managing the interface with government. There is no consensus among NGOs on how to pressure government on development issues. An exception are the networks of social action groups that are effective in addressing the government and are able to demand attention for the causes they espouse. The government response to these networks is often of extreme caution or outright dismissal. Therefore:

- Inclusive networking is critical for sustained collaboration.

Management of Schemes for NGOs

There are many small, struggling NGOs who avail of government schemes. With the lack of transparent mechanisms, such agencies, whose competence and integrity is doubtful, have increasingly begun to feature as recipients of schemes. There is an increased sense of frustration in serious-minded NGOs at the rampant proliferation of bogus NGOs within the sector. As a result, the general credibility of the NGO sector has been eroded.

Aside from the phenomenon of low provisions, there are a number of problems related to the designing and administration of schemes for NGOs. These mainly relate to: (i) a lack of consultation with NGOs at the design stage, which results in the laying down of unrealistic goals and activities, and low participation by quality organisations; (ii) weak selection criteria and procedures for screening NGOs and their proposals; (iii) timely disbursement of funds; and (iv) inadequate monitoring and evaluation of schemes.

ROLE DIVISION

Role division – derived from the notion of comparative strengths – does not always work well in the context of institutional GO–NGO collaboration. In most instances NGOs are given the task of organising and mobilising the community, while the responsibility for implementation rests with the government. Often, physical execution and achievement of financial targets assumes a more central role, whereas village level processes that NGOs provide the lead on are jettisoned. There are also power connotations in this kind of role division *vis-à-vis* the community – government functionaries continue to enjoy the power derived from their control of resources and their discretion regarding the priority and pace at which the programmes are carried out. Delays and deviations often occur, which results in NGOs facing a crisis of credibility with communities.

In institutionalised collaborations, where the GOs and NGOs work together in different roles, there is often a decline in the NGOs' role and involvement in key areas. Experience suggests that once learning takes place within the context of the project, NGOs' participation becomes redundant or marginalised.

The Role of Donors

Donor agencies occupy an influential niche in the affairs of governments and NGOs. What is the present and potential role of donor agencies in the realm of GO– NGO relations? What aspects of GO–NGO collaboration merit the attention of donor agencies and are likely to be positively influenced by a more proactive and considered donor response?

Donors in Rajasthan are at least as heterogeneous a group as the GOs and NGOs they support. Donor agencies generally have specific mandates and resources that guide the intensity of their work with governments, NGOs, or both. The multilateral and bilateral agencies, by virtue of their origin in governments and size of resources, extend 'development cooperation' to national and state governments. They also have an 'NGO window' for direct assistance to NGOs, which is relatively small and often built in as a component of the awards to governments. Private donor agencies and charities often exclusively support NGOs.

The increase in the flow of resources to NGOs over the past decade has been a major factor in the increase of NGO presence and activity in domains that were once considered exclusive to government. The flow of external resources to governments has also increased in absolute terms, but questions have been raised regarding effectiveness, reforms, cost efficiency, sustainability and participation. The emphasis on provision for NGOs in externally funded government projects is increasingly marked. This is driven in part by the experience of northern NGOs and pressure from indigenous NGOs, regarding what southern NGOs can bring to large-scale development interventions.

Donors may bring their specific agendas and mandates, but there is little general consensus among them on issues of community involvement, cost effectiveness, coverage, equity and replicability in the context of the interventions they support. Bilateral and private donor agencies need to be much more concerned about the potential represented by GO–NGO collaboration with respect to these factors.

Differing Perceptions of NGO Roles

Donors see NGO roles in relation to government differently. At the risk of over-generalisation, we surmise that bilateral aid agencies tend to view the NGOs' role as an intermediary and, in some cases, a transitory one, in relation to the government's links with people. NGOs are involved in functions that will help the government to understand community needs more accurately and generally improve its linkages with government programmes. In some cases, they may be invited to perform such tasks in a programme that are not possible within government, because a high degree of flexibility, cost efficiency and proximity to the community is required. Thus NGOs are involved as instruments of improved service delivery and outreach.

Far too often, donors see their task as completed once NGOs are admitted as partners in a project agreement with the government. They do not support or supervise the processes of selection of NGOs, do not see the resistance to their entry by government staff, or the inability of the nodal government agency to listen to their field experiences. Donors have a key role to play in setting up support mechanisms – processes and structures – to bring NGOs in as partners. This will ultimately have a positive impact on service delivery, participation and decentralisation, which have largely eluded governments in the past.

Private, non-government donor agencies tend to be much more intensely involved with NGOs. NGOs are seen as *catalysts* of social and economic change, with an ability to innovate and articulate the needs of the community. Their work and intervention in an area is not seen to be dependent on the government, though there is an overall notion (often unverified by donors) that NGOs' work is filling a gap in government resources or programmes. These donors are, however, less likely to be concerned about the complementarity of their NGO funding support with existing government resources in an area. Some private donors have identified *advocacy* as a valid role for NGOs to play *vis à vis* the government. Though they do not fund the government, the (non-funding) links of private donor agencies with government agencies are rather thin.

NGO Capability

Whatever the role an NGO undertakes, NGO capability needs to remain a major donor concern. There is an assumption that NGOs will play certain roles in government programmes (setting up user committees, working with village based workers, engaging in participatory planning, etc.) while the capability of NGOs in other areas such as technical support and implementation remains limited.

Tokenism of community and participatory processes in large scale government projects is common and, if anything, is growing. How can external donors ensure that the elements of participation and equity are effective in the government interventions they support? In the context of government projects what is the experience of involving NGOs in these processes?

Private donor agencies need to be more concerned about the strategic relevance of their support to NGOs. Public systems, despite their inherent flaws, are too costly to society to be ignored. At a macro level, gains can hardly be made unless administrative inefficiency, unresponsiveness, corruption and chronic inability to reach the poor is overcome by the development apparatus of the state. Can private donor support to NGOs help them to negotiate better resources from government for the communities of their concern? Would it be worth considering the ability or willingness of an NGO to engage with public systems as a criterion for support? What kind of non-funding roles is it possible for NGOs to play in order to improve GO–NGO relations.

CONCLUSIONS

Drawing on practical experience, this paper has attempted to provide lessons on how to build constructive collaborative relationships between governments and NGOs. The following conclusions can be drawn:

- The type and form of collaboration needs to be based on a clear understanding of project or programme objectives. Different objectives imply different roles for NGOs. Hence in projects promoting innovation and participation, NGOs need to give more parity, flexibility and space than those that want NGOs to provide a pre-determined service.
- Different outputs require different forms of relationships between NGOs and government. Pre-determined service delivery needs at least a dyadic relationship with enforceable instruments such as MoUs. Participation and empowerment in programmes requires space for NGOs and government to negotiate and interact and cannot be driven purely by targets – which is a characteristic of service delivery.
- Different forms of relationship require different organisational structures. Existing structures need to be modified if they are to administer even the simplest form of relationship, namely a dyadic one. Institutional relationships, which entail coalition, require specific support structures and processes, which autonomous structures are suitable only for the administration and

management of innovation within the confines of a project's organisation and activity. Often, a project can get better results under autonomous structures, which can create a snowball effect and force government department/agencies to respond. A less disjunctive way of mainstreaming innovation would imply embedding change units within the organisation to be changed.

- Arguments supporting the above statements are couched in terms of increasing the inclusion of the stakeholders in the design and management of interventions. Giving appropriate voice and agency to stakeholders requires project structures and procedures which allow and enable the evolution not only of organisations, but also of the rules which govern collective behaviour.
- There is little general consensus among donors on issues of community involvement, cost effectiveness, coverage, equity and replicability in the context of the interventions they support.

2

Indian Banking and Poultry Policy

INTRODUCTION

Role of Poultry in Livestock Revolution

A revolution is taking place in global agriculture, mostly due to large-scale transformations in the developing countries like India. Like in other developing countries, population growth, urbanization and income growth in India is fuelling demand for food of animal origin.

The changes in diet, income growth opportunities, particularly of rural populace in developing countries like India are triggering what is termed as "Livestock Revolution", which unlike "Green Revolution", is demand-driven. In India, Poultry is one of the fastest growing segments of livestock/agriculture and contributes a major share in terms of protein supplementation, from eggs and poultry meat. Amongst the animal products, which are, by and large substitutable in the diet, it is found that input-output ratio for poultry is most favorable. With 10 Kgs. of similar feed in each case, chicken (both meat & egg type) gives more protein than swine, cow milk, beef and sheep. Therefore, it is evident that poultry contributes a major share in this revolutionary process.

Livestock production in general in India is primarily the endeavor of the small holders and the sector is extremely livelihood intensive. However, poultry activity is characterized by a very wide range of operations with livelihood & subsistence farming at one end of the spectrum to highly viable & commercial operations at the other. All different operations are crucial for players of different strata it caters to, and no section can be ignored. The requirements of different sections are also varied and any policy accordingly has to make separate provisions are different levels, which will enable poultry to take livestock revolution to newer heights.

Poultry in Rural Development

In true terms 'livestock revolution'aims at not merely increasing the quantum of production but to have an holistic approach wherein problems of malnutrition, gender inequality and depraved socially-backward sections of the society are also dealt with. Poultry, due to its least demanding nature in terms of infrastructure in the backyard set up, has been widely accepted by the rural poor.

More than 50% of the landless and marginal farmers at the bottom end of the smallholder spectrum eke out their living from poultry & small ruminants. Poultry thus has been one of the core support system to subsistence farmers, providing supplementary income and is taken care of by the family, especially the women folk. Further, with some of the farmers earning from surplus production, the trend has been to keep larger flocks for more profit. Their inputs and requirement increase, which eventually make them dependent on other people in the allied sector like feed suppliers.

With Government & institutional support/financing, groups of such farmers are also organizing themselves through societies, cooperatives and self help groups for facilitating backward and forward linkages. Therefore, such activities bring about other developmental progress with increasing awareness, women's participation, literacy, health care etc. propelling an holistic improvement. Poultry rearing has also been seen as a popular activity among the tribal people who have been associated with it since ages. Their preference for indigenous birds, liking for colored plumage, tinted eggs etc. and traditional wisdom of raising the birds has also helped in *in situ* propagation of local birds. Unfortunately low productivity has been the hallmark of this rural backyard poultry, leading to lower returns.

Therefore, to give the necessary impetus to the rural development in general, poultry may be used as an effective tool with some crucial technological applications like increasing the productivity and decreasing the mortality rates etc.

Role of Women

Management of poultry has been associated with women for various historical and social factors. In developing countries, including India, women dominate most activities and are slowly also participating in the work like shelter construction and marketing, which were hitherto considered male domain.

Family poultry is easily managed within homesteads, and in rural areas this is the main resource which women farmers have more access to benefits accrued. With the recent emphasis on gender in development activities, there has been a tendency for poultry production to be seen as means of reaching women's group. With targeted training, gender based constraints such as poor access to information by women, division of labor/heavy workloads and fewer roles in decision making in the household are envisaged to be overcome. This also has been shown to lead to their greater empowerment if they are able to participate as poultry advisors, extension workers/ vaccinators, and for providing advice and support to other poultry owners.

Employment

As income and employment in crop reached saturation, the non-crop sector including dairy and poultry underwent an upward shift significantly. With the demand for poultry increasing and production reaching nearly 41 billion eggs and 1.4 billion broilers, this sector now employs over 2.0 million people. At least 80% of employment in the poultry sector is generated directly by farmers, while 20% is engaged in allied activities like feed production, pharmaceuticals, equipment etc. Additionally there may be a similar number of people engaged in marketing and other channels servicing the poultry sector. It may also be noted that as backyard poultry is not a full time occupation and taken care of mostly by family members, it is difficult to account for people engaged in this venture, which may also run into hundreds of thousands. It is also estimated that for increase in per capita availability of one egg of 50 gms. of poultry meat, an additional 20,000-25,000 job opportunities are created.

Output and Contribution

The value of output at current prices is steadily increasing for eggs and poultry meat during the last few years and during 2003-03 it was nearly Rs.16,000 crores. This is equivalent to nearly 10% of the total output from livestock and 2.8% of total agriculture. The value of exports is also increasing slowly with over Rs.200 crores during 2003-04 from a mere Rs.11 crores, ten years back.

POULTRY PRODUCTION SYSTEMS, CONSUMPTION TRENDS AND PERSPECTIVES

Production and Growth Rates

The provisional estimate of 2003 poultry population is around 489 million. The annual egg production is in the vicinity of 41 billion pieces (around 2.2 Million Metric Tonnes) and Chicken meat is around 1.65 Million Metric Tonnes. This put India on the global map for egg production among the top 6 countries (nearly 4% world share) and for chicken meat production among the top 5 countries (with nearly 3% of world share). The growth rate is pegged at nearly 6% for eggs and 10% for broilers. However, for sustainable doubling of egg production to 52.0 billion numbers by 2011-12(from base year 2001-02) a conservative estimate of 4.4% required growth rate is fixed for eggs. The share of egg production from desi birds is around 25% and improved birds nearly 75 percent. However, desi layers comprise nearly 41% with average yield of 104 eggs/annum and improved layers, 59% with average yield of 254 eggs/annum.

Regional Variations

One important aspect of poultry development in India is the significant variations in production across regions. Only 4

States of Andhra Pradesh, Tamilnadu, Maharashtra and Punjab account for over 60% of total egg production.

The per capita eggs and chicken meat availability is highest in southern states, followed by Northern & Western States and lowest in Eastern & Central States. The cost of production is also lowest in the southern region for both eggs and meat largely due to contract farming/integration in the sector.

It is also seen that though the rural distribution of poultry production is much higher(92%) than urban areas(8%), the markets are predominantly in the periurban areas and metropolitans.

Poultry Products Availability

The per capita availability for eggs and chicken meat is presently around 41 numbers and 1.6 kg. respectively which is very low compared to the National Institute of Nutrition's recommendation of 180 eggs and 11 kgs respectively. There is again a major divide in rural and urban areas with per capita egg availability varying from 45 to 170 in major cities and small tons; from less than 5 to 20 in underdeveloped and developed villages.

Similarly poultry meat consumption varies from 0.24 kg. in rural areas to 2 kgs in urban areas. Studies show that there has been a slow change in consumption habits of the people with a gradual shift towards animal protein like meat, fish and eggs, besides milk, which was already consumed by vegetarians. The income and price elasticity also indicate that there is a promising scope for raising demand for poultry products in rural areas, besides urban areas.

Structure of Poultry Sector

The poultry sector in India cover a broad range of operations varying in activities and scales, catering to different state of farmers, from the poorest of the poor to the wealthy. Broadly, the sector is considered two-pronged, as organized & unorganized sector. However, a 'need based'classification is more pragmatic and may be described briefly as follows:

Family Poultry System for Food Security

In this extensive backyard rearing system, the family members, especially the women take care of the stocks, which are very small in numbers, averaging 20 birds per family. The produce is consumed by the family and are distributed as gifts or occasionally bartered for other commodities. There is no commercial application here as there is hardly any surplus left for marketing. The major inputs required for this sector are locally adaptable improved variety of stocks with better productivity and low mortality, health care, trainings & extension. Formation of self-help groups, societies, cooperatives etc. will increase awareness about nutrition and also help the farmers realize surplus production through proper technological adoption, thus adding to their income as a supplementary source.

Small Holders

This group of farmers practice extensive to semi-intensive rearing which help them address the issues of food security and also enable surplus production for marketing. The size of flocks may vary from a few hundreds to few thousands in clusters. This sub sector requires some minimal infrastructure like poultry sheds and equipment, intensive training of farmers in chick rearing, health care, inputs like balanced feed and good quality stocks of both improved desi and commercial variety along with micro-credit for produce collection & marketing. Self Help Groups/ Cooperative set up for facilitating inputs acquisition and marketing helps this sub sector to become economically viable. Linkages with District Rural Development Agencies (DRDAs), Banks, Krishi Vigyan Kendras (KVKs) and Non-government Organizations (NGOs) will help technology & credit to flow to the farmers. Trained Poultry Link Workers are required in this section to disseminate services like basic health coverage and skills.

Commercial Operations

This is a highly organized and viable sub-sector employing intensive farming and sophisticated breeding systems. High productivity of the birds are their main feature, requiring high inputs and giving high output with nearly 315 + eggs per annum and Feed Conversion Ration (FCR) of less than 2.0. This sub-sector is also going through a paradigm shift from individual operations to integrated ones. Contract farming by large breeders is also one of the emerging features, to cash on the economies of scale. Stress is on marketing, health care, processing, achieving standards for food safety and exports. These operations range from thousands to hundreds of thousands of stock for breeding and millions for rearing. The major requirement of this sub sector are high yielding birds, health care, huge infrastructure for hatchery, housing, transport, cold chain, marketing intelligence and export standard compliance. Training for skilled manpower and infrastructure like laboratories for feed & product testing, disease monitoring and technology for Good Manufacturing Practices (GMP) and Hazard Analysis Critical Control Points (HACCP) implementations are the other indispensable supports needed by this sub sector.

ISSUES AND CHALLENGES

Low Production Potential

This is the major constraint in the rural poultry production system where the stocks maintained by the backyard farmers and small holders have low productivity. The local birds attain maturity slowly and laying age, is delayed as also the weight gained. This has been due to lack of taking the technological up gradation to the grass root level. Proper feeding and other manage mental aspects will also help improve the productivity of the birds. However, the up gradation has to be gradual as the birds need to retain their hardiness, required for their scavenging nature and survivability in harsh rural conditions.

Feed Availability and Feed Price

The major feed ingredients like maize, soya and oil cakes are presently produced adequately to meet the demand of poultry sector, but given its growth rate, chances are that they may fall short of the requirement in near future. Further, availability of these ingredients vary seasonally and due to lack of storage godowns the price fluctuates. The transportation costs also add to hightened price of feed. Feed alone constitutes about 60-70% of the cost of production and any hike in feed price leads to lesser remuneration to the farmer.

POULTRY HEALTH AND BIOSECURITY

This is one of the most formidable challenges for both the rural and commercial set up. Health coverage to the birds in the rural areas need a deep health service delivery system not adequate presently, to counter the high mortality rates particularly in birds of young age. In the commercial sector, the health requirements are even more stringent and demanding with the emergent and reemergent disease situations. The highly intensive production system also subjects the birds to a lot of stress, making them susceptible to diseases. Timely vaccinations and medication, coupled with strict biosecurity measures are needed to cope with this. Availability of vaccines and drugs, as also their safety in terms of acceptable levels in end products for human consumption are other issues needed to be tackled. Disease diagnostic laboratories with skilled manpower for diagnosis, monitoring and surveillance of important poultry diseases are needed to commensurate with the level of production. High level of biosecurity and surveillance is also needed to keep exotic diseases like Highly Pathogenic Avian Influenza (HPAI) at bay. There is a need to strengthen the quarantine measures also, in this regard.

Infrastructure and Marketing

In the rural poultry production system, investment for some minimal infrastructure requirement like sheds for mother units which will raise birds to certain age before distribution, is needed. In the commercial sector, banks usually finance large hatcheries/ poultry houses required, eagerly. However, huge infrastructure needs to be created for storage of feed and products cold storages, refrigerated vans, state of the art laboratories for feed and product analysis etc. commensurate with the increasing level of production. This will help facilitate marketing and cope with the seasonal fluctuations in prices due to undulating demand, like low demand in summers. Special emphasis is needed for marketing of rural poultry produce coming from the backyard and small flocks.

Extension and Training

There is a dire need of imparting basic training to the rural farmers to take up poultry activity and give them the needed confidence to successfully rear the birds. Usually the failure of first cycle leads to its being the last due to lack of training. On the commercial side, trained and highly skilled personnel are required for whom advance training like in laboratory methods, GMP and HACCP applications etc. are needed. Poultry science needs to be given the necessary importance at all levels of veterinary education, especially graduation. An extension activity for transfer of technology from the lab to the farmers' doorstep has to be intensified.

Quality Control

With food safety being one of the major areas of concern, quality control of feed, stock, biologicals, drugs and the product assume great importance. So far, focus has been on the end product quality but now it is of prime importance that as far as possible, quality has to be monitored through out the entire food chain so as to ensure safety from 'farm to the fork'. This entails huge investment and the major constraint is its application in rural production where stocks are widely distributed in small units and traceability is an issue.

Fiscal support, Institutional Credit and Incentive to Producers/farmers

There are many rural banks which are financing small farmers but in the rural areas backyard farmers are not organized and educated enough to even approach these banks for financial help. However, with schemes of rural development, self-help groups are coming forward to avail micro credit. The poultry activities also need to be defined clearly for giving optimum benefit to farmers. Ministry of Commerce and Ministry of Food Processing Industry are also having schemes for commercial sectors to encourage scaling up both primary and post harvest production: Support for freight, human resource development, market exploration, quality management, infrastructure development, backward and forward integration, promotional activities etc. for both domestic and export purposes are also extended. However, these need to be expanded in scope and finance to accommodate the requirement of the commercial sector.

Exports

Compliance with the standards of importing countries is the largest hurdle to be covered for which standards have to be set and implemented in consonance with Codex and WTO norms. Market explorations and brand promotion are other areas of thrust needed to increase exports. Innovative processing and value addition also need to be encouraged. The quantum of trade/export has to be increased from present global share of 0.4 percent.

Animal Welfare and Environmental Pollution

These issues have been of increasing concern in developed countries like United States & European Union. Considering globalization and the international trade in poultry products, these issues are assuming significance. Besides, with intensive production, environmental pollution abatement and bio-waste management strategies have to be worked out in advance.

PRINCIPAL POLICY OBJECTIVES

- To foster the cause of holistic development for the rural and socially backward communities, gender empowerment, poverty alleviation and nutritional nourishment, especially of the rural poor, using poultry as a tool.
- To increase per capita availability of poultry products by stepping up sustainable production using suitable technology.

- To build participatory institutions of collective actions for small scale farmers which will allow them to vertically integrate with input suppliers and processors.
- To crease an environment through training and extension to enable farmers to adopt technology for improving productivity and management of the birds.
- To promote creation of infrastructure like laboratories etc. and boost processing and distribution facilities along with commensurate export promotion to enable increase in exports.
- To promote effective regulatory institutions for dealing with environmental and health crises arising out of poultry and poultry products.

POLICY IMPLEMENTATION STRATEGIES AND OUTCOME

Breeding Policy

India is recognized as mega diversity zone and it is necessary foremost that the seed or the stock is chosen, suitable to the agro-climatic condition of the region. Impetus is needed for the development and adoption for the low input technology birds suitable for training at village conditions. To survive at the farmers' door, natural refractoriness to common diseases should also be an attribute of the birds. The States should get the evaluation of the performance of the existing stocks done and replenish them wherever needed and phase out wherever not. The breeding policy for such State requires specific attention to the local birds.

The indigenous birds have been researched in most of the regions and based on their production, adaptability to the environment, disease resistance, selection should be made for their propagation. The indigenous breeds are like genetic insurance, which may be needed in future and is also closer to the masses due to sentimental value. The diversification of poultry by taking up breeding of ducks, Japanese quails, turkey and guinea fowl will be given thrust. The inputs and marketing facilities for these shall be geared up prior to ensuring their popularization. Ostrich and Emu shall also be considered for introduction on commercial scale, keeping in view the environmental implications. Establishment of a gene pool or bank for indigenous breeds and threatened breeds as a conservation strategy will be considered. Studies and conservation of Red Jungle Fowl, the progenitor of modern day fowl will be undertaken as its native tract is believed to be the Indian sub continent and the knowledge may be used to our advantage in future.

An "Avian Genetic Resource Task Force: shall be set up to popularize propagation of already recognized indigenous breeds like Aseel, Ankaleshwar, Buser, Brown desi, Chatting (Malay), Daothigir, Denki, Frizzle, Phages, Haringhata, Kalasthi, Faverolla, Naked neck, Punjab Brown, Tellicherry, Titni, Teni, Nicobari and duck breeds like Indian Runner, Nageshwari, sythetmete etc. The nutritive/special characteristics of the poultry products from indigenous birds, if any, shall be scientifically validated and documented for wide publicity. In the commercial sector, nearly 15% of the production is dependent on production of stocks from imported grandparent stocks, certain lines of which have to be continually imported. The safety of import of these stocks in terms of prevention of ingress of exotic diseases shall be ensured, through compliance of sanitary requirements. There are presently no benchmarks regarding the field performances of the improved indigenous low input technology stocks, may be because other attributes like colored plumage, tinted eggs etc. complement for lower production. However, a threshold field level output will be studied and documented.

Besides laying stress on traits for improvement in breeding program, additional traits like improvement in carcass quality and dressing yield for broilers along with improvement in egg mass and egg quality characteristics for layers should also be considered by the breeders, in the commercial sector.

Feed Requirement

The rural poultry production, especially backyard ventures have minimal requirement of feed as the birds thrive on by scavenging but some supplementary feeding with home grown grain/by products is needed. The need for this sector is for non-conventional and locally available feed resources, which may be used by the farmers. Research on the nutritive value of these ingredients and extension of this knowledge will be intensified through documentation of regional availability, quantity to be used in ration, limiting factors, if any, etc. The low cost feed formulations using locally available raw material shall be standardized so as to have wide acceptability and accessibility by the small-scale farmers.

Feed availability, especially ingredients like corn and soya are the primary concern of the commercial sector. The Technology Mission on oilseeds, pulses and maize (TMOPM) shall be urged to intensify research and development in terms of increasing yield, oil content etc. of these ingredients to cope up with the unprecedented demand, mostly by the poultry sector, to the tune of 16-17 MMT for maize alone, by 2010 and Soya to merely 5 MMT. Multi exchange commodity trading for maize will be publicized along with its information on auction, which shall be made available by Food Corporation of India (FCI). Contract farming by poultry integrators for maize production will be encouraged. Use of alternate cereals as feed substitute and palletized feed may be encouraged to avoid wastage. Instead of antibiotic growth promoters, use of enzymes, pro and pre-biotics etc. will be encouraged and the farmer shall be phased out slowly.

Health Coverage and Biosecurity

The requirement of health coverage is as crucial to the commercial sector as to the rural/small scale sector. Whereas the requirement for rural poultry is availability of basic health care, the commercial sector needs more intensive disease monitoring, application of biologicals, drugs and diagnostics to cope up with the increased susceptibility of the birds due to stress of industrial production. Provisions shall be made to ensure the above. If need be, States may demarcate backyard/ core rural production pockets from commercial production pockets so that they do not pose any risk to each other. For instance commercial sector may be at risk from free range rural flocks due to their lack of biosecurity measures and rural production may succumb to commercial methods like indiscriminate use of vaccines even when they are not needed. Doorstep delivery of health services to the rural poultry farmers shall be bought about through the trained link workers who are decentralized and self-sustaining. Cold chain and thermo-stable vaccines are other requirement, which shall be considered along with continuous supply of biologicals drugs.

Ethno-veterinary medicines shall be encouraged in this sector and the knowledge will be widely disseminated, after validation and documentation. It is of utmost importance that the surveillance for important diseases particularly vertically transmitted diseases like salmonellosis are put in place strictly. Bio-informatics, epidemiological studies and interpretation of serious poultry diseases are indispensable in the present scenario in the commercial sector mostly. A Poultry Disease Surveillance and Information system shall be considered for creating a database for disease situation for further forecasting etc. or the ADSIS will be strengthened in terms of poultry diseases. Biosecurity measures be stepped up in light of HPAI in neighboring countries and other exotic diseases and any imports shall be scrutinized in detail for risk. Imports allowed, especially of germplasm shall be subjected to foolproof quarantine measures, which will be further strengthened. Imported biologicals shall be subjected to strict quality control testing.

Quality Control/standards for Safe Feed, Biologicals and Poultry Products

To ensure safe food, it is imperative that all the inputs that go into the poultry production have to be tested for quality. The standards for feed for poultry has already been set and the next phase is its implementation by the States in a regulatory manner. Feed additives like most bacterial inhibitors or antibiotic growth promoters are playing truant due to residue problems and all such products have to be phased out eventually. The maximum residue limits (MRLs) and Acceptable Daily Intakes (ADIs) of various additives/ drugs are being fixed, but mostly for the purposes of exports. The same levels have to be adopted for domestic production to purge out their injudicious use from the system. Also the level of inclusion of drugs/additives shall be ascertained so as to define therapeutic and prophylactic use.

The biologicals, imported and domestically produced, will be evaluated and tested for their safety, potency and efficacy before being released in the market. Farmers spend a fortune on health care products and we must ensure their worth. More laboratories will be accredited so as to meet the demands of testing, setting up of more Regional Referral Laboratories will be considered besides the National Institute of Animal Health at Baghpat, UP, which is in the pipeline.

Poultry products are considered high-risk commodities, which may cause food- borne diseases, and evaluation of all such risks, especially microbiological, will be covered. The Integrated Food Law, "Food safety and standards bill" encompasses such measures for all foods including poultry products.

Information inputs for this law shall be furnished to eliminate any risk of poultry meat products or egg-borne disease. Ninety five per cent of the market for poultry is wet market and therefore, it is necessary to have some standards for in-shop slaughtering and operating procedures shall be laid down for strict implementation. Standards for biosecurity including all aspects of locational, infrastructural, and operational aspects will be reviewed in the present context also and benchmarks for parameters like bird density and effluent reduction will be fixed and eventually regulated.

In the commercial sector, starting from breeding operations, feed milling to processing, good manufacturing practices (GMP) and Hazard Analysis Critical Control Points (HACCP) will be urged to be adopted voluntarily.

A package of practices for extensive and semi-intensive small-holder poultry production with due consideration of agro climatic conditions will be drawn up and guidelines for modern hatchery and farm management practices will also be prepared for reference by commercial sector. The package of practices for other species (besides chicken) will also be drawn.

INFRASTRUCTURE AND TECHNOLOGY

To cope with the targets set for augmenting rural production, infrastructure for central resource units, mother units and farmers unit will be created. Using kits and linkages will meet challenge of sero-surveillance of major diseases in rural conditions. Infrastructure is also required for setting up laboratories for feed analysis, disease diagnosis, residue monitoring etc. Even though partial requirement is met presently with accredited labs, but more infrastructure and equipment with cutting-edge technology shall be set up to ensure desirable quality of the products. Infrastructure in the commercial sector in terms of effluent treatment, waste management etc. shall also be urged to be set up to cope with the environmental issues, especially by the intensive commercial sector.

Establishing infrastructure for storage of feed, eggs and poultry products especially cold storages and refrigerated vehicles for the latter will be encouraged and this will also help in allaying the seasonal price fluctuations. Infrastructure like retail outlets will be set up to help stabilize markets for rural produce. Infrastructure for processing and value-addition will also be encouraged to be set up on a large scale, including egg graders, packaging equipment etc. Adoptive technology shall be employed using informal networks through computers and other communication devices to enable accessibility of information especially in the rural areas. Problems of farmers are proposed to be solved through trouble shooting and allowing them to interact with experts. Technology shall also be coupled with the traditional knowledge of the land and help in participatory approaches for social organization in rural areas. This will greatly help the extension and outreach programs.

Processing and Value Addition

In near future, the shift will be towards processed and value-added products due to its convenience and safety assurance. Besides infrastructure the major requirement will be compliance to standards viz. microbiological, chemical, antibiotic, pesticides, packaging, storage etc. and brand promotion etc. but considering a boost in processing from present 5% to 20% by 2011-12, the investment requirement will be mammoth and accordingly provisions will be urged to be made. Recommendations will be made to give thrust to the Post Harvest Technology and Total Quality Management through ISO, GMP and HACCP certifications shall be given for all processing units.

Training, Extension and Information System

Sources of rural poultry programs lies in the training of farmers in basic rearing and of poultry link workers for disseminating health services and importing skills to the farmers. Farmers'training shall be undertaken at large scale to give technical information about farming, mostly basic chick rearing and create awareness about benefits of poultry with respect to economics and nutritive value of egg products. The other aspect of training will also look towards developing skills of farmers for social organization to enable them to involve themselves in participatory way. The training of farmers shall also including taking up diversified farming, wherever required. Kukkut melas, seminars, workshops involving farmers from block to national level at regular intervals will also help crate awareness about poultry farming.

Provision for poultry training is also be made for advanced and latest technologies to the personnel in the commercial sector. Basic training in hygiene and sanitation shall be urged to be imparted to personnel handling meat/egg products in slaughter houses and processing centers, mostly by commercial sector. The poultry science departments of the veterinary colleges shall be strengthened and inclusion of rural poultry farming during graduation will help the veterinarians understand its importance once they are in the field. A center for excellence for training is also being envisaged by upgrading the Central Poultry Training Institute into International Avian Tropical Management Institute where even commercial sector person shall be imparted training as per their requirement and suitable training modules will be prepared for rural poultry programs.

Institutional Financing and Incentives

The Indian poultry sector does not accrue any direct or indirect subsidies /incentives barring for export purposes like freight subsidy, export promotion capital goods scheme, standard input output norms, Vishesh Krishi Upaj Yojana etc. However, for rural development and poverty alleviation some Central and State Governments schemes provide assistance to marginal farmers involved in poultry production but the amounts are very small in total investment and is declining over time.

The Agriculture sector gets some direct and indirect subsidies for fertilizers, pesticides, electricity etc. Though the poultry sector is an integral part of agriculture, it faces restrictions on use of agricultural land, attracts higher electricity tariffs and sales tax than agriculture and is subjected to different land/labor laws. Neither like other industries does it get benefits like the holidays. Therefore, it is obvious that for the required poultry development, this sector should be treated as agriculture in terms of all the benefits accrued by the latter, States have been requested to consider the issue favorably. National Bank for Agriculture and Rural Development (NABARD) and rural banks are playing a major role for availing finance to the poultry sector. Initiative will be taken for allowing micro-credit financing to small holder and rural farmers and giving loans at Prime Lending Rates (PLR) to the commercial sector. The Rural Infrastructure Development Fund of NABARD will also go a long way in helping create the requisite infrastructure for rural development.

Marketing

Marketing is on of the weakest link in the rural poultry development program. Presently market for poultry products is concentrated in peri-urban and urban areas. The overall impression of the market is that of not well organized and there is exploitation by middle men, reducing the margin of profit for farmers who are under threat by vagaries of weather, price fluctuations and productivity. Agencies like National Egg Coordination Committee and Bromark are declaring prices for eggs and poultry/broiler based on market dynamics and has participation of farmers, which helps tackle the problem of middlemen to some extent.

Infrastructure like cold storage and retail outlets will help stabilize the market in terms of price fluctuations. The other major requirement for marketing is to develop the marketing intelligence wherein information of surplus and deficit areas shall be assessed so as to strategize the logistics accordingly. This shall be developed in collaboration with all stake-holders and Geographical Information System (GIS) will be employed for the purpose.

Generic campaign for awareness of poultry products shall be intensified to apprise the consumers of its benefits and for dispelling some common myths. Brand development shall be encouraged to be taken up by the commercial firms. The rural produce shall be given wide publicity for its near-organic and non-synthetic nature. This will help create a niche market for the rural products.

Exports

India has a strategic advantage in terms of competitive cost of production, cheap labor, proximity to some potential markets and HPAI-free status making forays into global trade. However, our Achilles Heel is the inability to give matching incentives for exporters like the EU & US does and failure to promote processing to the level required.

International market exploration, brand promotion and ability to comply with the often-stringent standards of importing countries are areas which will be given fillip. There are schemes of Ministry of Commerce and Ministry of Food Processing Industry which cover the above but the funds are miniscule compared to the present day requirement and will be used for reviewing upwards. Besides poultry products, poultry equipment exports will be given encouragement and they should also be classified as farm/agriculture equipments. Further, the value-added and specialized poultry products like Tandoori chicken, kebab etc will be encourage to go 'glocal'i.e. to have global appeal with local taste.

The Task Force constit ted for overlooking promotion of poultry products should continue as it gives a suitable platform for the exporters, inspection agencies, government and other related institutions to interact and sort out the bottlenecks from time to time.

Export Inspection Council of India (EIC) and Agriculture Processed Products Export Development Authority (APEDA) are doing the tedious exercise of getting country approval for export of poultry products. The commercial poultry sector should be urged to cooperate and give necessary information inputs for hastening the process.

Convergence and Synergy

Poultry operations span over a wide range of activities, which come under the purview of many different sectors. The Central and State Government agencies like Rural Development, Human Resource Development, Animal Husbandry, ICAR, Agriculture, Food Processing, Commerce and Finance, Financial institutions like NABARD, NCDC etc. are actively involved and play their part. However, it is necessary to synergize activities with these agencies so that concerted effort is made for progress without overlapping objectives. Therefore, there is a need for better linkage and coordination between the agencies so as to collectively pool the resources and effectively implement the poultry development programs.

Synergy should also exist with the commercial sector, who should assist in areas of generic promotion of poultry products, consumer education etc. and help create public-private partnerships.

In the commercial sector, the integration and contract farming shall be encouraged and this convergence will also be fuelled with necessary forward and backward linkages to ensure good remuneration for farmers'produce and production of hygienic and wholesome food.

In the rural sector, the convergence of activities of different agencies is required to ensure proper functioning of central resource and mother units. Provisions will be made to ensure coordination with other agencies to ensure smooth flow of inputs and steady dissemination of outputs.

If required, poultry corporations/federations or other state agencies will be nominated to overlook the work of facilitator.

POLICY OUTCOME

The National Poultry Policy through appropriate programs and investment will help achieve the objectives of rural poultry development as well as concurrent development of commercial sector. The high growth rates of egg and broiler production are expected to be sustained through assured inputs like feed. The programs in consonance with the policy objectives will help increase household nutritional security, per capita availability of eggs and poultry meat with reduction in gap of rural and urban availability, increase in employment in the commercial sector and increase in household income of rural poor through supplementary earnings. Eventually, in the long run, the vision of holistic rural development through community development, women empowerment and poverty alleviation will be realized. On the global trade front, the measures will help India in getting a sound footing on international arena and help in increasing her share in trade.

3

Agricultural Policy and Long-term Agricultural Growth

INTRODUCTION

Agriculture plays important roles in economic development, such as provision of food to the nation, enlarging exports, transfer of manpower to nonagricultural sectors, contribution to capital formation, and securing markets for industrialization. Improvement in agricultural productivity is key to the realization of each of these roles and herein lies the importance of agricultural policies.

Historical records have shown that agricultural productivity has been growing due to introduction of modern technologies, commercialization of agriculture, capital deepening, factor shifts from agriculture to nonagricultural sectors, etc., none of which occurred in isolation from the policy settings of each agriculture. This paper, therefore, attempts to associate long-term trends in agricultural productivity in India and Pakistan with changes in political institutions and agricultural policies. The use of a very long time series that corresponds to the current border of India and Pakistan distinguishes this paper from the existing studies on South Asian agriculture.

At the same time, when discussing the effects of policies, the fictitious treatment of "India" and "Pakistan" that refer to the areas delineated by the current international border becomes more problematic. Because of this reason, we use the pre-1947 performance as a benchmark to normalize the post-1947 performance and discuss the policy impacts during the post-1947 period only.

DATA

This paper employs an updated version of the dataset compiled by the author (Kurosaki 1999, 2002). We cover a period from 1901/02 to 2001/02. The addition of the 1990s distinguishes this paper from the previous studies (Kurosaki 1999, 2002). We cover geographic areas that correspond to the current international borders of India and Pakistan. The data compilation procedures for the colonial period is explained by Kurosaki (1999). We basically subtracted areas and production corresponding to the areas currently in Pakistan and Bangladesh from the data base compiled by Sivasubramonian (1960, 1997). Information included in district-level data in *Season and Crop Reports* from Punjab, Sind (or Bombay-Sind), the NWFP (North-West Frontier Province), and Bengal was utilized in this exercise.

Because historical data on agriculture are less detailed than the current ones, we cannot compile production statistics for several crops. Therefore, we focus on production of principal crops, which are important in contemporary India and Pakistan, and for which detailed data on production and prices are available from the British period. For India, eighteen crops are included: foodgrains = rice, wheat, barley, jowar (sorghum), bajra (pearl millet), maize, ragi (finger millet), gram (chickpea); oilseeds = linseed, sesamum, rapeseed & mustard, groundnut; other crops = sugarcane, tea, coffee, tobacco, cotton, and jute & mesta.

These crops currently occupy more than two thirds of the total output value from the crop sector and more than a half of the total output from agriculture, and their contribution was higher in the colonial period. For Pakistan, all twelve crops included in the major crops subsector are covered, i.e., rice, wheat, barley, jowar, bajra, maize, gram [foodgrains]; rapeseed & mustard, sesamum, sugarcane, tobacco, and cotton. These crops currently occupy about 70 percent of value-added from all the crops and about 40 percent of value-added from agriculture, and its share was higher in the colonial period.

The gross output values from these crops are aggregated using 1960 prices. Ideally, the sum of value-added evaluated at current prices and then deflated using some price index would be a better measure, but the sum of gross output values at constant prices is used as a proxy due to the absence of reliable data on input prices and quantities before independence. The results reported in this paper are insensitive to the choice of other base years (1938/39 and 1980/81). We call the gross output value thus compiled *Q*. As measures for partial productivity, we divide *Q* by *L* (official population estimates of India and Pakistan) or by *A* (the sum of the acreage under the eighteen or twelve crops).

PRODUCTIVITY AND CROP MIX IN AGRICULTURE IN INDIA AND PAKISTAN

With the dataset described above, we updated tables and figures reported in Kurosaki (1999, 2002). Since the data revisions in the period already covered in these studies are minor, the discussion in this section focuses on the latest decade. Namely, we investigate whether or not trends in agricultural productivity and crop mix have changed during the 1990s.

Productivity

Growth performance in Indian agriculture is plotted in Figure 1. Table 1 shows statistical results to quantify the level of growth rate, its significance, and its variability in India. To smooth out short-term fluctuations, we estimate a time series model for Yt in the form of

(1) $\ln Yt = a0 + a1\ t + ut,$

where t is measured in years and ut is an i.i.d. error term. We estimate equation (1) for the logarithm of *Q*, *Q*/*L*, and *Q*/*A*, by the OLS for each decade and then for the periods before and after independence. The first column of Table 1 gives coefficient estimates for $a1$.

The total output value (*Q*) grew very little up to the Partition and then grew steadily since then. The growth rate in the 1990s was 1.7%, which is less than the post-Partition average of 2.8%.

Table 1: Growth Performance of Indian Agriculture

Period	Q (Total output value)		Q/L (Output per capita)		CQ/A (Output per acre)	
	Growth rate	Coeff. var.	Growth rate	Coeff. var.	Growth rate	Coeff. var.
1901/02 – 1910/11	1.04%	11.8%	0.39%	11.8%	-0.26%	9.8%
1911/12 – 1920/21	-0.88%	13.0%	-0.97%	13.0%	-0.40%	8.0%
1921/22 – 1930/31	-0.08%	2.6%	-1.09% ***	2.6%	-0.41%	2.4%
1931/32 – 1940/41	0.24%	4.0%	-1.16% **	4.0%	0.10%	3.0%
1941/42 – 1950/51	-0.53%	4.2%	-1.78% ***	4.2%	-1.45% **	4.0%
1951/52 – 1960/61	4.24% ***	5.1%	2.28% ***	5.1%	2.34% ***	4.2%
1961/62 – 1970/71	2.53% **	8.8%	0.32%	8.8%	1.89% **	7.2%
1971/72 – 1980/81	2.62% **	7.1%	0.41%	7.1%	2.12% ***	5.6%
1981/82 – 1990/91	3.21% ***	6.2%	1.09%	6.2%	3.23% ***	3.7%
1991/92 – 2000/01	1.68% ***	3.5%	-0.26%	3.5%	1.65% ***	2.3%
1901/02 – 1946/47	0.48% ***	8.5%	-0.34% ***	9.6%	-0.01%	6.3%
1947/48 – 2000/01	2.80% ***	6.5%	0.68% ***	6.7%	2.21% ***	6.3%

Source: Kurosaki (1999) and update estimates by the author.

Note: "Growth rate" shows a parameter estimate for the slope of the log of Q (or Q/L or Q/A) on a time trend, estimated by OLS (see equation (1)). The parameter estimate is statistically significant at 1% ***, 5% **, or 10%* (two sided t-test). "Coeff. var." shows the coefficient of variation approximated by the standard error of the OLS regression.

Table 2: Growth Performance of Pakistani Agriculture

Period	Q (Total output value)		Q/L (Output per capita)		CQ/A (Output per acre)	
	Growth rate	Coeff. var.	Growth rate	Coeff. var.	Growth rate	Coeff. var.
1901/02 – 1910/11	4.32% **	15.1%	2.75%	15.1%	0.99%	10.9%
1911/12 – 1920/21	-0.33%	14.6%	-1.18%	14.6%	-0.19%	6.6%
1921/22 – 1930/31	-0.64%	10.3%	-1.73%	10.3%	-1.15%	7.4%
1931/32 – 1940/41	2.81% ***	5.8%	0.97%	5.8%	1.86% **	5.1%
1941/42 – 1950/51	0.05%	6.7%	-2.92% ***	6.7%	-0.19%	3.4%
1951/52 – 1960/61	3.44% ***	5.2%	1.00%	5.2%	1.66% ***	3.3%
1961/62 – 1970/71	5.85% ***	5.2%	2.99% ***	5.2%	3.93% ***	4.5%
1971/72 – 1980/81	3.24% ***	3.7%	0.09%	3.7%	1.75% ***	3.3%
1981/82 – 1990/91	3.50% ***	5.2%	0.85%	5.2%	2.65% ***	5.3%
1991/92 – 2000/01	2.30% ***	5.3%	-0.35%	5.3%	1.61% ***	5.5%
1901/02 – 1946/47	1.30% ***	12.8%	-0.03%	11.9%	0.38% ***	8.6%
1947/48 – 2000/01	3.58% ***	7.3%	0.77% ***	7.5%	2.34% ***	6.3%

Source and notes: See Table 1.

The column for "Variability" shows how variable was the output around the fitted values in terms of the coefficient of variation.

The 1990s was associated with less variability. In the 1990s, output per capita (*Q*/*L*) did not grow while output per acre (*Q*/*A*) grew at a rate similar to that of *Q*. In other words, the source of growth in the 1990s in India was exclusively the improvement in aggregate land productivity.

Similar changes were observed in Pakistan but with higher growth rates throughout the period. The growth rate of *Q* before the Partition was smaller than the post-Partition period but still statistically significant at 1.3%.

The growth rate declined in the 1990s to 2.3% against the post-independence average of 3.6%, but its level was still higher than that of India. Unlike in India, the variability of *Q* was similar to the previous periods and the source of growth was not only the improvement in aggregate land productivity but also the expansion of total acreage in Pakistan. The growth rate of output per acre (*Q*/*A*) was positive and significant but smaller than that of *Q*. in the 1990s in Pakistan.

Crop Mix

An important aspect of agricultural transformation is changes in crop composition and diversification/specialization (Timmer 1997). Even when there is no change in land productivity of individual crops in each location, aggregate land productivity can grow through spatial shifts of crops, which reflect the development of more efficient rural markets (Kurosaki 2003).

The spatial shifts are the result of farmers' attempts to diversify farming activities towards non-traditional, high value-added crops such as fruits and vegetables and towards livestock activities (Chand 1999).

To capture the long-term changes in crop mix, the Herfindahl Index of crop acreage was calculated. Let *Si* be the share of crop *i* in the sum of the principal crops covered in this paper, in terms of acreage. Then the Herfindahl Index is defined as

(2) *H* .... “*iSi*,

which has an intuitive meaning of a probability of hitting the same crops when two points are randomly chosen from all the land under consideration.

To investigate whether or not these changes in crop mix were consistent with those indicated by comparative advantage and market development, changes in aggregate land productivity were decomposed into crop yield effects, static inter-crop shift effects, and dynamic inter-crop shift effects (Kurosaki 2003). Let *Yt* denote per-acre output in year *t*, i.e., *Q/A*. Its growth rate from period 0 to period *t* can be decomposed as

(3) (*Yt-Y*0)/*Y*0 = [“*iSi*0(*Yit-Yi*0) + “*i*(*Sit-Si*0)*Yi*0
+ “*i*(*Sit-Si*0)(*Yit-Yi*0)]/*Y*0,

where subscript *i* denotes each crop so that *Yit* stands for per-acre output of crop *i* in year *t*. The first term of equation (3) captures the contribution from productivity growth of individual crops. The second term shows ‘static’ crop shift effects since it becomes more positive when the area under crops whose yields were initially high increases relatively.

The third term shows ‘dynamic’ crop shift effects because it becomes more positive when the area under dynamic crops (i.e., crops whose yields are improving) increases relative to the area under non-dynamic crops. Decomposition results for India are reported in Table 3. Throughout the post-Partition period, the contribution of both static and dynamic crop shift effects were substantial. More interestingly, during the 1990s, the growth due to improvement in crop yields was reduced while the growth due to static crop shifts maintained the level of the 1980s. As a result, relative contribution of static shift effects was as high as 31% in the 1990s. This is the highest among the post-independence decades. Therefore, we can conclude that the changes in crop mix in the 1990s were indeed consistent with comparative advantages of Indian agriculture so that the aggregate land productivity was improved.

Table 3: Contribution of Crops Shifts to Land Productivity Growth in India

Annural growth rates of land productivity (%)		Contribution share (%)
Period	Pure yield effects Static shift effects Dynamic shift effects Total	Pure yield effects Static shift effects Dynamic shift effects
1901/02 - 1911/12	0.90 0.00 -0.04 0.85	105.1 -0.1 -5.1
1911/12 - 1921/22	-0.35 -0.07 0.26 -0.17	209.5 43.8 -153.3
1921/22 - 1931/32	-0.34 0.14 0.05 -0.14	234.6 -97.2 -37.4
1931/32 - 1941/42	-0.36 0.30 -0.06 -0.12	290.9 -239.7 48.8
1941/42 - 1951/52	-1.48 0.30 -0.01 -1.20	124.0 -25.1 1.1
1951/52 - 1961/62	2.76 0.14 -0.01 2.89	95.3 5.0 -0.3
1961/62 - 1971/72	1.55 0.15 0.20 1.90	81.6 8.0 10.3
1971/72 - 1981/82	1.83 0.35 0.09 2.28	80.6 15.4 4.0
1981/82 - 1991/92	3.10 0.44 0.14 3.68	84.2 12.1 3.7
1991/92 - 2001/02	1.06 0.48 0.02 1.56	67.7 31.1 1.2
1901/02 - 1947/48	-0.24 -0.05 0.23 -0.06	423.5 82.2 -405.7
1947/48 - 2001/02	2.45 0.25 0.63 3.33	73.5 7.5 19.0

Source: The author's calculation. Note: Annual growth rates were estimated by the method explained in the text (see equation (3)). Since both the model to estimate and the data treatment for smoothing are different, the total growth rates of land productivity in this table is slightly different from those shown in Table 1.

Table 4: Contribution of Crops Shifts to Land Productivity Growth in Pakistan

Annural growth rates of land productivity (%)		Contribution share (%)
Period	Pure yield effects Static shift effects Dynamic shift effects Total	Pure yield effects Static shift effects Dynamic shift effects
1901/02 - 1911/12	1.84 -0.19 0.09 1.74	105.4 -10.8 5.4
1911/12 - 1921/22	0.06 -0.05 0.02 0.02	254.3 -226.2 71.9
1921/22 - 1931/32	-0.35 0.03 0.02 -0.31	113.4 -8.5 -4.9
1931/32 - 1941/42	1.51 0.16 0.32 1.99	75.8 8.2 16.0
1941/42 - 1951/52	-0.80 0.18 0.03 -0.58	136.6 -30.6 -6.0
1951/52 - 1961/62	1.03 0.85 0.03 1.92	53.8 44.4 1.8
1961/62 - 1971/72	3.37 0.52 0.28 4.16	80.8 12.5 6.7
1971/72 - 1981/82	1.72 0.63 0.13 2.49	69.2 25.4 5.4
1981/82 - 1991/92	2.35 0.07 0.21 2.63	89.3 2.5 8.2
1991/92 - 2001/02	0.85 0.28 -0.02 1.11	76.6 25.4 -2.0
1901/02 - 1947/48	0.55 -0.03 0.22 0.74	74.5 -4.0 29.6
1947/48 - 2001/02	2.32 0.47 0.63 3.42	67.8 13.7 18.5

Source and notes: See Table 3.

In contrast, the crop concentration index in Pakistan did not show acceleration in the 1990s. Rather it remained at the highest level, which was already reached during the 1980s. This seems to indicate that acreage shifts toward crops with comparative advantages occurred earlier in Pakistan than in India, possibly reflecting Pakistan's earlier attempt to liberalize agricultural marketing during the early 1980s. Decomposition results for Pakistan in Table 4 show that the contribution of both static and dynamic crop shift effects were substantial and their shares were larger than in India, throughout the post-Partition period.

This indicates that crop shift effects are more important in a smaller economy. During the 1990s, the growth due to improvement in crop yields declined substantially while the growth due to static crop shifts recovered. As a result, relative contribution of static shift effects was 25% in the 1990s, which was higher than the post-independence average (14%). Here is a similarity between India and Pakistan — in both agricultures, the crop shifts were an important source of land productivity growth in the 1990s.

LONG-TERM TRENDS AND AGRICULTURAL POLICIES

The empirical results in the previous section has shown a discontinuation at the Partition, both in India and in Pakistan. Total output growth rates turned from zero or little to significantly positive levels, which were sustained throughout the post-independence period; crop mix changed with increasing concentration since the mid 1950s.

Therefore, as far as the data suggest, agriculture in both countries has been experiencing one-way concentration of crops since the mid 1950s, when agricultural transformation in terms of output per agricultural worker was proceeding. According to Timmer's (1997) stylization, this is a stage before a mature market economy with diversified production and consumption at the national level. Against our initial expectation, these trends were not reversed in the 1990s in the direction of more diversified production if we focus on major crops.

The trends were strengthened in India during the 1990s while they became less significant in Pakistan. The performance in the 1990s suggests that agriculture in India has remained in the phase of diversification where concentration into high value-added crops is strengthened.

To investigate the impact of institutional and policy changes in the 1990s, we compare major changes in political institutions compiled in Table 5 with long-term trends in production discussed in the previous section. The colonial period in the early twentieth century was associated with free trade of agricultural commodities. Under this institutional setting, public investment into irrigation contributed to the rapid expansion of production, especially in regions currently belonging to Pakistan. The colonial period ended with increasing state control on trade and marketing under the war pressure. This period was associated with stagnation in agricultural production.

Policy shifts in agricultural development after independence were indeed similar in India and Pakistan if we look back from a long-term perspective. In the early 1950s, the focus was on land reforms on the one hand and on irrigation development on the other hand. Land reforms were, however, not implemented thoroughly, leaving the disparity between the landed and the landless almost unchanged. Since the late 1960s, the policy emphasis moved to technological innovation called the "Green Revolution" in both India and Pakistan. The rapid increase in land productivity of wheat and rice thanks to the Green Revolution is well documented. As emphasized by Kurosaki (1999, 2002), it is of interests to note that a substantial increase in aggregate land productivity occurred *before* the introduction of high-yielding varieties of rice and wheat, mainly through crop shift effects quantified in the previous section.

These periods were followed by institutional and policy changes in the direction of liberalization, deregulation, and privatization in India and Pakistan, which are continuing today. However, if we look at the individual components of the policy reform, there are several contrasts between India and Pakistan in the 1980s and 1990s.

Table 5: Changes in Institutions and Policies in Indian and Pakistani Agriculture

Period	India	Pakistan
1900s	Irrigation Commission established (1901)	
1910s	Completion of "Triple Canal Project" in the Indus Basin of Punjab (1917)	
1920s	The Great Depression (1929)	
1930s		
1940s	Bengal famine followed by the introduction of rationing of foodstuff in major cities Independence with partition of Bengal, Punjab, and Indus canal networks (1947)	
1950s	First 5 Year Plan (1951-56): emphasis on irrigation investment	Establishment of Water and Power DevelopmentAuthority [WAPDA] (1958)
	Land reform legislation to abolish intermediaries and guarantee tenants' security (1905s)	Ayub Khan's "Land Reform" (1959)
1960s	Indus Water Treaty with Pakistan (1960)	Indus Water Treaty with India (1960)
	Bad harvests in 1965-66 followed by the "Green Revolution with wheat and rice HYV (1966/67-)	Green Revolution with wheat and rice HYV(1966/67-)
1970s	New guideline for land reform: land ceiling and distribution of surplus land (1972)	Z.A. Bhutto's "Land Reform" (1972, 1977) Nationalization of fertilizer industries (1972)
	Integrated Rural Development Programme [IRDP] (1976-)	Pakistan Agri. Storage and Services Corporation [PASSCO] established (1973)
1980s	National Rural Employment Programme [NREP] (1981-)	Agricultural Prices Commission established (1981)
	National Bank for Agri. and Rural Dev. [NABARD] established (1982)	Rupee: fixed -> floating (basket) system (1982)
		Abolition of wheat and sugar rationing system (1987)
		IMF SAF agreement (1988)
1990s	Start of "Economic Reforms" (1991)	
	Unification of exchange rate. Floating Rs. System (1993)	Abolition of fertilizer subsidy (1993)
	Implementation of WTO agreement on agriculture (1995)	Liberalization of marketing and export of rice and cotton (abolition of export corporations, 1996).
	Reform in Public Distribution System [PDS]: Targeted PDS (1997)	

Source: Compiled by the author.

In India, policies to promote rural employment and reduce poverty were in force since the late 1970s. Most of them were not abandoned but revised under the Economic Reforms since 1991. In contrast, major liberalization policies in agriculture were adopted since the early 1980s in Pakistan with little emphasis on rural employment or poverty eradication policies.

Re-examining figures and tables in Section 3 with these differences in mind, the contrast in crop mix dynamics in the 1990s in India and Pakistan is suggestive. As already discussed, the crop concentration index did not show acceleration in the 1990s in Pakistan while it accelerated in India, but the concentration indices of both countries were at the highest level in the 1990s in the whole 20th century. The similarity could be attributable to the general effects of liberalization, deregulation, and privatization policies in agriculture. The contrast could be attributable to the earlier adoption of these policy reforms in Pakistan. Pakistani farmers were exposed to international relative prices earlier than Indian farmers were. In other words, Indian agriculture seems to have more room for productivity growth through crop shifts today than Pakistani agriculture has. In this aspect, the implementation of WTO agreement on agriculture in India since 1995 is expected to reinforce this advantage. However, as shown by Chand (2003), the WTO implementation has worsened the overall terms of trade for agriculture in the late 1990s, thereby blocking the full exploitation of this advantage.

The comparison of our results with those reported by Misra and Rao (2003) is also interesting. They showed that agricultural export was the main source of growth for Indian agriculture in the 1990s, which was facilitated by trade liberalization policies and the devaluation of Indian Rupee. Their finding is reinforced by our results since we have shown that crop shifts are an important source of productivity growth in the 1990s and shifts to export crops are consistent with out results.

Although our analysis has shown the importance of crop shifts in improving aggregate land productivity, it is an underestimate of their true impact because our measure only covers eighteen major crops. Under the Economic Reforms, contract farming is gaining its importance in India in the 1990s (Singh 2002). Similar changes are observed in Pakistan as well, although not so strong as in India. Our measures of the impact of liberalization policies on output growth in the 1990s should be understood as an underestimate because the growth in non-traditional crops such as vegetables or horticultural crops was not captured.

CONCLUSION

Based on a production dataset that corresponds to the current border of India and Pakistan for the period c.1900-2000, we investigated the performance of agriculture in the two regions and associated it with changes in political institutions and agricultural policies. Through examining the growth records of agricultural production and changes in crop mix indices, we showed that institutional and policy changes have significant effects on agricultural growth in India and Pakistan. Farmers have responded to these changes, adjusting their crop mix and production technology. The crop concentration indices were at the highest level in the 1990s both in India and in Pakistan, suggesting that liberalization/deregulation/privatization policies in agriculture in these countries led to an increased role of crop shifts in enhancing aggregate land productivity.

To quantify structural determinants of these changes and net effects on the welfare of rural population, further research is needed, such as analysis of production costs, investigation of minor crops and livestock activities, etc. These are left for future study. Instead, implications for agricultural policies in the 21st century are explored to conclude this paper. First, institutional and policy changes are likely to have significant effects on agricultural production in India and Pakistan. This is confirmed by the fact that the sustained growth in the total output began just after the Partition, well before the introduction of the Green Revolution technology, and also by changes of these trends in the 1990s. The current controversies in India and Pakistan on contract farming, corporate farming, and land ceiling legislation should be viewed from this historical perspective.

Second, farmers in India and Pakistan have responded to the changes in market conditions so that they not only adopted new technology with high-yielding potentials but also adjusted their land allocation toward high value crops. The importance of the effects of land re-allocation should not be ignored. For example, the effects of reforms in the price support system of major crops cannot be isolated from their interactions with crops whose prices are not under the support price system.

Third, although not discussed fully in this paper, existing evidence suggests that public investment in/for agriculture were reduced in the 1980s and 1990s. This occurred both in India and Pakistan under the banner of "Economic Reforms" or "Structural Adjustment." It should be emphasized that the sustained growth during the post-colonial period was achieved when substantial public investment was implemented. With reduced public investment without simultaneous improvement in investment efficiency, the boom experienced during the 1990s in response to newly opened opportunities would not last long. The importance of production-oriented infrastructure in increasing productivity of agriculture and in reducing rural poverty cannot be overemphasized (Hayami 2003). Rather, considering the public-good nature of such investment, its importance should rise under the context of globalization and trade liberalization.

4

Credit Flow to Small and Marginal Farmers in India

The facilitating role of credit in agricultural development has assumed special significance in today's context when Indian agriculture with contribution of about a quarter to the GDP and about two-third in terms of employment of the rural population is confronting a number of fresh problems like limited scope for area expansion, unsteady and retarded growth, tremendous fragmentation of land, stagnating productivity, decreasing profitability, erosion of the economic conditions of small and marginal farmers, lesser employment opportunities, reduced capital investment, decreasing efficiency of resource use, increased competition and poor quality of produce. Obviously, the need of the hour is not merely an increase in quantum of credit, but rapid increase in quality of credit to tackle the above-stated problems.

The pertinent question in today's juncture is therefore whether and how agricultural credit will be able to play this desired role.

The issues confronting institutional suppliers of agricultural credit at this stage are simply too many lending to agriculture viewed as very risky with near-absence of risk-management measures, unattractive lending rates on loans below Rs. 2 lakhs, high transaction and monitoring costs, constraints in availability of latest technology, inputs and extension services, general absence of effective marketing tie-up for recovery and too much reliance on government policy support in the form of direct subsidies, concessional interest rates, liberal recovery policy, strong infrastructure support etc. Rapid erosion in the credit position of vulnerable sections of the rural population, however ridiculous it might look after 55 years of the country's Independence, is therefore a natural consequence of the underlying trends and features.

It is against this backdrop the present study is undertaken following the recommendations of the Parliamentary Standing Committee on Agriculture to study the credit flow problems of only small and marginal farmers in getting easy and cheap credit from the rural financial institutions, in general and from cooperatives, in particular.

Although the study was not originally stipulated to include farm labourers, the fact remains true that the distinction between small and marginal farmers, on the one hand, and farm labourers, on the other, is somewhat blurred. Thus small and marginal farmer households may include not only pure cultivating households depending exclusively on cultivation of their operational landholdings, but also impure cultivating households, who sell a part of their labour power in the market. Moreover, in statistical terms, the latter category seems more numerous as compared to the former one. Therefore, the study has proceeded on the premise that the credit problems of the latter category are often very similar to those of pure wage labour (i.e., landless) households.

The current study therefore aims to capture the problems of the landless category as well. As a significant part of the landless and wage earners is serviced by micro-finance institutions, the study has attempted to include inputs from that sector as well. The inclusion of micro-credit institutions is necessary to find out whether and how far such new generation institutions are making a difference to the flow of credit to this target group of farmers. Given the frequently observed limitations of traditional financial institutions, attempts have been made to include a comprehensive list of the new generation financial institutions under both formal and informal segments of the market.

Thus, the study examines the credit flow problems of not only pure cultivating households owning less than 2 hectares of land but also of landless rural households. Although landless households and households operating on 2 or more hectares of land are not the target of the study, it was found to be useful to include a small sample of such households as control.

This was done not only for providing a contrast to the credit flow problems of the latter groups, but also for examining if there is any 'crowding out' effect of credit between small and marginal farmers, on the one hand, and medium and large farmers, on the other.

The study was undertaken by 14 Agro-economic Research Centers/Units across various parts of the country and covered a period of 3 years – that is, 1997-98 to 1999-2000. The present work attempts to consolidate and supplement these individual centre studies.

Objectives of the Consolidated Study

The consolidated study has the following five objectives:

1. To review the credit experiences of traditional financial institutions-namely, commercial banks, RRBs and cooperatives and also new generation institutions engaged in micro credit activities like NBFCs, SHGs etc. specifically with respect to the vulnerable sections of the farming community (i.e., small and marginal farmer households and labour households) based on the existing literature and available documents in the country;
2. To document through a summary of case studies the innovative credit experiments of new generation rural financial institutions, especially in private and cooperative sectors in India, with respect to the same target group;
3. To summarize and consolidate the findings of AER centres/units on flow of credit to vulnerable sections of the farming community;

4. To identify and analyse the existing credit flow gaps and the reasons thereof for the same target group based on the pooled data of 14 AER units/centres on the experiences of suppliers of credit as well as borrowing households across the country; and
5. To suggest measures at both macro level and enterprise level to ensure smooth flow of credit on sustainable basis to this group.

Study Design, Methodology and Major Hypotheses

For achieving the first objective of the study, a critical evaluation is made of the functioning of traditional as well as new generation credit organizations, besides that of NABARD, the apex organization for agriculture and rural credit in the country. To fulfil the second objective, an attempt is made to summarize and consolidate the findings of individual centres' case studies on new generation credit institutions, with a view to highlighting the processes being followed by these organizations to tackle the usual problems associated with credit.

The third objective is fulfilled through preparation of a summarized and consolidated view of the descriptive results reported in individual centre studies. However, this consolidated study has performed two additional functions. First, under the fourth objective, it has performed an independent analysis of the pooled sample of 94 lending organizations across 13 states of the country. Second, under the fifth objective, it pooled sample data of 700 borrower households (collected by the participating centres) spread over 12 states to bring out the stylised facts about flow of credit to the vulnerable sections of the agricultural community. To fulfil the final objective, policy lessons have been extracted at both macro level and enterprise level for sustainable use of credit.

As failure of credit flow may be caused because of failure of either the demand side or the supply side or both, at the conceptual level the study involves understanding the credit needs of the target group (in both quantitative & qualitative terms), and examining whether the supply organisations are able to sustain the demand levels on reasonable terms.

The two major hypotheses of the study are:

Hypothesis 1: Borrower credit experiences are significantly different across villages with and without micro-credit exposure.

Hypotheses 2: Borrower credit experiences also vary across borrower households in different landholding status groups-that is, depending on whe her the borrower household is a marginal/small farmer, a landless one, or a medium/large farmer.

In order to test these hypotheses, information is collected using structured questionnaire on:

- borrower's socio-economic identity,
- lender's socio-economic identity;
- credit & non-credit activities of both borrower & lender;
- borrower's credit needs;
- borrower's transaction costs;
- lender's capacity to supply credit & credit-complementary activities;
- lender's transaction costs;
- the terms and conditions of credit;
- default on credit 1; and
- the broader economic context (including village infrastructure), in the background of which the credit transaction is taking place.

In the process of testing these two major hypotheses, attempts are also made to highlight the features of the selected villages and of the sample households, besides providing a glimpse of the lending institutions providing credit to these households.

Ideally, the default rate should have been expressed as percentage of loan demand, rather than as percentage of loan outstanding. Inadvertently, this point was missed at the beginning and could not be corrected, when detected at a later stage. It must also be pointed out in this context that different lending organizations have different practices with respect to definition of 'default' and 'overdue'. Ideally, these two terms should boil down to the same, meaning any due loan amount, which is not repaid by the due date, becomes defaulted or overdue as soon as the stipulated due date is over. However, many lending organizations treat defaulted loan amount (with reference to the due date) as overdue if it is not repaid within a stipulated time period (usually 90 days).

Hence the difference in default rate and overdue rate in our exposition of the matter.

Sampling Design followed by Individual Centers to Collect Primary Data

In order to test the two above-stated hypotheses, study areas representative of overall credit in a state were selected in consultation with NABARD regional offices. The analysis of a sample of 700-borrower households spread over 12 states has been done. The sample households are selected following a multi-stage stratified random sampling process. In the first stage, two representative villages are purposively selected from each of the selected states – one where micro finance has made a beginning and the other where micro finance is yet to make a mark.

In the next stage, information on landholding status of each household within these villages is collected from local panchayat bodies to facilitate drawing of a random sample of 25 households as per the following stratification: 5 landless households, 5 medium and large farming households (these two groups acting as two separate control groups), and 15 households spread between the two categories of marginal and small farmers in the same proportion as they occur in the population of selected villages.

The total borrower household sample includes 148 landless households, 235 marginal farming households, 171 small farming households and 145 medium and large farming households. As previously mentioned, the consolidated study also analyses the data collected from 94 lending organizations across 13 states of the country. It includes 28 commercial banks, 5 RRBs, 27 cooperatives, 2 LDBs, 2 NBFCs, 1 NGO, and 29 SHGs.

The lending organizations were requested to report the loan amounts delivered to five types of households – medium and large farmer households, small farmer households, marginal farmer households, and households engaged exclusively in non-farm activities, as well as the number of borrowers under each category for each of the three years – 1997-98, 1998-99 and 1999-2000. The purposes of loans were categorized as crop loan, other (medium & long-term) agricultural loan, off-farm loan, non-farm loan and purely consumption loan. The lending organizations were also requested to share the extent of default (as percentage of outstanding loan amount), and the extents of recovery and overdue of the defaulted amount, besides indicating the overdue figures for different categories of borrowers.

Organisation of the Study Report

The results of this study are presented in five parts. The first part reviews the experiences of rural credit institutions – commercial banks and RRBs, cooperative credit system, new generation credit institutions based on the notion of micro-credit, and NABARD, the apex organization for agriculture and rural credit. The second part summarizes the conclusions from 14 individual centre studies. The third part summarizes the processes being followed by new generation micro-credit institutions. The fourth part summarizes the results obtained from pooled data of 94 lending organizations and 700 borrower households across the country. The final part brings out the policy recommendations of this exercise.

Review of Experiences of Rural Credit Institutions

A review of the experiences of commercial banks and RRBs reveal that the infrastructure for reaching out financial services to the poor does exist in the country. There is, however, an increasing recognition that it is access to services rather than the cost that is the bottleneck in this sector. Even the RBI now admits that access to adequate credit is of more importance than the cost of credit. The softer aspects or repayment ethic, governmental intervention in the sector leading to erosion of banker-borrower trust and the system-wide dependence on low-cost capital and operating subsidies has created a lot of noise factor for the formal financial system to effectively operate. This has led to looking at financial services to the poor more as an obligation rather than as an opportunity. The recent policy changes and the thrust on growth do not seem to recognise the need to leverage the existing infrastructure. Instead it is moving towards an alternate structure of "micro-finance".

The following are the positive landmarks that have happened in the decade of the 1990s helping the rural credit sector. Since the financial crisis of the early 1990s, some significant reforms in the formal financial sector have been introduced:

- Focus on integrating micro-finance with the banking sector by the SHG linkage program;
- Restructuring of the RRBs and freeing of some interest rates;
- The self-employment schemes have been consolidated into the SGSY;
- A new private sector promoted initiative of Local Area Banks has been encouraged; and
- There is learning from countries such as Bangladesh, Indonesia, and Thailand, which indicates that institutional culture of state-owned financial institutions can be changed, given the right policy environment and incentive structures. This learning is brought into the country by the micro-finance fraternity – which is constantly lobbying with the government to ensure involvement of the mainstream structure in this activity as well.

From a review of the evolution and functioning the cooperative credit structure in this country it appears that although a great deal of emphasis and investment have been made to evolve a mammoth cooperative credit structure covering both short-term and long-term requirements, they seemed have been good in quantity and poor in quality. In other words, they simply failed to meet the high demand and expectations placed on them. So, alternatives routes to cover the domain of rural credit have been tried through creation of RRBs and rapid expansion of commercial bank branches in the rural sector. But they too failed to produce enough results. So, since the 1990s, the country has quite justifiably embarked on a course of financial sector reforms. In the process, the cooperative credit structure has been thoroughly examined and its weaknesses brought out for possible remedial actions, especially by two recent committees – one, Capoor Committee appointed by the RBI and the other, Vyas Committee appointed by NABARD. Though there is a lot of similarity in the approaches, observations and recommendations of these two committees, it is probably important to reiterate their major recommendations, as they are quite exhaustive and require a lot of efforts in the coming years to implement.

The Capoor Committee advised re-engineering around four major points – namely, member-driven cooperatives, strengthening of their resource base, especially capital, structural changes and improved management – that is, professionalization. The Vyas Committee, on the other hand, recommended (1) government financial support; (2) replacing State Cooperative Acts by Model Act to achieve effective cooperative governance; (3) fuller applicability of BR Act, 1949 to cooperative banks; (4) steps to strengthen PACS; (5) promoting SHGs as cooperatives within cooperatives for the short-term structure; (6) reforming deposit insurance as per recommendations of RBI committee of 1999; (7) selective de-layering of cooperative credit system; (8) integration of long-term and short-term structures; and (9) relaxation of norms for refinance support to cooperatives.

A review of the growing literature on new generation micro-credit institutions reveals that micro-finance has existed in India for a long time, though in other forms. It has been only in the past two decades that some particular processes of delivery have come to be formally recognised as "micro-finance". It has been recognised that there is enough scope to carry out micro-finance related activities in the country due to existence of a huge unfulfilled demand. The major debates in the field have been on the issue of sustainability versus access. Micro-finance sector has some models, which provide both high sustainability and access.

While the most important models of micro-finance in India pertain to the self-help groups, we find two other models also taking root in some parts of the country – these are named as the Grameen model and the Individual Banking model. There are concerns about the lopsided geographical growth of the micro-finance movement, which has triggered off largely in South India. There is also a general consensus that micro-finance does not solve the problems of the credit needs of small and marginal farmers. It only provides a bridge to the small and the marginal to access mainstream institutions. Therefore, strategies for embedding micro-finance organizations in mainstream credit institutions deserve urgent policy attention.

Based on an review of its functioning over the last two decades, the study has also attempted to provide an overview of NABARD – highlighting its major achievements as well as the issues for its future development. Its major achievements are: • In organizational terms, NABARD has developed a vast network over the last two decades. It has now regional offices in all state headquarters, besides 319 DDM offices in most of the district headquarters and 5 training establishments. As of August, 2002, it has a share capital of Rs. 2000 crores, total working funds to the tune of Rs. 38,816 crores, and a staff strength of 5400, of which about 2900 (54%) are professionals.

- During 1996-97 to 2000-01, total financial support from NABARD increased from Rs. 12,003 crores to Rs. 17,999 crores. During the same period, short-term credit support increased from Rs. 7,023 crores to Rs. 8,486 crores, whereas the same under medium/long-term structure and RIDF increased from Rs. 3,893 crores to Rs. 6,336 crores and from Rs. 1,087 crores to Rs. 3,177 crores, respectively. Thus, support under the last two categories increased at a much faster rate than in the first one.

- RIDF disbursements till 30 th September, 2001 are believed to have made a large impact on the economy through completion of sanctioned government projects. The total contribution to GDP is estimated at Rs. 7202 crores. Irrigation potential is reported to have increased by 59.62 lakh hectares; direct recurring employment generation has been of the tune of 35.33 lakh man-days, besides addition of another 8,868 lakh non-recurring man-days. 1,04,014 kilometres of road length and 1,95,109 meters of bridge length with additional 9,437 lakh man days of non-recurring employment have also been created as a result of RIDF disbursements.
- Micro-finance, Kisan Credit Card (KCC) scheme and watershed approach are some of the important development initiatives of NABARD in recent years. The SHG-Bank Linkage Program providing micro-finance access to 53 lakh poor households through 3.11 lakh SHGs and with an outreach nearly 2.5 times the same of the Grameen Bank of Bangladesh is now the world's largest micro-finance program. With 1.54 crores KCCs issued till June 2001, the KCC scheme has also been well received. Under the watershed approach, 95 projects covering 88,000-hectare area have been functioning under IGWDP scheme of NABARD. Another 63 projects have been sanctioned in 6 states till August, 2002 out of Watershed Development Fund.
- Other important development initiatives of NABARD include restructuring of RRBs. It has resulted in 172 out of 196 RRBs in current profits, and 79 of them have wiped out their losses. With support from Cooperative Development Fund, NABARD has started Development Action Plans (DAPs) and Organization Development Initiatives (ODIs) to sensitise cooperative banks on viability issues. In the rural non-farm sector, 52 lakh persons have been employed till August 2002 in 15 lakh micro enterprise units, as a result of refinance support

to the tune of Rs. 10,010 crores. 23 districts in the country have been covered under District Rural Industries Project (DRIP). 80,700 rural youth have been covered till August 2002 under entrepreneurship development programs. 4921 Farmers' Clubs have been functioning in 418 districts of the country as a result of direct encouragements from NABARD.

In spite of its vast network and such an impressive record of performance, concerns are expressed in various quarters about the functioning of NABARD as the apex organization of this country with respect to rural and agricultural development in general and with respect to rural credit in particular. At a conceptual level, such an apex organization is expected to develop a thorough understanding and a perspective on both demand and supply sides of credit in relation to development, such that not only innovative credit and related financial products are produced and supplied at low costs as per clientele requirements (thus shifting to the right the supply curve of such services), but also pro-active steps are taken to boost up its effective demand (i.e., demand backed up by willingness to repay and make further use of credit in the future to expand business), thus shifting to the right the demand curve for such services. If both demand and supply curves for credit are progressively shifted to the right, it is certain that an increasingly larger quantum of credit (in real terms) will be absorbed by the economy, resulting in continuous expansion of business of not only NABARD, but also of its clients all over the country. If this shift to the right of the supply curve of credit happens to be stronger than the rightward shift in the demand curve, not only consumption in quantum of credit will jump, but also price of credit will fall in real terms, thus improving competitive edge of any project supported by credit. A futures perspective of NABARD must aim at undertaking action plans so as to move in that direction.

Credit being a means to support another transaction rather than an end in itself, demand for credit is essentially a derived demand, which is derived from the client's demand for an underlying product or service. So, unless pro-active steps are taken by credit supplying organizations to promote clients' projects involving demand for goods and services, demand for credit would not be boosted up and even if boosted up, it will fail to be an 'effective' demand backed by strong willingness to repay and make further use of credit – the typical problem this country is facing today.

In other words, the role of an apex credit organization is far more than mere deliver of credit, or mere supervision of credit. Although promotional activities of NABARD are still there, it appears that over time NABARD is being progressively overburdened by governmental supervisory functions, as if like a part of the Finance Ministry of the Government of India, whereas its pro-active role as promoter of demand for credit and also as leader in delivery of cheapest line of credit refinance is taking a back seat. The pro-active role of a financial institution can be elaborated with the example of the background for New Generation Cooperative (NGC) development in North Dakota during 1980s, where the bankers played the role of a leader in a partnership with governmental departments and local cooperatives to turnaround existing enterprise structures and re-vitalize the area's economy.

Issues Brought out by Individual AER Center/Unit Studies

The issues brought out by individual AER Center/Unit studies can be broadly divided into five groups: (1) Defects in credit schemes/projects; (2) Defects in the credit delivery system; (3) High borrower transaction costs in accessing credit; (4) Insufficient credit-complementary services; and (5) Inadequate monitoring of credit.

These points are elaborated below.

The following defects, identified in existing credit schemes and projects, need to be removed:

(1) Lack of integration of credit schemes meant for target groups in rural areas resulting in inadequate flow of credit to small and marginal farmers;

(2) Inadequate provision for marketing finance to small and marginal farmers, leading to distress sale of production soon after harvesting of crops;

(3) Inadequacy of scale of finance to meet prevailing price of inputs;

(4) Non-availability of credit for non-farm sectors like dairy, poultry, fisheries to small borrower from formal sources because of lack of security;

(5) Non-availability of consumption credit from formal institutions – forcing poor to go to informal sources at a high interest rate;

(6) Activity-wise distribution of loan does not provide much help to small and marginal farmers in getting loan from formal institutions;

(7) Provision of subsidy in SGSY scheme has been harming the formation of SHGs;

(8) Credit support for only traditional cropping pattern;

(9) Absence of special credit schemes to tackle seasonal unemployment; and

(10) Lack of villagers' participation.

Defects in the credit delivery system include: (1) Lack of well-versed staff in the coop sector at branch level; hence time taken in processing and approving of loans is more; (2) Lack of regular interaction between staff and borrowers, leading to apprehension and fear to seek loans from formal sources; and (3) Inadequate and untimely availability of crop loan from coop banks are causes for unbalanced use of inputs in crops of small and marginal farmers.

High borrower transaction costs seem to be arising from (1) Inflexibility in terms of loaning design in formal institutions is a constraint to approach the banks; and (2) Demand for security and collateral for small loans from formal institutions. Besides this, documentation is elaborate and troublesome for small/marginal farmers. On the other hand, absence of suitable credit-complementary services is found to be reflected in

(1) Absence of provision for rescheduling of loan in formal institutions puts borrowers in hardship; (2) Lack of infrastructure facilities and conducive atmosphere, NGOs and micro-finance institutions are unable to spread their financial activities in rural areas and weed out professional moneylenders; (3) Poor recovery of money and recycling of funds; and (4) Interference of State Govt. creating hurdles for bankers in their efficient functioning.

At the same time, inadequate monitoring of loans gets reflected in lapses on proper maintenance of loan record and extension services on the part of financial institutions to make borrowers fearless to divert the loans to other purposes.

Highlights of the Processes followed by New Generation Institutions

A review of the cases and case-lets prepared by various AER Centers and Units in course of this study reveals certain distinctive features of the processes followed by these organizations.

Findings from Pooled Data of Lending Organizations and Borrowers

Although the pooled sample data of 94 lending organizations across 13 states of the country is not drawn at random, nor does it cover all lending institutions in the areas of this study, the results derived out of this fragmented data seem to be quite indicative of the ground realities:

- As expected, the average annual loan amount and the average number of borrowers handled annually are considerably larger for traditional (around Rs.180 lakhs and about 2000 borrowers, respectively) as compared to non-traditional lending organizations (Rs.11 lakhs and 110-150 borrowers, respectively).
- The traditional lending organizations have a tendency to concentrate on medium and large farmers, and small farmer categories (their joint shares being about 66% in terms of loan amount and about 57% in terms of

borrower coverage), whereas their non-traditional counterparts seem to be concentrating more on marginal farmers and landless categories (their corresponding shares being 68-71% in terms of loan amount and 68-70% in terms of number of borrowers).

- Except in cases of NGOs and SHGs, borrowers from medium and large farmer groups have managed to corner a disproportionately large share of loan as compared to their importance in total number of borrowers. As is normally expected, non-farm households have usually a higher loan share than their share in the number of borrowers with respect to most loan sources.
- In the commercial bank and RRB category. states like Maharashtra, Haryana, Punjab and Gujarat seem to have a much larger average annual lending activity compared to the rest, and especially vis-à-vis AP, Assam, Bihar, MP, UP and West Bengal, which are on the lower end. In the cooperative group, not only developed states like Punjab, Haryana, Maharashtra and Gujarat, but even relatively backward states like Assam, TN and UP appear on the higher end of the spectrum in terms of average annual lending operations. In contrast, states of AP, HP, Karnataka, MP and West Bengal (of course, after leaving out one large DCCB from the WB sample) have much smaller lending operations per unit. Average annual loan figures for NGOs and SHGs are highest in Karnataka, moderate in Gujarat, Assam and HP, and are especially small in AP, Haryana and Maharashtra. Although the sample is far from a representative one, it seems to reflect at least a part of the reality.
- While both traditional and non-traditional lending institutions concentrate on crop loans, non-farm loans and to a lesser extent on other agricultural loans, the latter too has smaller percentage shares in all three types of loans, thus reflecting considerable competition between these two broad types of lending institutions in these loans. Given negligible share of traditional lenders as compared to as much as 26-30 percentage

share of non-traditional lenders in consumption loans, the relation between the two broad categories of lenders appear to be complementary rather than one of competition with respect to consumption loans. Thus, if a credit package needs to contain both production and consumption loans to meet the overall demand for credit by smaller farmers, there is tremendous need for coordination between these two types of lending operations when demand for these loans are met by separate organizations.

- While default rates (as % of outstanding amount) have steadily come down over years for traditional lenders, this is far from the case with respect to non-traditional lenders (though these figures are considerably lower for them – only 5-7%). • While default rates (about 19-27%) and overdue rates (about 22-39%) are fairly comparable across commercial banks, cooperatives, RRBs, LDBs, NBFCs and NGOs, they seem to be slightly lower for the last four categories. These rates are considerably lower for SHGs (a maximum of 4% and 12%, respectively). While there is a tendency for these rates to decline over the three-year period under consideration, the pattern is far from uniform and consistent. In fact, the overdue rates seem to have gone up for cooperatives and RRBs between 1997-98 and 1999-00.

As mentioned earlier, the study has also attempted to bring out the stylized features of rural credit based on analysis of three-year (namely, 1997-98, 1998-99 and 1999-2000) credit experiences of a sample of 700 borrower households drawn through a multi-stage stratified random sampling process from 12 states. Although 74 of the sample households didn't borrow during the study period, the study treats all the 700 sample households as potential borrowing households to determine how their village and household characteristics influence their credit experiences.

Credit being a package of service with multifarious dimensions like borrower's access, purpose, explicit interest rate, collateral, borrower transaction costs, extent of shortfall in supply of credit, default on loans, duration of borrower's relationship with lending institutions, nature of interest charges (whether upfront or later alongside instalment payments), extent of flexibility allowed to borrowers in loan repayment, borrower's comfort level vis-à-vis lending institutions, borrower's recommendation (to other customers) index for the lending institutions, and the expressed interest of borrower to leave certain lending institutions and shift to some others based on past experiences, statistical tables are used to explain variation in these credit attributes in terms of borrower characteristics, especially in terms of holding size of borrower households.

Access to credit: On this aspect, as much as 37% sample households are found to have borrowed from only formal source, 17% from both sources, 35% from only informal sources, and about 11% from neither source. Among landless borrowers, only 24% are found to have borrowed only from formal source. On the other hand, as many as 33% of landless households depend on both sources of credit, whereas the corresponding figures are only 16%, 11% and 9%, respectively, for marginal farmers, small farmers and their larger counterparts. It is important to note in this context that about 41-42% of marginal and small farmers seem to have developed exclusive dependence on formal sources. As we have saw about 81% and 58% of borrower households have accessed formal and informal sources of credit to claim, respectively, 71% and 29% of credit shares. In terms of numbers, local informal lenders have maximum clientele group among the borrowers (58%), followed by cooperatives (52%), commercial banks (34%) and SHGs (21%). The corresponding shares of loan of these four major sources are 29%, 35%, 32% and 4%, respectively. Obviously, average loan size per borrower is the largest for commercial bank group, moderate for cooperative group and relatively small for informal lenders and SHGs.

While testing whether households with access to credit and especially to formal source of credit have distinctive characteristics (in terms of four types of household characteristics: (a) educational and demographic characteristics, (b) agricultural production characteristics, (c) asset holding status, and (d) income earning capacity) as compared to their counterpart without such access, it is found that only households with such stronger socio-economic-political power have got better access to formal sources of credit.

Impor ance of Lending Sources in Borrowers' Loan Por folio: While examining the relative importance of different loan sources, it appears that the share of the commercial bank group enters prominently in the loan portfolio of landless and small farmer borrowers (about 64% and 50%, respectively). The cooperative group enters prominently in the loan portfolio of marginal farmers (33%), medium and large farmers (29%) and small farmers (only 18%), with very little coverage of the landless group, for understandable reasons (namely, their emphasis on landed collateral). Local informal lenders have a fairly uniform presence in the loan portfolio of landless group and marginal/small farmers (with share varying between 18% and 21%), but their weight is considerably higher (36%) in the loan portfolio of the largest group of borrowers. As expected, SHGs have made their presence felt in the loan portfolio of landless (12%) and marginal farmers (13%), whereas NBFCs have made some dent in the loan portfolio of small farmers and medium/large farmers (with 12% shares in each case). Chit funds have a negligible role in the loan portfolio of the present sample of borrowers.

Purpose-wise Distribution o Loans

Among loans for different purposes, it is found that the importance of production loan varies within a range of 68-88% for the four borrower groups, whereas the incidence of consumption loan is rather low-less than 0.5% for the two largest size groups, less than 1% for marginal farmers and about 2% for the landless group. The incidence of human capital investment loan is relatively high for landless, marginal farmers and small farmers (varying within 15-31%), and rather low for the largest land holding group (about 1%).

Though it may not be by design, but in practice, formal sources are found to have met 100% of consumption loan needs of small farmers, 83% for landless people, 57% for marginal farmers and 56% for the largest land holding group. Commercial banks are the main source of such consumption loans for landless households (64%), whereas cooperatives constitute the main source for other three classes of households (44-80%).

So far the incidence of consumption loan needs of various groups met by SHGs is a meagre 1%, 13% and 28%, respectively, for landless, marginal farmer and small farmer households. It is probably high time to legitimize accommodation of a reasonable percentage of consumption needs in the loan portfolio of major formal sector lenders – namely, commercial banks and coops.

Formal sources meet 85-98% of production credit needs of the four size groups of borrowers, the highest figure being observed in case of medium and large farmers. The main contributors to formal sources of production credit are commercial banks (49%), NBFCs and SHGs (17% each) for landless households, commercial banks (35%), cooperatives (32%) and SHGs (20%) for marginal farmer households, commercial banks (43%), cooperatives (20%) and NBFCs (17%) for small farmer households, and NBFCs (86%), cooperatives and commercial banks (6% each) for the largest land holding group. Informal lenders contribute only 9-15% of production loans for the first three size groups of borrowers, and a mere 2% of production loans for the largest size group. While the role of informal lenders, NBFCs and SHGs in production credit may look supplementary in percentage terms, criticality of their intervention in meeting credit needs of especially landless, marginal and small categories of households ought not to be lost sight of. High importance of NBFC lending in meeting production credit needs of the largest land holding group deserves special mention in this context.

Informal lenders seem to be playing a very critical role through supply of human capital loan (for meeting educational and health needs) to the order of 24-44% for the sample households. The role played by SHGs deserves special mention in this context. It seems formal sector institutions like commercial banks and cooperatives are yet to tap this potential fully.

Explicit Interest Rates

On explicit annual interest rate charged as price of credit, the observed variation of formal sector interest rate across borrowers is to be attributed to variation in the composition of loans across borrowers. This is especially true of commercial bank and cooperative categories, which are subject to interest rate regulations. Interest on informal sector loans, however, varies more across individuals and even irrespective of size and purpose. The observed average pattern is as follows. Very high average annual interest rates are observed on loans from Chit funds (27%), local informal lenders (25%), NBFCs (20%), and SHGs (19%). Considerably lower interest rates are observed for loans from cooperatives (13%) and commercial banks (11%). As expected, informal sector loans attract much higher interest rates as compared to formal sector loans (25% as compared to 13%), and this is true of all size classes of borrowers. For both formal and informal sector loans taken together, interest rate variation is found to be larger, the smaller the size group of borrowers' land holding – only 12-24% for medium and large farmers, 11-27% for small farmers, 9-25% for marginal farmers, and 10-42% for landless households.

Type and Incidence of Collateral Used

The relative importance of different types of collateral in terms of their use is found to follow the following descending order: personal guarantee (49%), group guarantee (20%), interlinked contract (16%) and tangible collateral (15%). Within the category of interlinked credit transactions, the incidence of input purchases from the lender (12%) far outweighs the incidence of labor or output sale (3% and 0.38%, respectively). While group guarantee is used in nearly 30% cases as a collateral by formal credit institutions, it is hardly used by the informal segment (its incidence being only 0.36%). However, informal sources of credit use all other forms of collateral more intensively as compared to their formal counterparts. A significant difference is observed in percentage usage of interlinked form of credit between informal and formal sources of credit (29% as compared to only 9%). Landless household borrowers are found to be using tangible assets and interlinked labour transactions as collateral much more intensively than an average borrower in the entire sample. Marginal farmer households use group guarantee and interlinked labour and output sale as collateral more intensively than an average borrower. While personal and group guarantees are more favoured as collateral by both small farmer and medium/large farmer groups, the former group seems to have a stronger bias in the choice of interlinked input purchase transaction as collateral against credit.

Borrower Transaction Costs

In terms of monetary and non-monetary transaction costs borrowers incur per loan (the former estimated as the monetary value of documentation cost, application cost, and cost of foregone opportunities while undertaking trips to the lender for loan approval, besides bribing cost, while the latter estimated as the average number of days taken between filing of application for a loan and its disbursement on approval), various lending institutions can be ranked in the following descending order: commercial banks & RRBs (Rs.538), chit funds (Rs.160), cooperatives (Rs.144.27), NBFCs (Rs.76), local informal lenders (Rs.60) and SHGs (Rs.52). When ranked in terms of monetary transaction cost per rupee of loan this ranking changes slightly: commercial banks & RRBs (0.05), cooperatives (0.04), NBFCs (0.02), informal lenders (0.02), SHGs (0.02) and chit funds (0.01). Formal sources have higher monetary transaction cost than informal sources both per loan (Rs.322 versus Rs.65) and per rupee of loan (0.04 versus 0.02).

For commercial banks and RRBs, monetary transaction cost per rupee of loan is highest for small farmers (0.07), moderate for the largest landholding group (0.04) and smaller for landless and marginal farmer group (0.01-0.02). For cooperatives, this figure is highest for the landless group (0.08), moderate for small and medium/large group (0.02-0.03) and lowest for marginal farmers (0.01). For informal lenders, it is highest for small farmers (0.03), moderate for landless and marginal farmer group (0.02) and negligible for the largest size group of borrowers (0.003). For SHGs, this figure is only a bit lower for the two larger size groups as compared to the same for the landless and marginal farmers, thus displaying a high degree of uniformity around a figure of 0.02.

Non-monetary transaction cost per loan (in terms of days taken by lender to disburse a loan after application is filed) is highest for commercial banks and RRBs (23.1), second highest for SHGs (22.6), third highest for cooperatives (16.4), lower for NBFCs (11.3), chit funds (10.3), and the lowest for local informal lenders (5.5). This figure is consistently lower for all informal lenders than for formal lenders for all four size groups of borrowers. Non-monetary transaction costs are also the highest for medium and large size group of borrowers and considerably lower for the other three groups in case of loans from commercial banks and RRBs. This is also true for loans from all formal sector loans, loans from SHGs and loans from chit funds. The pattern is exactly the opposite for cooperatives. There is no clear pattern for informal lenders.

Because of conscious efforts being made in this study to avoid confusion between notional and effective demand for credit at the prevailing market rate of interest, the resulting percentage gap between demand for and supply of credit has turned out to be quite moderate and fairly comparable between formal and informal sources (8% and 9%, respectively). This figure however varies between 4.63% for SHGs and 27.33% for chit funds. While the extent of shortfall between demand and supply seems to be relatively more for landless and marginal farmer group of borrowers as compared to the other two groups for loans from cooperatives and also for SHGs (though to a lesser extent), the pattern is a mixed one for loans from commercial banks and RRBs, and also for traditional informal lenders.

Default on Loans

The overall loan default rate (as percentage of loan outstanding) is found to be around 19%, though it is a bit higher for landless borrowers (22%) and a bit lower for the largest size group of borrowers (17%). Default rates for marginal and small farmers are fairly close to the overall average. Between formal and informal loan sources, default rates are always lower for the former and higher for the latter category except for medium/ large farmer group. Although it may appear counter-intuitive, the exposure of informal credit sector to borrowers in general and to borrowers of smaller means in particular over a longer period of time as compared to the same for formal sector credit probably explains this phenomenon.

Continuity of Borrower-Lender Relationship

Regarding various borrower households' past credit experience in years with various loan sources, it appears that it is a monotone increasing function of borrower's landholding status. Moreover, informal lenders have consistently longer period of credit experience with their borrowers than their counterparts in the formal sector. For the entire sample of 700 borrowers, informal lenders have on average about 12 years of credit history with respect their borrowers. The corresponding figures are 8.45, 4.65, 4.57, 2.50 and 1.33 for cooperatives, commercial banks and RRBs, chit funds, SHGs and NBFCs, respectively.

Incidence of Upfront Interest Payments

Incidence of interest payments upfront rather than later (along with repayment of principal in instalments) seems to be highest for loans provided by chit funds (57%), followed by traditional informal lenders (33%), SHGs (23%), NBFCs (15%), cooperatives (5%) and commercial banks and RRBs (2%). It is also consistently higher for informal lenders (as compared to the figures for formal lenders). It is however important to point out that even within the category of informal loans, the incidence of upfront interest payment is much higher for landless, marginal farmer and small farmer borrowers (varying between 34 to 40%) than for the largest size class of borrowers (only 17%).

Flexibility in Loan Rescheduling

In terms of flexibility of loan rescheduling as permitted by lenders, the highest figure is reported for chit funds (100%), followed by traditional informal lenders (76%), SHGs (46%), cooperatives (42%), NBFCs (33%) and commercial banks and RRBs (19%). This flexibility index is consistently higher for informal lenders vis-à-vis formal lenders, irrespective of the size class of borrowers. However, for all types of loans taken together, this flexibility index is lowest for landless borrowers (66%) and highest for the largest size group of borrowers (81%). The corresponding figures are 73% and 75% for marginal and small farmer borrowers.

Borrower's Comfort with Loan Source

In terms of borrower comfort level with respect to alternative loan sources, the highest comfort level (equal to 1) is found to have been enjoyed by the maximum percentage of clients of SHGs (87%), followed by clients of cooperatives (69%), NBFCs (50%), commercial banks & RRBs (47%), traditional informal lenders (23%) and chit funds (14%). For this group, the worst experience (i.e., a comfort level of 5) is confronted by 35% of customers of traditional informal lenders, 29% of chit fund borrowers, 14% of commercial bank/RRB borrowers, 7% of cooperative borrowers and 2% of SHG borrowers.

Borrower's Recommendation Index for Alternative Loan Sources

In terms of borrower recommendation level (to friends, based on past experiences) for each loan source, which varies between 1 (best recommendation) and 5 (poorest recommendation), it is found that SHGs have the best recommendation index (1.38), followed by commercial banks and RRBS (1.45), cooperatives (1.48), traditional informal lenders (3.49), chit funds (3.50) and NBFCs (4.50). This recommendation index is invariably better for formal lenders as compared to the same for informal lenders, irrespective of the size group of borrowers. In fact, this index always varies between 1 and 2 for commercial banks & RRBs, cooperatives and SHGs, whereas it invariably exceeds 3 for informal lenders. This is true of all size groups of borrowers in the sample.

Borrower's Desire to leave Specific Lending Source in favour of Another: From the frequency distribution of borrowers of different categories, who have revealed their desire to leave specific lending institutions in favor of others, it is found that the extent of desired net inflow of customers is nearly 26% for commercial banks and RRBs, 22% in favour of cooperatives, and only 3% for SHGs, whereas the order of net outflow of customers is 49% and 1%, respectively, for traditional informal lenders and chit funds. Moreover, the tendency to move towards commercial banks and RRBs is much stronger for landless and medium/large size groups of borrowers as compared to the same for marginal and small farmers. Similarly, small, medium and large farmers are more keen to join cooperatives as their desired source of credit (around 33% and 29%, respectively) than landless and marginal landholding class of borrowers (13% each). All size groups of borrowers want to move away from traditional informal lenders in terms of net outflow of customers from this source. However, this tendency is much stronger for small farmers (-72%) and medium/large farmers (-63%) than for the other two groups (-38% and –31%, respectively). In terms of net flows of customers, 7% of borrowers from landless group and 2% from marginal farmers seem to like to move away from SHGs, whereas 17% of small farmers and 4% of medium/large farmers want to get into the fold of SHGs.

Factors explaining quantitative attributes of loan: Four types of quantitative attributes are considered: (i) total size of loan from all sources, (ii) percentage of loan received from formal credit sources, (iii) percentage of consumption loan, and (iv) extent of gap between loan demanded and supplied. The major and statistically significant findings are summarized below:

Role of Village Attributes

- Proximity of Panchayat office to the borrower's village seems to have boosted up his credit share from the formal sector and reduced percentage gap between demand and supply of credit to him.
- Proximity of market place and bus route to the borrower's village is found to have contributed to an increase in the overall size of loan to him.

- Borrowers from villages with larger incidence of non-farm employment seem to have attracted a smaller loan size, smaller demand-supply gap, but a larger share of consumption loan.
- Borrowers from villages with higher incidence of upper caste population are found to have attracted a larger share of formal sector credit and a smaller share of consumption loan.
- Borrowers from villages with higher male literacy rates have generally taken a smaller share of consumption loan.

Role of Household Attributes

- A larger family size of borrower household is found to have ended up with a larger demand-supply gap in loan.
- Borrower households with a larger percentage of working population, as typically found in poorer households, are found to have enjoyed a smaller share of formal credit, but a larger share of consumption loan.
- Borrowers with a larger size of operational holding are found to be incurring more than average amount of expenditure on purchase of agricultural inputs.
- Borrower households involved in local level organizations seem to have captured, as expected, a larger than average loan size.
- Borrowers with a larger incidence of cash crops on their agricultural land seem to have ended up having a larger demand-supply gap in loan and a larger share on consumption loan. This is expected as putting more land on cash crops tends to increase demand for loan proportionately more than increase in supply (due to built-in inflexibility of stipulated scale of finance for crop loans), besides increasing demand for consumption loans to meet consumption expenses before such crops are marketed.
- While familiarity with important local personalities is found to have increased borrower's share of formal credit,

it has increased the gap between credit demand and credit supply – apparently because it has increased credit demand proportionately more than credit supply.

- The borrower family's access to official extension service channel seems to have helped reduce demand-supply gap in credit and increase the family's share in consumption loan.
- As expected, borrower families having a larger share of income from trade and services (which is generally more stable as compared to agricultural income), are found to have enjoyed a larger share of formal credit and a larger share of consumption credit, as compared to an average borrower.
- A longer period of association with lending institutions has similarly contributed to achieving a larger loan size and a larger percentage of consumption loan.
- Borrower families having comparatively larger (relative) comfort/recommendation levels based on their past experiences for formal sources of credit have naturally got a larger share of formal credit.
- While access to either source of credit (formal or informal) has positive effect on the total size of loan enjoyed by the borrower, this impact coefficient is larger and statistically significant for the informal source, while it is smaller and far from statistically significant for the formal source of credit. Similarly, while access to both sources of credit tends to increase share of consumption loan, the impact is larger and statistically significant only for the informal source of credit. Exactly the opposite is observed for these access variables with respect to demand-supply gap in loan – the impact is negative, larger in absolute terms and statistically significant only in case of access to formal source of credit.
- Total loan size equation seems to have a larger intercept term for all other size groups of borrowers, as compared to the same for the largest size group.

- The share of formal credit, while it tends to be less for all three smaller landholding groups of borrowers as compared to the largest group, it is significantly only in case of landless borrowers.
- The demand-supply gap in credit has a tendency to be larger for all three smaller landholding groups (as compared to the same for medium and large farmer households), but it is statistically significant in none of the cases.
- The share of consumption loan seem to be the highest for the landless group of borrowers, higher for marginal and small groups, and the smallest for the largest landholding group of borrowers.

Role of Other Loan Attributes

- Total loan size is found to have a negative and significant effect on the demand-supply gap in loan.
- The negative and significant effect of informal sector interest rate on the share of formal sector loan signifies complementary rather than competitive relation between formal and informal-the two broad sources of credit.
- Percentage of monetary transaction cost for formal source of credit has a natural negative and significant effect on the total size of loan, but overall non-monetary transaction cost has a positive and significant association with the same variable.
- When more flexibility is imparted in loan repayments, it tends to significantly increase demand-supply gap in credit.
- Greater incidence of monitoring and counselling of loans by lender leads to significantly reduce the extent of demand-supply gap in loans and the incidence of consumption loans.

Factors Determining Borrower Transaction Costs

Two different measures of overall transaction costs are constructed – monetary transaction cost as percentage of total loan size, and number of days' gap between application and approval of loan, which is probably the most important determinant of the non-monetary efforts a potential borrower has to put in order to get a loan. They are found to be influenced by the following factors:

Role of Village Attributes

- The location of the borrower's village in a place where micro-financing has made a beginning has a positive and significant effect on the measure of non-monetary transaction costs for the simple reason that micro-finance organizations generally follow a rigorous process of verification of the borrower's credentials between application for and approval of a loan.
- Proximity of Panchayat to borrower's village or higher incidences of upper caste population in borrower's village are found to pull down borrower's monetary transaction costs in a significant way.

Role of Household Attributes

- Borrower's household size, annual household expenditure on purchase of provisions, incidence of use of tangible collateral and access to formal source of credit are found to have significant negative impact on monetary transaction costs, whereas incidence of cash crops being grown by the borrower household and number of years' association of borrower family with credit institutions are observed to have significant negative effects.
- Monetary transaction costs seem to be smaller for households with smaller rather than larger size of land holdings, but this effect is found to be significant for only landless group of borrowers.
- A larger order of extension of borrower household, a higher incidence of use of tangible collateral, and greater access to formal source of credit seem to have positive and significant impact on the measure of non-monetary

transaction costs, whereas a higher incidence of irrigation on borrower's agricultural land, a higher incidence of production of cash crops by the borrower's household, a larger number of years' association of borrower with credit institutions and a greater access to informal source of credit, too, have significant but exactly the opposite effects.

- The three smaller size group of borrowers incur significantly lesser non-monetary transaction costs as compared to their larger counterpart (and this is more so for the landless group of borrowers).

Role of Endogenous Loan Attributes

- Total loan size and incidence of monitoring and counselling are found to have significant negative effects on monetary transaction costs, whereas greater flexibility provided in loan repayment clauses is found to have exactly the opposite effect.

Factors Explaining Interest Rates on Loans

Three types of annual interest rates are considered: those on formal sector loans, those on informal sector loans and overall interest rate (which is an weighted average of the first two). The interest rate on formal sector loans, however, due to government interest rate regulations. The determining factors are identified below:

Role of Village Attributes

- Proximity to nearest market place seems to have the effect of significantly pulling down interest rate across the board, while villages with higher male literacy rates – apparently through influencing the term structure in favor of longer-duration loans-seem to have attracted statistically significant higher interest rate on formal credit.
- Borrowers living in villages with larger bovine stock per head and a larger percentage of working population

engaged in non-farm business and services seem to have confronted significantly lower overall interest rate.

Role of Household Attributes

- Household size has a positive and significant effect on formal sector interest rate • Incidence of cash crop on borrower's agricultural land has significant negative effect on both informal and overall interest rates.
- Incidence of borrower's loan being adjusted against borrower's sale of output to the lender – a prominent feature of informal credit – has a significant negative effect on informal sector interest rate.
- Percentage of borrower family income arising out of trade and services has significant and negative effect on both formal and overall interest rates.
- Borrower family's access to official extension services – probably through its influence on size and term structure of loans-seems to have significantly raised interest rates across the board. Apparently for similar reason, incidence of deposit holding by borrower seems to have significantly increased interest rate on formal credit.
- Incidence of use of tangible collateral by borrower household has for understandable reasons significant negative effect on interest on formal credit.
- While longer duration of association between borrower and lending institution has a negative and significant effect on formal sector interest rate, the relation is exactly the opposite in the informal credit sector.
- Borrowing household's involvement in local level organizations – apparently through its influence on size and term structure of loans) – seem to have both positive and significant effects on informal and overall interest rates.
- While annual per capita family income has a negative and significant effect on the interest rate on informal credit, incidence of child labor in borrower household has exactly the opposite effect on the same variable.

- While access to both formal and informal credit tends to raise the overall interest rate on loan, the effect is larger and statistically significant only in case of informal sector loan.
- Compared to the largest landholding group of borrowers, landless and marginal farmer households pay significantly higher interest rate on formal credit (the additional interest payment is again higher for landless group as compared to the case of marginal farmers). The overall interest rate is however consistently and significantly higher for the three smaller size groups of borrowers as compared to the largest size group of borrowers. While this interest rate is on average 4.11% higher for the landless group, this difference is only 2.8% for marginal farmer group and 1.95% for small farmers. Contrary to the common belief, interest rates are not significantly higher (as compared to the same for medium and large farmers) in the informal credit market for the smaller landholding groups of farmers, nor are there any consistent hierarchy of interest rates, as observed in case of formal sector credit.

Role of Endogenous Loan Attributes

- Total loan has a positive but statistically insignificant effect on the overall interest rate.
- A higher percentage of production loan (i.e., a lower percentage of consumption loan) has a negative and significant effect on the overall interest rate.
- Less flexibility in loan repayment procedures is found to have generated a lower interest rate on formal credit.
- In the informal market for credit, a greater incidence of upfront interest payment, a larger incidence of monitoring by lender and a higher default on loans are found to have led to a higher interest rate on informal credit.
- Factors explaining incidence of upfront interest payments, monitoring/counseling of borrower, extent of

flexibility permitted in loan repayment provisions and percentage of default on loans: To explain the first two attributes, single-equation logistic regressions have been tried, whereas regular OLS regressions are tried to explain the rest.

Role of Village Attributes

- The incidence of upfront interest payments is found to be significantly less in villages, where micro-finance has made its appearance.
- Proximity of borrower's village to local Panchayat office seems to have given a boost to the overall default rate, which is also found to be a statistically significant result.
- Distance of the borrower's village from the nearest market place seems to have encouraged incidence of upfront interest payment, increased flexibility in loan repayments – apparently under government policy influence, and reduced the default rate on loans.
- Borrowers from villages with higher incidence of upper caste population seem to have confronted a lower order of flexibility in loan repayment, but exactly the 6
- It may be recalled that the flexibility parameter varies from 1 to 5, with 1 in cases of perfect flexibility and 5 in cases of perfect inflexibility in repayment provisions. opposite seems to have happened to borrowers from villages with a higher percentage of male literacy rates.
- Greater bovine stock per head in borrower's village has apparently increased the risks involved in loaning and consequently increased the incidence of upfront loan payments and loan monitoring.

Role of Household Attributes

- Household size has significant and positive effect on percentage default and flexibility in loan repayment, and it also significantly reduces the incidence of upfront interest payments.

- Increase in size of operational land holding significantly increases the incidence of monitoring and counseling of loan and decreases the extent of loan default (though not statistically significantly).
- Availability of greater irrigation facilities on borrower's land also significantly increases the incidence of loan monitoring.
- Both greater incidence of cash crops on borrower's land as well as greater borrower's access to official extension service channel reduce the extent of loan default, but whereas the former significantly increase flexibility in loan repayment, the latter does exactly the opposite – that is, borrowers enjoying government extension services confront lesser flexibility in loan repayment.
- Borrowers with higher values of crop output per hectare and with greater familiarity with local bureaucracy enjoy greater flexibility in loan repayment. Such familiarity index also significantly reduces the incidence of upfront interest payments and monitoring of loans.
- Longer association with credit institutions reduces the default rate (and significantly so).
- Incidence of use of tangible collateral is found to be associated with lower incidence of upfront interest payments, but lesser flexibility in loan repayments and a higher rate of loan default.
- Access to both sources of credit significantly reduces incidence of upfront interest payments and loan monitoring, though the effect is much stronger for informal credit. Access to formal credit reduces flexibility in loan repayment, whereas access to informal credit does exactly the opposite. Access to both sources has a tendency to raise the default rate, but this impact is statistically significant only for borrowers of informal loan.
- The incidence of loan monitoring is consistently and significantly higher for borrowers with smaller land

holding size (as compared to the same for medium and large farmers), and other things remaining the same, it is the highest with the landless group.

- Only the landless group of borrowers has comparatively and statistically significantly lower default rate as compared the reference group – borrowers with medium to large landholding.

Role of Endogenous Loan Attributes

- Total loan size has a positive and significant effect on the incidence of upfront interest payments, but negative and statistically insignificant effect on loan default rate.
- Percentage of consumption loan has positive and statistically significant effect on loan default rate.
- Higher overall interest rate on loan seems to have contributed to a lower (and significantly so) incidence of upfront interest payments and loan monitoring.
- While incidence of upfront interest payments has a positive and significant effect on loan default rate, exactly the opposite is the effect of monitoring variable.
- Imparting greater flexibility in loan repayments seems to have an encouraging effect (and significantly so) on loan default rate.

POLICY ACTIONS

Given the general failure of formal sector credit to meet the needs and aspirations of vulnerable sections of the rural population in this country, as detailed above, three broad types of policy actions are called for. First, the country must be bold enough to push further financial sector reforms to drastically cut down on the cost of credit and to ensure competition, transparency, accountability and people's participation in the functioning of our rural financial institutions.

A number of expert committees (especially, Capoor and Vyas Committees) have already suggested several reform packages to boost up the functioning of our commercial and cooperative banking system, and the sooner their recommendations are implemented, the better.

Second, contrary to common belief of the credit supplying agencies, creating, nourishing and boosting up the demand for credit and credit-worthy projects is no less important task than the task of fine-tuning the supply side of credit and related financial services.

Thus, the task of promotion of leadership and entrepreneurship qualities cannot be shied away by our formal credit organizations and left to be mercy of the existing market system and a few inefficient players providing under-quality training and education in isolated manners here and there. This means our formal credit sector has to perform a pro-active leadership role to generate strong and sustainable effective demand for credit.

Handling the various pre-contractual and post-contractual problems commonly associated with credit requires continuous evolution of systems and processes, which our traditional banking system seems to have ignored. Fortunately, the informal lenders and modern micro-credit organizations in the private sector are quite aware of the underlying issues and are continuously investing their time and energy to evolve suitable systems and processes to handle issues like adverse selection of borrowers, adverse use of credit and moral hazard of borrowers, credit-complementary services including de-risking strategies, etc.

The formal credit sector must be prepared to build up suitable bridges and linkages with the vast and expanding micro-credit organizations and also to learn from their experiences. Although the entire study is full of suggestions of these three broad types, it might be useful to spell out a few of them, even at the cost of repetition.

Reform Packages

Besides the reform packages already suggested by several expert committees including those headed by Mr. Jagdish

Capoor and Prof. V. S. Vyas, a few more need to be considered by the Finance Ministry, RBI and NABARD:

- There are built-in disincentives, for example, in the cooperative structure to cut down on the cost of credit operations. With built-in margins of 0.5% to be appropriated by Apex Bank, 2% by DCCBs and another 3% by the PACS, the cooperative credit system, often in connivance of politicians and the bureaucracy, finds it easier to over-invest in poor quality human resources. The existing monopoly power of these organizations in the local market for credit simply allows them to pass the burden of costly credit on to their captive customers, rather than looking for various innovative steps to augment repayments. So, total freedom in interest rate determination is necessary to create an urge to cut down on these cost margins.
- Bankers must have incentives to perform necessary homework so as to educate and empower the borrowers such that the borrowers can continually augment their productivities and thus absorb at least partly the higher cost of credit.
- With the present value of shares remaining very low (Rs.10=00), there is hardly any member-stake in the credit-supplying organizations. Nor is there any scheme for compulsory savings of the members. This is especially true for the cooperatives, which must be immediately corrected.
- Bold and innovative steps to improve loan recovery like avoidance of public loan waiver, postponement of recoveries and granting of interest subsidies, exclusion of defaulters from voting rights and contesting of elections, establishment of debt recovery tribunals, introduction of compromise/settlement procedures for closing long-pending overdue loans etc. are missing in this structure.
- Institutional protection fund along the lines of the German Cooperative Banking System, wherein

contributions by participating organizations could be determined on the basis of performance ratings is also missing in this system.

Based on the study team's interaction with NABARD officials and their understanding based on this interaction and review of the relevant literature, Table 1.6 has attempted to develop a supply-side perspective to improve NABARD's functioning and its role in the years to come.

Pro-active Steps by the Financial System to boost up Demand for Credit

Most of the suggestions made to improve functioning of rural credit system are in the nature of cautions and regulations on the supply side of credit. There is no denying that there are supply side problems. But probably the more pressing and fundamental problem is inadequacy or lack of demand for products or services being supported by credit.

Generating demand for products and services being supported by credit requires far reaching and innovative changes in both technological and organizations dimensions covering such areas as processing, value-addition, delivery and marketing, diversification of agriculture and allied activities, various risk and insurance products, infrastructure development, competitiveness analysis etc., which go far beyond establishing or fine-tuning a good financial management system.

So, the question is not merely of developing the requisite manpower, training and MIS system to strengthen the supply system of credit, but also and more importantly of creating visionary leaders and entrepreneurs, capable of boosting up demand for products, services and activities to be supported by credit.

It seems the entire cooperative credit system as well as the cooperative structure in general has done very little to strengthen the demand side for credit. Given the fact that most suppliers of credit lend others' resources rather than their own, besides being protected from competitive pressures, it is not surprising that the former would look for short-cut supply side measures, rather than undertaking elaborate and innovative measures to promote credit-worthy projects and ensure high repayments.

Evolving Internal Processes, like New Generation Financial Institutions, to handle both Pre-contractual and Post-contractual Problems of Credit: Steps need to be taken to resolve adverse selection of borrowers and their credit projects, adverse use of loanable funds, and both wilful and non-wilful defaults.

5

Expansion in the Agricultural Exports

COMMON CONSTRAINTS OF AGRICULTURAL EXPORT

Restictive & ad hoc trade policy towards agricultural products.

High cost of production & export transactions.

Lack of sound and efficient infrastructure for post harvest.

Quality aspects neglected Inadequate efforts in market development & brand building Over-dependence on few markets The scope of the study has been determined in this background, which may be summed up as follows-

- To analyze the present scenario and visualize the future requirement from point of view of exports.
- The study aims at flagging various interventions including policy reforms, Institutional reforms, infrastructure support etc.
- HRD needs to carry out the action plan.

PRESENT SCENARIO

Maharashtra is one of the States not favored by nature in terms of soil type and rainfall. Agriculture on light soil and drought prone areas has not been remunerative for the farmers. The benefits of green revolution, which took place in 60's, could not benefit the farmers of the State substantially as the paddy growing areas of the State are rain fed and the State is not very suitable for wheat production. The introduction of hybrids in kharif sorghum resulted into increased production of the grain. But the grain was of poor keeping quality, which had the further problem of blackening in event of late rains in Sept-Oct. The marginal increase in farmers' income was not enough to sustain the interest of farmers in these crops only. Therefore, the farmers of the State always looked for diversification of agriculture.

Diversification of agriculture towards seed production in most of the parts of central and eastern parts of Maharashtra in late 60's and 70's was marked by diversification towards sugarcane-based cropping system in western Maharashtra. The next phase of diversification was marked by introduction of soybean as commercial oil seed crop and planned introduction of wide range of horticulture crops under Employment Guarantee Scheme (EGS).

Though, oranges of Nagpur, banana from Jalgaon and grapes from Western Maharashtra do not get overshadowed while making the milestones of diversification of agriculture of the State.

Above mentioned diversification of agriculture has, at all points of time, paid dividend to the farmers of the State, though the sustainability pattern of each phase has been different. Due to increased role of private seed companies-who were always looking for low cost of seed production, invented the preferential suitability of parts of Andhra Pradesh and Karnataka States for seed production, which resulted into decrease in seed production activities in the State. International prices of soybean. Import policy for edible oil has adversely affected the soybean production and soybean based industries in the State.

Sugarcane, banana and orange based cropping systems have resulted into depiction in ground water resources and therefore have its own limitations. The area expansion under horticulture crops of wide ranging varieties have provided a sound base of production of fruits like pomegranate, cashew, mangoes, sweat oranges, lemon, sapota. custard apple, tamarind, amala and what not Common constraints on exports of agricultural exports:

1. Restrictive and ad hoc trade policy towards agricultural products;
2. High cost of production and export transactions;
3. Lack of sound and efficient infrastructure for post harvest;
4. Management such as storage, cold storage, and bottlenecks at mandies
5. Insufficient & inadequate storage & handling facilities at ports of shipment
6. Absence of adequate & timely market intelligence for producers & exporters;
7. Poor quality of the products & absence of standard, presence of high level of pesticide residues;
8. Poor quality assurance system & absence of certification system to conform to international requirements;
9. Lack of modern & technologically sound certification agencies & laboratories;
10. Absence of appropriate technology protocols for handling, storage, and transportation;
11. Inadequate efforts in market development & brand building;
12. Over-dependence on few markets.

STRATEGY FOR 10TH PLAN PERIOD

The State's policy for the 10th plan period is marked by increased emphasis given to technology transfer to farmers for globally competitive production in terms of quality and cost. The post harvest handling, value addition, processing, scientific storage, modem marketing system and export promotion are the main features of the policy. The State is sensitive towards the need of techno-infrastructure and market intelligence, product development and product promotion.

During this period the identified problems are being handled by adopting the following strategy-

- Undertaking studies to scientifically define the constraint and identify the alternative solutions
- Making gap analysis in infrastructure, technology and trained manpower
- Identify areas requiring policy and institutional reforms
- Organizing awareness campaign for the farmers of the State for the new regime of WTO
- Removing the structural barriers in tackling the issues of production, PHM, processing and marketing
- Diversification of agriculture towards horticulture, medicinal and aromatic plants, spices etc
- Application of IT in agriculture for addressing mass of farming community for transfer of technology
- Capacity building for extension workers
- Giving due importance to frontier technology as R & D policy.

LONG TERM STRATEGY

Long-term strategy towards agri-exports may be defined, in view of terms of reference of the Committee, as strategy, which visualizes long-term problems and suggest solutions accordingly.

Following are the milestones for long-term policy in this regard-

- Setting quality parameters for various agricultural produce on scientific lines,
- Standardization of production technology for export quality production at globally comparative prices to serve dual purpose of protecting domestic market from imported farm produce and getting increased access to export market,

- Mapping of PHH infrastructure such as cold chain, sorting and grading / pack houses, packaging, transport and storage and marking gap analysis.
- Identifying the need for varietal changes in crops from point of view of requirement of end user,
- Identification of technology gap in production, plant protection, PHH, processing etc.
- Market sector reforms for domestic marketing system,
- Setting a system for market survey, market intelligence, market information, product development, product promotion in place-especially with respect to transit markets (domestic) and export destinations,
- Application of IT in agriculture extension and information dissemination,
- Assessment of HRD needs in changed scenario,
- Increased participation of private sector and women

INFRASTRUCTURE REQUIRED

Post harvest handling by scientific methods not only reduces post harvest losses of farm produce but also makes quality material available for agribusiness and raw material for value addition and processing.

Agriculture engineering wing of the sector of agriculture in public sector, has remained almost stagnant so far as development of latest infrastructure in terms of plants and machinery is concerned.

Even the 'minimum technical specifications, performance parameters of such equipment do not match the actual requirement of farmers. Except for the segment of items reserved for SSI units others have undergone a lot of technological upgradation by private sector's effort.

Road, water and power are other important infrastructure whose support is required for increase in agribusiness. Out of these road development plans are better implemented than irrigation and power sector.

Cold chain, pack houses, scientific storage, advance markets are some other essential ingredients of infrastructure.

Access to rail-head, port and cargo terminals of air-port are of equally high significance. In case of the State of Maharashtra the farm mechanization is of moderate nature. Road, water and power availability is better than many other States. Except the liberal water and power policy for irrigation water has adversely affected our valuable land resources.

The state has too many cold storage, which are not economically viable. There is strong need to do the mapping of cold chain infrastructure and have a policy to make them viable by getting them business for minimum of 300 days in a year. Controlled atmospheric storage system are still not standardized for tropical fruits grown in the State.

The state has international air-port at Mumbai and sea ports at BPT and SNPT, which puts it in advantageous position. However, small ports can be developed in mango producing area to save cost on transport. Air cargo terminal at Sahar (Mumbai) is not yet provided with cold chain of adequate capacity.

Following infrastructures are required to be developed as a long term strategy.

- Cold chain as per requirement identified after proper mapping as discussed above (at present there are about 161 cold storages in the state but majority of them are concentrated in Western Maharashtra and hence there is no uniform distribution of them leading to under utilization of this facility in some areas and cut throat competition in other area)
- Minor ports in Sindhudurg and Ratnagiri districts to facilitate direct exports cutting down transport cost
- Cashew processing units in Konkan (With rapid increase in area under cashew cultivation under EGS linked Horticulture Development Programme, need for promotion of cashew processing in the state itself was given main thrust. Today under workplan so far more

than 400 cashew processing units have been established and around 450 units will be established during 2002-03. Thus the 70% of the state's cashew production which otherwise was going to other states like Kerala, will gradually processed in the state, providing employment opportunities and scope for value addition. Such as project is also promoted by NABARD at Gopuri (Dist. Sindhudurg) in the form of cashew cluster.)

- Food parks for processing of major fruits, which requires expensive and hi-tech common facilities such as oranges, sweat lime, pomegranate, and mangoes (the state has already established one food park at Butibori, Dist. Nagpur.)
- Bio-technology park to facilitate availability of expensive infrastructure to industries
- Fully developed agri-export zones for grapes, mangoes, cashew, onion, pomegranate, oranges, banana etc. (Maharashtra State Agricultural Produce Marketing Board and Maharashtra Industrial Development Corporation (MIDC) have taken initiatives and has identified few areas as Agri Export Zones such as Aurangabad for kesar mangoes, konkan for Alphonso mango, Grape and Grape wine at Nashik and Sangli. Besides this vapour heat treatment plant is set at APMC, Washi for control of fruit fly in mango)
- Modern flower auction house (Considering the growing area under floriculture and especially inhouse cultivation, the State Government has taken initiatives to establish flower auction centre at Goregaon, Mumbai on the lines of Dutch auction market.)
- Air cargo terminal with cold chain at Mumbai and Nagpur • Rural godowns for storage of non perishable farm produce
- Farmer level Onion Storage System and Market level Hi-tech treatment system for enhancing self life such as irradiation (Maharashtra is a major state producing onions. To minimize losses in storage, assistance for

erection of improved onion storage structures is given. So far 988 such structures are erected in farmers fields and 1180 will be erected during 2002-03.)

- Advanced and developed markets-on concept of NDDB markets for F & V
- Web based Market Information System and information Kiosks (The State Government has launched website "phalbazar.com" on which market rates of all APMC s is available. In future this type of facilities will gain momentum. Besides this the department is promoting Agri-information centres through which the farmers will have access to world market.
- Video conferencing facilities for farmers-researchers-extension workers interface
- On farm vegetable and fruits storage /processing / preservation and packing facilities
- Post harvest technology department should be established in Agriculture University for horticultural crops
- Setting up Agri export zones the crops having export potential like grapes, banana, mango, onion, pomogranate, cashew, chilli and orange.
- Multi chamber cold storage on large scale to be established
- For quickest transport of horticultural commodities special railway wagon should be developed incunsultation with railway dept.
- Crop wise commodity board for mango, santra, onion, banana, sapota cahew to be established in maharashtra to have coordination between various dept. like Coop, Agril. Universities MIDC Industry etc.
- To promote the precision farming concept to the farmers.
- For promotion of vegetable production concept of shed net cultivation should be promoted.

- Agro Horticultural cropping system should be promoted
- To promote monsoon harvesting techniques for horticultural crops.
- Promote the concept of Integrated Pest Management (IPM) and Integrated Nutrient Management (INM)
- Intercropping concept should be promoted in dry land farming
- Beekeeping from horticultural production point of view to be promoted
- To finalize the export oriented production standard
- To carry out study on the crop competitiveness in international market
- To develop alternative traditional mango verities against Alphanso
- To establish the food park facilities processing of major fruits which requires expensive and hi-tech common facilities
- Setting a system for market survey, market intelligence, market information, product development, product promotion with respect to transit markets (domestic) and export destination

TECHNO-INFRASTRUCTURE GAP

In WTO regime non-tariff barriers are going to be more difficult to counter than the tariff barriers. Techno-infrastructure help us in maintaining quality of farm inputs and output.

Following are major techno-infrastructure required for maintaining quality of inputs and quality of production in context of the State.

- The laboratories should be established for testing of genetic purity, Eliza test and other important Tests.
- Tissue culture laboratories should be established for production of quality planting material by using tissue culture i.e. micro-propagation techniques.

- Development of facilities for production of disease / virus free planting material
- Leaf and Tissue Analysis labs
- Residue testing labs at Nashik, Thane, Aurangabad and Sangli.
- Facilities for VCU testing of planting material under new (draft) Seed Act
- Creation of facilities for DUS testing as per National Guidelines under Plant Variety Protection Act 2001
- Phytosanitary labs at the level of phytosanitary certificate agency
- Modernizing of quarantine testing facilities
- Short term and medium term Weather Forecasting Facilities
- Pest and Disease Forecasting Centres
- Bio-technology park to facilitate availability
- Bio-agent labs
- Advance Fertilizer, Pesticide and Seed Testing Labs
- Food Testing labs-to check quality standards of food material targeted for exports (In addition to test the samples of fruits, flowers, vegetables and processed foods imported in India)
- Upgraded Virology labs
- Advanced Soil & Water Testing labs

TECHNOLOGY AND R&D NEEDS

- Varietal changes in F & V to meet the requirements of end users (Majority of the available varieties of horticultural crops are not suitable for processing on account of low TSS contents, colour, pulp ratio etc. Unless varietal changes are made this sector can not be exploited properly.)
- Scanning of planting material from various sources all over the world in F & V for selective imports for

multiplication in public sector till public sector R & D has yielded desired results (Contribution of public sector in releasing varieties is very migre. Considering the international market trend, market potential for India, relevant germ plasm from all available resources must be screened to become self sufficient in getting varieties of International quality)

- Advanced Technology for food processing including fruit processing for citrus, banana, pomegranate, sapota etc. for making RTS (Ready to serve) drinks etc.
- Technology for advance packaging
- Technology for CA storage of tropical fruits (The controlled atmosphere storage facilities today available are not tuned to the need of tropical fruits. There is also need for multi-crop, multi-chamber type of cold storages. This technology should be environmentally friendly.)
- Application of bio-technology in food processing and plant genetics
- INM and management of micro nutrients to crops with special reference to horticulture crops (Integrated nutrient management is still in its childhood. Except for few crops such as grapes, it is not yet thought of The basic limitation is non availability of proper fertilizers. Maharashtra has recommended few grades of liquid fertilizers. The department has extended assistance to SAU's for setting up of leaf and tissue analysis laboratories)
- Complete IPM package in horticulture crops, maize etc.
- Further R & D for varietal development of hybrid seeds in paddy for Vidarbha region, tur, pulses and oilseeds including need base Breeder seeds.
- Improving efficacy of bio fertilizers
- Short term and medium term weather forecasting system
- Pest and disease forecasting
- Crop health monitoring and area survey by satellite imageries for kharif and horticulture crops

- Technology for leaf and tissue analysis for making recommendations for INM
- Preparation of Crop wise Good Management practices should be made available to the farmers.
- Guide to the farmers for maintained of GMP record for export purpose
- To finalize the packaging standard for all horticultural commodities which have export potential
- To finalize the codex standard for exportable horticultural crops like grape, mango, onion, pomegranate, cashew etc.
- Establishment of Vapour Heat Treatment plant at sindhudurgh district for export of Alphanso Mangoes.

STRENGTHENING OF MARKETING FACILITIES

- Marketing cooperatives should be established in horticultural areas. This would link producer with consumers.
- Rayat Bazars on the lines of Andhra Pradesh should be organized all over Mahrashtra. All municipal bodies should create necessary in fracture for that.
- Weekly bazaars for sale of vegetables, fruits and lowers should be organized in every village. The village panchayt should be creating necessary in fracture for weekly bazaars.
- The village woman are given training in scientfic preservation fruits and vegetables,
- The micro-credit Groups movement whish is known as 'Bachat Gats' has been widely spread all over Mahrahshtra. This movement has empowered women both rural and urban areas. Self-employment for women would be generated both in rural and urban areas.
- Co-op marketing societies to be established in each villages

- On the basis of mother dairy NDDB project in New Delhi. The fruit and vegetable marketing center at metropolitan city like Mumbai, Pune Csolapur,Nagpur, Nasik, Aurangabad etc. Credit facilities for horticulture/ Agriculture produce should be given by NABARD on 5 to 6 % interest rate.

HUMAN RESOURCE DEVELOPMENT

Maharashtra has satisfactory infrastructure for human resource development.

The state has 4 agricultural universities with 4 colleges of horticulture under them and around 6 private colleges of horticulture affiliated to them.

Besides this there are 3 NRC's in the state i.e. for grapes, citrus and onion and garlic. One more NRC is proposed by the state for pomegranate. The state has renouned institute viz. Water and Land Management Institute at Aurangabad rendering training and education to the staff as well as farmers about water and land management.

The state has established hi-tech floriculture unit at College of Agriculture, Pune to demonstrate inhouse cultivation of flower crops, vegetables etc. to the farmers. One Centre of excellence is established for tissue culture at SAU, Parbhani. The state also has renouned institutes like Vasantdada Sugar Institute, at Pune, which guides sugarcane growers as well as factories about cultivation of sugarcane and making its bio-products.

The state has one Open university i.e. Yashawantrao Chavan Open University, at Pune.

The Maharashtra State Agricultural Research and Education Council conducted massive programme of training on minimal qualification regarding various aspect of floriculture, processing, flower arrangements etc. The state department started refreshing course for its staff The department has seven training institutes of which two are designated for horticulture and the third one is for agribusiness.

Though the state is having basic infrastructure and facilities for human resource development in the state still much more is yet to be achieved.

There is need for expertise in many fields such as

- Micro irrigation services (layout, installation, maintenance etc.)
- IPM, INM consultants
- Green house (project preparation, erection, planting and aftercare, market assessment etc.)
- Controlled atmosphere for storage of fruits and vegetables (Controlled atmosphere unit should be environment friendly, designed in a multi-crop multi-chamber etc.
- Capacity building
- Agro information centres
- Agencies for certification of the produce as agricultural produce/organic etc.
- Export promotion agencies (assessment of international market, developing brand for Indian produce, promotional campaign for Indian commodities in international markets, facilities for residue testing laboratories etc.) Need for human resource development to support the above mentioned actions is self-explanatory. The HRD program may be classified into following categories

  1. HRD for Enabling Undertaking Research in the Field of Identified Frontier Technologies,
  2. HRD for Other Priority Research and Adoption of Imported Technology,
  3. HRD for Capacity Building for Technology Transfer to User Groups, In public sector In private sector In User's Group
  4. For Capacity Building for Undertaking Self-employment in this Sector

5. HRD of Application of IT in Agriculture
6. HRD for Managerial Capacity Building-Review, Evaluation and Monitoring
7. Human resource development is very crucial for promoting horticulture development.
8. Organiszation of short term course oriented foe self employment
9. Promotion of women participants in Agriculture
10. Special development programme for tribal area by doing micro level planning
11. Separate Dept. of Food Processing industries in Maharashtra State as per directives of Government of India should be established
12. The producer farmer will have to be given intensive training in handling horticultural products for exports.
13. Establishment of separate Directorate for effective monitoring of Agri business and export
14. To organise awareness campaign for the farmers of the State for the new regime of WTO

For undertaking HRD program of above mentioned magnitude and dimension, a multi-agency approach has to be followed. State has already endorsed to this view and Institute of Agriculture Extension Management has recently been set up. PHM is being taken care by MSAMB.

For undertaking R & D in hi-tech agriculture SAUs and Director of Horticulture have been provided with model training centres dedicated to F & V, mushroom cultivation and floriculture.

The State has four SAUs to meet the varied demands of different agro-climatic conditions, three NRCs, one training centre of CFTRI at Mumbai, Indian Institute of Packaging in Mumbai. The State has set up separate university of Animal husbandry, dairy and fisheries at Nagpur.

POLICY AND STRUCTURAL REFORMS

- Introduction of New Seed Act and setting up support system for VCU testing
- Finalization of subordinate legislation's for PVP Act 2001 and Setting support system for DUS testing in Order
- Market Reforms-APMC Act
- Public sector investment in non profit making key infrastructure
- Reorganization of DoA on Farming System Approach
- Tax policy for food processing industries
- Tariff policy for Hi-tech agriculture
- Tariff policy for imports to be sensitive to domestic producers' protection
- Import policy for planting material in F & V in public sector for making new hybrids available to common farmers SSI related policies
- Labour laws-amendment
- Market Access Initiatives-New Role of Indian Consulates Abroad
- Synergy of DoA, Marketing
- Synergy of ICAR and CSIR
- Interface between MoC and MoA
- Forum for Coordination among Air Port Authority, Customs, Air Lines and Exporters, railway.

WTO regime has provided opportunity to get better access to world market but at the same time imposed a challange on the front of quality and cost of production.

The state is facing with multiferrous problems relating to its agriculture. It witnesses almost stringent production of food grains, wide fluctuation of production of some of the perishable cash crops, problems relating to procurement of cotton, dipliting ground water resources and major threat of land degradation due to imbalamced use of farm inputs. In this context hopes have been provided by the sound production base for horticultural crops.

Fortunately the diverse agro climaitc conditions of the state are very congenial for cultivation of various horticultural crops.

Agriculture on light soil and draught prone areas is not remunerative for the farmers, Therefore, the innovative and progressive farmers of the state always looked for diversification. This includes seed production, horticulture plantation etc. Sugarcane, banana and orange based cropping system have resulted into duplication in ground water resource and therefore have its own limitation.

The area expansion under horticulture crops of wide ranging varieties have provided a sound base of production of fruits like pomegranate, cashes, mango, sweet orange, lemon, sapota, tamarind, custared apple, amla etc.

However, important constraints like restrictive and ad-hoc trade policy towards agricultural product, his cost of production and export, transactions, lack of sound and efficient infrastructure for post harvest, cold storage and bottle necks at mandis, insufficient and inadequate storage and handling facilities at ports of shipment, absence of adequate and timely market intelligence for producers and

exporters, poor quality products, presence of high level of pesticide residues, absence certifications systems to confirm to international requirements, absence of appropriate technology protocols for handling, storage and transportation, inadequate efforts in market development and brand building and over dependence on few markets needs to be addressed.

For this purpose strategy and needs to be formulated for globally competitive production in terms of quality and cost. The post harvest handling, value addition, processing, scientific storage, and modern marketing systems and export promotion are the main feature of the policy. Development of latest infrastructure, techno infrastrucutre, HRD and policy issues enlisted below needs to be addressed properly.

Major Recommodations

Infrastrutural Requirements.

- Post harvest handling by scientific method.
- Food, water and power.
- Cold chain, pack houses, scientific stroages and advance markets.
- Access to rail heads, ports and cargo terminals of air ports.
- Processing units.
- Food parks, Bio-technology parks.
- Fully developed agri-export-zone.
- Modern flower auction house.
- Air cargo terminal with cold chain at Mumbai and Nagpur.
- Rural godowns for storage of non perisheable farm produce.
- Farm level improved onion storage structures.
- Advanced and developed markets.
- Web based market information system and formation of kiosks
- Video conference facilities.

Techno Infrastructure

- Leaf and tissue analysis labs.
- Residue testing labs.
- Facilities for VCU testing for planting material under new (Draft) seed act.
- Facilities for DUS testing as per PVP act.

- Phytosanitory labs at the level of Phytosanitory certification agencies.
- Modernization of quarantine testing facilities.
- Wheather / pest and disease forecasting centers.
- Bio-technology park to facilitate availability.
- Advanced fertilizers and seed testing labs.
- Food testing labs.
- Up-graded virology testing labs
- Advanced soil and water testing labs.

Human Resource Development.

- Development of expertise in various fields.
- HRD for enabling undertaking research in the field of identified frontier technologies.
- HRD for other priority research and adoption of imported technology.
- HRD for capacity building for technology transfer to user group.
- HRD for capacity building for undertaking self-employment.
- HRD for application of Information technology in agriculture.
- HRD for managerial capacity building.
- HRD for review, evaluation and monitoring.

Policy and Structural Reforms

- Introduction of new seed act and setting up support system for VCU testing.
- Finalization of subordinate legislation for PVP act 2001 and setting support system for DUS testing.
- Modification of APMC act.
- Public sector investment in non-profit making key infrastructure.

- Tax policy for food processing industry.
- Tariff policy for imports to be sensitive to domestic producer's protection.
- Import policy for planting material in fruits and vegetables in public sector for making view hybrids available to common formers.
- SSI related policies.
- Labor laws amendments.
- Markets access initiatives and new role of Indian consulates abroad.

Forum for coordination among sea, air port, authorities, custom, airline, exporters, railway, public and private research and development institutes, etc.

6

Technology Development and Delivery System in Agriculture

Owing to globalization and liberalization, agriculture in India need to change and change for better than the best. Diversification of production is fast happening along with widespread dietary evolution. Commodity based production is giving way to system based production and there is a paradigm shift using farming system to production to consortium system of operation. Private sector participation is increasing. Agriculture is becoming more and more knowledge-intensive and market-driven. Hence for more innovative research, efficient policies and effective delivery of services, supplies and markets are imperative. Agriculture is no more closed and protected, but globalized and open.

THE CHALLENGES

Against the anticipated annual growth rate of 4% plus, the agricultural sector grew only at 2% p.a. during the X Plan. National Commission on Farmers in its 3 rd Report suggests attention to soil health care, water harvesting and management, credit and insurance, quality and safety, technology and inputs and farmer-friendly marketing in order to help our hard working farm families to help the country achieve 4% plus growth rate in agriculture. Suggesting to measure progress in agriculture by the growth rate in the net income against the current measure of physical production of foodgrains and other farm commodities, the NCF recommended review and reform of the service, support, research, extension and input supply and market system. The suggestions of the mid-term review of X Plan by the Planning Commission are not much different. Thus, to achieve a growth rate of 4% plus p.a. in agriculture as well as to serve framers and save farming from increasing distress, a new model for technology development and delivery system in agriculture is necessary.

The Role of R&D in agriculture

Since Science and Technology are the drivers of change, the agricultural revival / renewal has to be basically knowledge-intensive, technology led and resource based. Stagnating productivity growth in the sector and declining total factor productivity in agriculture are major challenges to meet the needs of a market-driven, competitive regime. In this context, R&D assumes more importance because it is a cost-effective method for promoting sustainability and attaining competitiveness. Harnessing advances in frontiers of science in selected priority areas with larger spin-off benefits by focusing on basic and strategic research also assumes significance. There is also a need to revisit the existing public extension system which is considered to have been weakened over the years at the state, districts and block levels. Hence, there is a serious search for alternatives to the present public agricultural extension system in the country.

A Critique of the Existing Agricultural Research and Extension System

We have a good network of agricultural research institutions in the country, which is facing serious resource crunch to meet the existing and emerging challenges. The National Agricultural Research System (NARS) has although significantly contributed to the agricultural progress since independence, but the situation has changed and challenges foreseen in future are complex and the system has to prioritize and focus itself to the jobs for which it has a mandate as also competitive advantage. A clear-cut delineation of roles at the Central and State level is to be defined. Similarly, the technology delivery system requires an immediate re-look. Technology development and delivery need to be in a continuum and should be interactive. The research system has to forge linkages with the public extension system at all levels, particularly at the district and below levels where the actual uptake and impact happens.

It is resolved to establish one KVK in each of the rural Districts of the country by the end of the Tenth Plan. ATMA model is developed and tested in 28 Districts of the country under NATP and now as a successful model is replicated in 252 districts of the country as a plan programme of Department of Agriculture and Cooperation.

Keeping in view the needed change in technology development and delivery system discussed earlier, at the same time utilizing the existing system, a framework for technology development and delivery is suggested. It is realized that far greater emphasis on basic and strategic research is essential in pursuit of effective technology development. With the new tools and techniques available now, it is possible what was considered impossible in the past *viz.*, with the new tools, designer genotypes could be developed as indicated sequentially by Prof. V.L.Chopra, Member, Planning Commission, in the flow diagram.

Suggested Framework

In the proposed Framework for Technology Development and Delivery System, it is envisaged that basic and strategic research will be substantially carried out by the ICAR institutes, while region-specific strategic research will be done by SAUs and AICRPs.

The strategic research of AICRPs will also feed other areas of the country and a generic model for the purpose is presented and the working of this generic model in some selected representative individual sectors / cases is illustrated through. Applied and adaptive research will substantially be carried out by the SAUs and AICRPs where location, situation and system-specific technology generation, testing and refinement will take place. In this task, private sector involvement will be mutually beneficial. As regards private sector research, proprietary technologies can directly go to farmers and others as per agreements/understanding, can also flow to SAUs/ATMAs for integration.

Technology transfer will be through ATMAs (registered societies) located at the district and bodies at district-subsidiary levels. It is a focal point for integrating research and extension complemented with development supplies and services. ATMA is a tested platform where all service providers will converge and share their strengths. It is an interactive backstopping system supported by research system, service providers like line departments, involvement of PRIs, NGOs, etc. ATMAs will decide on the kind of technologies to be transferred through which agencies. For example, if the technologies are commercial in nature, they will be transferred through private sector. If they are not commercial in nature, the help of NGOs or other civil society organizations will be sought with needed incentives. Knowledge empowerment of the whole system (research and technology transfer) will be through the proposed ICAR portal which is interactive.

Knowledge management includes HRD, policy, and national and international perspective related information and products. Training to extension functionaries will be provided by State Agricultural Management & Extension Training Institute. At the block level, there will be a Farm Information and Advisory Centre (FIAC) which is an extension planning and operational arm of ATMA. It would have two bodies, *viz.*, Farmer Advisory Committee (FAC) and Block Technology Team (BTT). FAC would review Block action plan, prioritize the activities and provide feedback. With high connectivity in terms of computers, Internet, telephone, etc., it would be linked to KVKs, ZRSs, SAUs, etc. BTT would consist of Block officers representing different Departments.

At the village level, there will be Farmer Interest Groups (FIGs) and Farmers Organization (FOs). The FIGs are informal, voluntary and self-governing associations of farmers and farm women, while FOs are federations of FIGs, mandated to support the cause and activities of member FIGs.

Technology Development and Delivery System in various Sectors of Agriculture

In different models, linkages will vary depending upon the nature of crop/ commodity/enterprise and technology service in involving relevant stakeholders to a specific technology-enabled zone/area/situation.

Such linkages will not only boost the production and productivity but also will create an enabling environment for job opportunities, rural marketing economy and export opportunities. Some sector-specific models for technology development and delivery system in crop, horticulture, livestock, fishery, farm mechanization, processing and value addition, and natural resources management have been described. Knowledge drives development, and today, investment in knowledge development is becoming more and more important along with investment in capital development.

The farmers need to connect with agri-business, production systems, research institutions, public administration, other farmers, open market both at domestic and global scale, and other numerous partners. Conventional systems of dissemination of farm information through face-to-face communication by the development functionaries, providing information in the form of printed publications, organizing agricultural exhibitions, etc. are becoming limiting propositions. A model of 'Agri-India Knowledge Portal' to serve as a single electronic gateway for providing information to all those engaged in the task of development of agriculture has also been described subsequently.

Development of High Yielding Seeds

Development of improved varieties and hybrids and availability of their quality seed is the most vital and critical input for increasing the productivity of crops. Appropriate seed ensures its suitability for adoption in specified agro-ecologies. It also ensures its acceptability for consumer quality preferences, trade and industry suitability for various products for domestic and international markets. There is a tremendous diversity of crops and agro-ecologies in the country. The Breeders, Geneticists, Plant Pathologists, Physiologists, Biotechnologists and others are engaged to work on basic, strategic and applied aspects in order to develop quality seed and associated production and protection technologies in various institutes / Directorates/National Research Centres (NRCs), All India Coordinated Research Projects (AICRPs) and State Agricultural Universities (SAUs).

These technologies are tested and demonstrated in the first instance. Breeder seeds are produced for production of foundation and certified seeds in the chain before it is made available to the farmers. For efficient development and delivery of improved seeds of varieties / hybrids and associated production and protection technologies, the following system is being suggested:

(i) The Institutes/Directorates/NRCs need to interact with various Advanced Research Institutes (ARIS), CGIAR Centres/ other international institutes and Centres of Excellence for exchange of knowledge, germplasm and human resource development and relate these developments to the national/regional requirements. Relevant basic and strategic research issues need to be identified and investigated by the institutes utilizing adequate resources.

(ii) Interfaces with relevant commodity (crop, horticultural, animal and fisheries) Institutes, Central Government Departments (DOAC, DAHDF, DBT, DST)/State Departments/SAUs/other Universities/Institutes and Industries to take up applied R & D related to production of varieties/hybrids, so that output reaches the intended stakeholders without loss of time and gets converted into outcome. An applied R&D effort must have a pre-identified stakeholder/public-private partnership to accept the output.

(iii) Frontline demonstrations, supply of mini kits and training by the ICAR Institutes/Directorate of Seed research/Private sectors for technology dissemination and feed back including the preparation of training manuals and organizing institute-stakeholder interface meetings.

(iv) Multidisciplinary commodity and multilocation/region specific technology development and testing by the AICRPs in a network mode in involving the local scientists, farmers, extension agencies and industries so that the output reaches the stakeholders without any gestation period. AICRPs will also undertake frontline demonstrations in collaboration with KVKs of the region to ensure technology absorption and awareness creation to the maximum extent.

(v) Production of breeder seed and test stock seed of varieties and parental lines of hybrids to be undertaken by the ICAR institutes/directorates/NRCs, AICRPs and SAUs, while the central/State seed developmental agencies/ private sectors/self help group/ farmers associations/ individual farmers will take up the production of foundation/ certified/truthfully labeled seed including delivery mechanism for availability of seed to the farmers/growers.

(vi) Production of truthfully labeled seed by the ICAR institutes/Directorates/NRCs/ AICRPs/SAUs at their own farm to a limited extent in addition to production of more parental lines of hybrids/other varieties to expand the base of availability of quality seed to the farmers. Besides, SAUs can also augment the production of foundation seeds.

(vii) Appropriate policy interventions by the central/state developmental departments/ agencies for ensuring the availability of critical quality inputs, adequate price support policies, market infrastructure development, agro-processing industries and other facilities for optimum utilization of potential of high yielding/hybrid seed.

(viii) Seeing is believing. Also in the fast changing technology domain, it is imperative that awareness is brought about without any loss of time. Hence, it is necessary to ensure stock seed production and ensure supply of a limited quantity of seed by breeder institutions as Centre/State supported development activity to each Panchayat which can serve as demonstration, demand generation as well as in inbred varieties farmer-to-farmer seed flow in the Panchayat in the shortest possible time. This new system is believed to bring much needed transformation by cutting the time lag. To avoid any misuse of precious seed, treated seed could be supplied which will also take care of seed borne diseases.

Cut and dry Flowers for Export

The country has diverse agro-climatic conditions for growing several cut flowers like rose, chrysanthemum, carnation, gerbera, lilium, tuberose, etc., which can effectively be grown in glasshouses and gladiolus in open fields.

The protected cultivation is presently undertaken by about 70 export oriented floriculture units, with an area, of about 1000 ha. Flower export has now grown worth more than Rs. 200 crores; however, the domestic market still plays a dominant role. Among the loose flowers, marigold ranks the first followed by chrysanthemum, jasmine, tuberose, gaillardia and crossandra. In a planned way, the cultivation and export of cut flowers will bring foreign exchange to the country manifold.

Besides cut flowers, there is a tremendous scope of dry flowers, which constitute 70% of the total floriculture export of the country. Many of the plant species having ornamental value include floricultural crops, horticulture crops, grasses, legumes and edible crops. Even wood carving and clippings are considered in this class of product. The added advantages of dry flowers are that the maintenance is easy and cheap and the product is durable.

The dry flowers as well as live flowers and cut leaves of certain plants may also be used for preparing floral crafts. There is therefore, a great need of production of fresh and dry flowers with novelty and strengthening the delivery system to promote the export of these products. The action points in this regard are suggested below:

- Identification of crop and product and quality requirement for export.
- Development of varieties/hybrids for cut flowers and their testing for region-specific adaptation.
- Development of protected cultivation for cut flowers
- Agro-techniques including substrate, integrated nutrient and water management and integrated insect pests and disease management for cut flowers.
- Post-harvest technologies including time of cutting, post-harvest handling and standardization of holding, storage, wrapping, transport, etc. for cut flowers.
- Facilitating production of quality cut flowers in greenhouses by the entrepreneurs with support of NHB, APEDA and NABARD.
- Institutional arrangement of collection and delivery mechanism of cut and dry flowers from entrepreneurs to the export point.
- Establishment of packaging houses by the exporters/ entrepreneurs with the technical guidance of APEDA.
- Establishment of cool chamber at the airport/sea port points by the Air/Sea Port Authorities of India and private exporters.
- Standardization of drying, value addition, packaging, moisture level in finished products and management of insect problems with dry flowers.
- Demonstration of technology/product of dry flowers by the research institutes to the entrepreneurs.
- Market research for destination of product and requirements.
- Policy support or incentive for export.

The model system for cultivation and commercialization/ marketing of cut flowers for trade is presented.

Dairying

The Livestock is a rapidly growing sector in Indian economy contributing 5.22% to GDP and 28% of the value of output of agricultural and allied sector. India is the highest producer of milk with an annual production 91 million tonnes. The milk production has grown @ 3.4% in the last few years, and the productivity @ 2.6% in last ten years. The productivity of milch animal is 987 kg per year as compared to world average of 2200 kg. The per capita availability of milk is 231 gm/day as compared to world average of 270 gm/day.

The true potential of Indian farmers was realized through Operation Flood which is a classic example of fusion between technology intervention and linkage with the end-user. The innovative technologies has the potential to revamp growth of dairy sector.

A number of technologies has been developed in the field of dairying including improved growth and reproduction; area specific recommendation on feed and fodder including mineral mixtures; diagnostics, vaccines and drugs; process of value addition, quality assurance and shelf life enhancement. There is a need to re-structure the mechanism of technology dissemination from individual to collective mode because common resources and its open access play a major role in adoption of dairy practices. The suggested steps of facilitating the adoption of dairying will be as follows:

(i) Addressing the research gaps in genetic improvement in cattle, area specific feeds and fodder including mineral mixtures, development of diagnostics, vaccines and drugs, and process improvement for value addition, quality assurance and shelf life enhancement.

(ii) Identification of high producing dairy animals

(iii) Supply of progeny tested semen/bulls from ICAR institutes and state livestock farms for upgradation of the breedable cattle

(iv) Organizing large scale training and demonstration through State DAHDF, KVKs and NGOs.

(v) Organizing milk cooperatives, federations and feed manufactures for supply of key inputs and credit from NABARD and other financial institutions.

(vi) Capacity building and networking for organizing collection centres, increasing shelf life and value addition with dairy cooperatives and unions, public/private sector milk chilling plants, local milk based business organizations

(vii) Certification of hygienic milk production procedures by APEDA and its franchise

(viii) Integrating the use of information technology

(ix) Providing enabling policy and environment

Aquaculture

Aquaculture provides for diversification of agriculture, as well as value addition in terms of higher returns from a unit area. Along with high potentials for ensuring domestic nutritional food security, it also generates high employment and contributes to export earnings. All the three segments, *viz.*, freshwater aquaculture, coastal aquaculture and mariculture have been showing high growth rates in the recent past. While freshwater aquaculture comprises mainly of carps, along with catfishes, giant freshwater prawn and ornamental fishes, shrimp has been singly contributing to coastal aquaculture production which is also the main export commodity in the fisheries sector. Mariculture has come up in the last ten years, with scope for enhancing the coastal economy.

A planned strategy of improved natural resource management, breed improvement, seed production and dissemination, better input delivery systems, cold chain and marketing and human resource development in the relevant aspects would enable realization of full potentials of the sector. This requires a mix of basic and strategic research to address the key issues of the biology of the species including growth and disease resistance, feed and health management measures. At the same time, aspects of scaling up of hatcheries, design of seed production systems for different species in varied ecosystem conditions are addressed in the applied research mode to develop and or refine technologies.

A key concern in aquaculture has been the ready access and availability of all quality inputs in one place that has hindered the development. The concept of 'Aqua-shops' is intended to provide the seed, fertilizers, feed, prophylactics, therapeutants and diagnostics, nets and implements along with advisory services in one place, with a number of Institutions involved in these areas joining hands. Further, in view of the remoteness of places of fish/shellfish production lacking infrastructure for transport and marketing resulting in low price realization, cold chains of different levels and dimensions linked to the collection centres and marketing is incorporated in the model for Aquaculture.

While research aspects pertain to the aspects of breed improvement, nutrition and health management, as ingredients of breeding and culture of fish/shellfishes, policy issues relate to leasing of water bodies and infrastructure development. Major inputs for enabling the farmers to enlarge the operations and realize the gains would be training and demonstration, quality inputs, information about markets, both domestic and export, for scheduling culture and marketing processes and valued information from production to consumption.

Farm Mechanization

Farm mechanization facilitates timeliness in operations, better placement of inputs, lower cost of production and reduction in drudgery of farm workers. It plays an important role in enhancing the productivity and profitability of agriculture by 20-30% reduction in cost of production and 5-20% higher cropping intensity. Mechanization involves development of tools, equipment and ensuring adequate power for carrying out the on-farm and off-farm agricultural activities. The technology development in farm mechanization begins with the identification of local needs and further design and development of tools, equipment and renewable power systems including market search through basic and strategic research by the ICAR institutes (eg. CIAE, Bhopal) in collaboration with SAUs and IITs. Based on the commodity and location-specific packages developed through multilocation trials by the R&D institutions and AICRPs, appropriate training modules and manufacturing drawings are prepared before developing interface with the entrepreneurs and industries for making the tools and implements available to the farmers on reasonable cost. The State Development Agencies, NABARD and other financial institutions need to provide necessary financial support for large scale promotion of farm mechanization.

Post Harvest Technology

Post harvest technologies are commodity and location-specific and appropriate basic and strategic research inputs including varietal characteristics of a particular crop, post harvest physiology, nutritional physiology, food biochemistry, and post harvest ecology are assessed before the intended products and processes could be developed by the ICAR institutes, SAUs and IITs. These research inputs are essential for developing products, processes and ultimately design of pilot plants. Based on the assessment of market response and consumer acceptance, standardization of product, process and equipment is undertaken to ensure the quality and safety of the output. These developments are then evaluated and demonstrated in different locations for the entrepreneurs, NGOs, self-help groups, and cooperatives for large scale promotion and adoption of the post-harvest technologies. Banks, State Development Departments and other agencies are given the exposure for enabling them to extend necessary financial support. Figure 8 provides the linkages of different activities of technology development and delivery and actors in the form of a flow chart.

Rainfed Farming through Watershed Management

The productivity of rainfed areas occupying 60 per cent of cultivated area in the country and supporting 59 per cent of population is still low and is a major concern of policy makers, planners and R&D investments portfolio. Even after achieving the full irrigation potential, nearly 50 percent of cultivated area will remain rainfed, constituting an important source of food and livelihood.

Therefore, integrated and holistic development of rainfed areas within the perspective of watershed management constitutes one of the key elements of increased production in the country. There is a need to develop appropriate technology to remove the production constraints of these areas and establish an effective system for the dissemination of the technology to the farmers.

The research back up concerning basic and strategic issues would be provided by the ICAR Institutes, SAUs and related National Institutes. Research is required to be focused on run-off and recharge modelling, soil-water-plant interactions, water harvesting, *in situ* moisture conservation, integrated nutrient and pest management, contingent crop planning during droughts and drip / sprinkler / fertigation systems. The socio-economic-environmental-market imperatives should be given due consideration while framing up technologies.

The technology generated is required to be further assessed and refined for different agro-climatic situations through AICRPs and SAUs and disseminated through State Development Departments (Agriculture, Horticulture, Animal Husbandry, and Forestry), ATMAs, KVKs, SAUs, SHGs, NGOs, Cooperatives and web-based Agro-advisory Services. The financial institutions like NABARD would need to provide financial support for development of infrastructure like water harvesting ponds and pressurized irrigation systems.

The cooperatives and contracting / leasing agencies could be associated in agro-forestry / bio-fuel plantations. The activities and functioning of the watersheds need to be in a participatory mode, ensuring transparency and equitable sharing of services and benefits among different stakeholders. The participatory watershed management will be facilitated through formation of watershed associations (Pani Panchayats, Van Panchayats, and Joint Forest Management Committees). The technological interventions would have deliverables in terms of water conservation, increased land productivity, enhanced employment, livelihood security, equitable sharing of benefits, and empowerment of women, environmental upkeep and better quality of life.

INTEGRATED FARMING SYSTEMS

Development and adoption of integrated farming system provides high opportunities of productivity enhancement, employment, income generation and nutritional security by diversifying and integrating different components of farming, *viz.* crops, horticulture, livestock and fisheries (depending upon location specificity). The systems based on multiple recycling of carbon, energy and nutrients would also help minimize environmental loading with pollutants. The different components of the system have complementarities with waste products of one component becoming source of food and energy for another.

The researchable issues encompassing analysis of nutrient and energy fluxes among system components, path analysis of bio-physical constraints, multiple uses of water, water harvesting and recycling, socio-economic conditions of people, internalization of ITK and market analysis, etc. are to be addressed through basic and strategic research by ICAR institutes and SAUs. The integrated technology would be developed integrating crops, horticulture, fisheries & livestock by ICAR Research Complexes having R&D facilities on different system components at SAUs.

Further assessment and refinement of developed farming systems to cater to region and location specific requirements would be accomplished through centres of AICRPs on Cropping/Farming System Research and SAUs. The technology would be disseminated through KVKs, SAUs, NGOs, SHGs, etc. with true participation of ATMAs and different functionaries of State Line Departments (Agriculture, Horticulture, Animal Husbandry, Fishery) at district and block levels. The backward and forward linkages between KVKs and state functionaries would provide the required feedback to SAUs and ICAR institutes on upgradation of technology. The KVKs would organize regular trainings on different aspects of technology to extension personnel and various stakeholders.

Establishment of Agri-India Knowledge Portal-A Single Electronic Gateway

The information on improving agricultural productivity and protection of crops, livestock and natural resources from damages caused by disasters and unsustainable activities is focal to the rural farming communities. This would require access to a wide range of information on new technologies, alternate varieties of crops, improved breeds of livestock, information related to soil, water quality, information on pesticides, farm implements, animal health, weather and other related aspects. Besides farm-activities, non-farm activities also constitute sources of income and livelihood for the rural farmers. Therefore information is also required on the means to produce food products required by markets and ability to sell them as also the markets, cold-chains, warehouses, processing and other avenue.

ICAR-ERNET network consists of 274 Institutions including National Agriculture Institutes, State Agricultural Universities including some of their colleges and Research stations, National Research Centres, Project Directorates connected through Leased line and VSATs. Besides, a VSAT-based network of Krishi Vigyan Kendras could be had. Both these networks will be linked through a high capacity leased line to make a unified high speed secured Intranet. Since the intranet of NARS institutions is built over the existing ERNET network, it is planned to host the core components of knowledge portal application at the ERNET Hub.

The Department of Telecommunications has set up several sub-groups on network expansion, broadband, telecom equipment manufacturing and R&D to examine various options to enhance growth. The sub group on network expansion has targeted that subscribers numbers must cross 250 million by 2007 and 500 million by 2010. Another target is mobile coverage of 85% of the country by the end of 2007. To boost the broadband penetration in the country, another sub-group will examine the ways to provide broadband coverage for all panchayats by 2010 and all secondary/ higher secondary schools and public health care centres by 2007. The Portal application will be constructed and deployed using suitable Portal management software. The core functional components of the portal application software are:

User Registration: The user registration process is a mechanism for acquiring the information related with the user of portal which is an integral part of the portal.

User Authentication: The user ID and the password pair generated as end result of registration process are authenticated through a carefully designed mechanism and form a basis for accessing the various resources of a portal.

User Access Control: Once the users are authenticated, an access control mechanism built into the portal determines which data and information can they see/manipulate, and how will it be displayed? The User Access Control mechanism is designed based upon the specific role that the particular user will perform in the portal.

Personalization: Personalization is a feature that enables a user to access targeted web content that meets a user's needs and preferences from the enormous web content on the portal.

Content and Document Management: Content and document management system in the portal application streamline redundant content development, publishing and management processes to increase operational efficiencies, and improve content quality.

Document/workflow: The various rules to manage the workflow and lifecycle of documents are established in a portal, which automates the manual, labor-intensive process and results in consistency and auditability in authoring and producing content.

Collaboration: The portal applications facilitate collaboration among the various stakeholders/ partners via online chat rooms, discussion groups, online document sharing, messenger applications, etc. The digital content of the portal will be developed through a peer review process. For this purpose, 15 Content Accreditation Centres, i.e. one each in the 15 Agro-climatic regions of the country could be had. Each accreditation centre will coordinate with other SAUs and agricultural institutions in their region for development of content in regional language as well as in English and also do its validation, which will be collected in the central data warehouse integrated in the knowledge portal.

The intranet network consisting of various stakeholders primarily ICAR institutes, SAUs and KVKs will facilitate the development of Central Agriculture Data warehouse, Content Development and Validation System, Agricultural Best Practices, Expert System for users, Multi-lingual content development and convertibility. The portal will also serve as a platform for facilitation of interaction among researchers and extension workers in KVKs through high speed secure intranet.

Various applications and services of the knowledge portal will be accessible to the users including farmers, entrepreneurs, private sector organizations, other participating government and non-government organizations, extension workers, etc. through Internet. The services include Agro-met advisory services, Market intelligence, Packages of practices, Agri-business consultancy, e-learning, knowledge on indigenous farming practices, and agriculture related FAQs. Besides, it will also act as information gateway for all agriculture related schemes and programmes etc. The Portal will also serve as a gateway for up-to-date websites of various agricultural research and education organizations accessed through Internet. The portal will provide a platform for facilitation of interaction among the end user communities through Internet also.

The Agri-India Knowledge portal will also provide for collaboration among other agencies related with agriculture like Meteorological Dept, Agricultural Markets, Banks and other financial organization, Input suppliers, Agricultural equipment manufacturers, Non-agricultural universities for providing services through Agri-India knowledge portal both through secure and high speed Intranet and Internet. The services proposed to be implemented in the collaborated mode include On-line education, Information on Market Prices, Weather Information including early warning system, Agricultural Input status information, Credit and crop insurance services, land record information, etc. The AIK Portal is neither intended to replace any agency websites nor any other government portal. This Portal will, however, provide additional means by which those sites might be accessed by a possibly wider and more varied client base. The AIK Portal will open opportunities for multiple agencies to participate in web delivery and development opportunities. The Portal would be able to integrate diverse interaction channels at a central point, providing a comprehensive context and an aggregated views across all information related to agriculture including *know-what* or declarative knowledge, *know-how* or procedural knowledge, and *know-why* or usual knowledge and *creation of new knowledge*.

REENVISIONING EXTENSION SYSTEM

The main extension system primarily responsible for delivery of technical messages is operated by the State Department of Agriculture (DOA), through the state, district and block level machinery. Other state governments departments, such as Animal Husbandry, Horticulture, Soil and Water Conservation, and Fishery have been providing very limited extension services. The main focus of the Departments of Animal Husbandry has been treatment of animals and for the Departments of Horticulture, distribution of seeds/seedlings (of fruit and vegetables) is the prime activity. While the Department of Soil and Water Conservation are mainly engaged in constructing soil and water conservation structures, the Departments of Fisheries is mainly engaged in providing fingerlings and some financial support to Fish Farmer Development Associations. The research centres and agricultural universities play a very limited role in extension service.

The system, however is more pre-occupied with implementation of a number of central and state sector schemes having input/subsidy delivery. The performance of the main extension system has been adversely affected by the difficulty in recruiting and retaining extension staff due to budgetary constraints, depleting operational support and inadequate technical background of the majority of the staff commensurate to the changing scenario of agriculture, resulting in the dependence of farmers on input dealers and others, as sources of information. Their role in technology up-scaling has been minimal and even non-existing. Through Centrally Sponsored Scheme on Support to State Extension Programmes for Extension Reforms, Agricultural Technology Management Agency (ATMA) has been established in 252 districts so far. The ATMAs are expected to support the state extension system by making it more broad-based and participatory for planning, implementing and monitoring the extension activities of a district.

Diversified nature of farming demands, against a background of the economic liberalization and globalization, is radically changing the spectrum of service providers to the farmers. Indeed, the private sector, farmers' organizations, cooperatives, self-help-groups, Para-professionals, non-governmental organizations, input suppliers and small agri-businesses are increasingly engaged in providing information and services. Increased reliance on private sector extension does not imply a complete withdrawal of the public sector, which must continue to finance public goods extension and information services and coordinate extension activities.

In view of the above, the basic concept of extension needs to be re-looked from persuasive technology transfer originally conceived, to the model of interdependence within specific innovation system framework of the stakeholders and institutional context based on the strengths of both public and private sector.

The Approach Perspective

The models for technology development and delivery system in various sectors of agriculture is essentially indicative of a pluralistic environment right from research institutions engaged in technology development, up scaling and integration of technology, and its adoption by the end users. The models can be modified as per the need for various states and districts for appropriate multi-agency extension arrangement with the state, district, block and village level functionaries of various development departments, including the farmers' organizations and the private sector. While in floriculture, there is an emphasis on quality production of cut and dry flowers with appropriate institutional arrangement for cold chain and collection centres; in dairying the emphasis is on the institutional arrangement for availability of progeny tested semen/ bulls, complete balanced feeds, shelter management, diagnostics, vaccines and drugs, post-harvest processing and value addition. Similarly, the emphasis in aquaculture is on establishment of Aquashops with cold chain and collection centres; there is need for formulation of location and commodity specific packages of tools and equipment and its availability through entrepreneurship development for manufacture and supply of those to the farmers at an affordable price or on custom hire service. There is a need for promotion of agro-processing centres in rural sector/ production catchments for value addition of agricultural produce including technological back-up support. The participatory resource management will be the key to watershed management. The pluralistic extension pattern requires that the programmes are jointly planned, implemented and evaluated by all service providers.

Unified Production System Approach

The activities of different agencies from technology development to its dissemination at the user level need to be unified. For example, once the production and protection technology of high yielding varieties / improved parental lines and hybrids are developed, its dissemination needs to be initiated through frontline demonstrations by the technology development institutions, and the mini kit testing of technology by the development departments, ensuring quality seed of improved variety/hybrid to each Village Panchayat in the region for which the variety is recommended/released. Breeder seed production and test stock seed production for Panchayats must be simultaneous to cut short the time lag and ensure demand for seed by the time breeder seed is converted to certified seed and it is ready for distribution.

The demonstration plot seed in each Village Panchayat of inbred variety would also move from farmer to farmer in each of the villages. Simultaneously, there is need for integrated programmes for production of breeder, foundation and certified seed by seed producing agencies including the production of parental lines for hybrid seed production, supported by marketing, transport, storage, credit and policy environment. Similarly, with the development of appropriate varieties, production technologies, post harvest technology for quality production of cut and dry flowers, the support for packaging and wholesale market/agencies for export is imperative. In aquaculture, along with aquashops for increased production, there is need for unification of processing plants and marketing both for domestic and export.

Knowledge Centric Approach

In knowledge-driven development, there is need for providing extension education keeping in view their diverse needs not only on production procedures, but also quality certification and reporting procedures, grading, packaging, storage, transportation and other requirements of both domestic and export markets. The farmers need to have knowledge about the whole range of agri-business, production systems, research institutions, programmes and schemes of the development departments, open markets both at domestic and global scale, and other unlimited partners is to be provided through training, demonstration, literature, and other human resources development support including interfaces at different levels. The development of Information Communication Technology (ICT) and Telecommunication Network have paved the way for creation of information network, knowledge pool and services on new agricultural technology, products and marketing of produce, which must be intensively used. It will be appropriate to develop farmer-friendly information network to provide whole range of information leading to delivery of knowledge of new agricultural technology, products, procedures, and related services to enable them to take control of their farming environment in near future.

Research-Extension-Farmer Interface

The strategy for technology development and the strategy for technology dissemination are not mutually exclusive. Agricultural extension is a process of bringing about innovation and change. There is an inherent degree of overlap among them; however, the fundamental point is that they are potentially useful in joint assessment, diagnosis, planning, implementation, monitoring and evaluation. The models presented in various sub sectors of agriculture have made it clear that research and extension are part of a continuum. While research-extension linkages were theoretically possible in inter-personal mode, in the new regime, effective linkages of production systems with marketing, agro-processing and other value added activities have acquired greater importance. In the present competitive environment, the research and extension service must be reoriented to overcome the exclusive focus on production that ignored market demand, profitability and institutional arrangement in the past.

Although a variety of farmers' organizations including cooperatives, farmers' club/self-help groups, and farmers' companies has been promoted in the past, there is lack of sustainability of their existence and the purpose for which they were promoted. These farmers' organizations need to be looked as a kind of business federation for undertaking primary processing and marketing of local products and to facilitate much needed organizational support for effective implementation of quality control and standardization of farm products.

The new mechanisms and protocol suggested for technology development and delivery system for various sectors of agriculture would need spatial and functional integration and complementarities and institutional arrangements in the context of creating an environment to encourage and assimilate results of innovativeness. There is need for introducing MBO based agenda and clear delineation of task components in the form of assembly line and also creating coherent synergy within and amongst state development departments, SAUs, ICAR institutes and all related functionaries. This would require policy support in terms of integration of efforts of institutions dealing with technology development, assessment and refinement, and dissemination including encouraging and accepting the contribution of corporate sectors, private sectors, cooperatives and farmers' associations in delivery systems.

Growth of Agriculture both in terms of GDP and livelihood security with social equity has been ever challenging and more so in the present context of inadequate public sector investment and services, and pressure of globalization of agriculture leading to a greater demand for highly knowledge-intensive services. Investments in present Indian agriculture need to be rationalized and appropriate knowledge driven institutional reforms have to be brought in. Appropriate framework for technology development and dissemination would be very much needed for transforming Indian agriculture from the present approach of its sustenance as a way of life to a vibrant economic activity with a sense of pride for future generations.

7

Agriculture, Irrigation and Food Security

AGRICULTURE

The agriculture in India is largely dependent on monsoon as only about 37 per cent of the Net Sown Area (NSA) is irrigated. During 1999 Monsoon (June to September), 81 per cent of the area received normal to excess rainfall. Moisture deficiency in some areas and floods in some other areas affected agriculture adversely and despite the record production of rice, foodgrains production during 1999-2000 is likely to reach a record level of 201.91 million tonnes (MT), as compared to 205.91 MT achieved during 1998-99. The sugarcane production is likely to reach a record level of 309.31 MT. But, the production of oilseeds and cotton has declined. For 2000-01 foodgrains production target has been fixed at 212 MT.

During the Ninth Plan, Regionally

Differentiated Strategy has been adopted with due emphasis on checking land degradation, encouraging expansion of minor irrigation, increasing fertiliser consumption, improving input delivery system, increase in credit flow and wider coverage under crop insurance scheme. To bring in convergence among ongoing programmes and to address the state specific issues a new concept "Macro Management of Agriculture-Supplementation/Complementation of State's efforts through Work Plans" has been approved for implementation from 2000-01. The new scheme will replace a number of ongoing centrally sponsored schemes and allocation to the States by the Department of Agriculture & Cooperation (DAC) will be based on the Work Plans.

FOODGRAINS

For Increasing Foodgrains Production, Various Schemes viz., Integrated Cereals

Development Programmes (in Rice/Wheat/Coarse Cereals based cropping System's Areas (ICDP-Rice, ICDP-Wheat and ICDP-Coarse Cereals), Accelerated Maize Development Programme (AMDP), National Pulses Development Programme (NPDP) and Seed Minikits Porgrammes are being implemented. The three ICDP Programmes are to be merged with the scheme of Macro Management of Agriculture from 2000-01. The AMDP and NPDP will, however, continue to be implemented as separate schemes under the Technology Mission on Oilseeds, Pulses and Maize (TMOP&M).

Ninth Plan Targets of Production of Foodgrains

During the first three years of the Ninth Plan foodgrains production targets could not be achieved and have remained about 200 MT only which is approximately the figure of

Strategy

- Convergence of on-going programmes.
- Adoption of macro-management approach, through "Work Plans" to supplement/complements the efforts of the States.

Merger of Schemes

Integrated Cereals Development Programme for Rice + Wheat and Coarse Cereals to be merged with schemes of Macro-Management. 1996-97 production (199.44 MT). However, the rice (88.55 MT) and wheat production exceeded the targets of 86.00 MT and 74.00 MT respectively during 1999-2000. If only the peak of production level of past were achieved during the current year, the foodgrains production would be 213.89 MT.

Taking account of this fact alone, the target of production for the current year 2000-01 is achievable.

OILSEEDS

For increasing production of oilseeds, under the Technology Mission on Oilseeds, which was introduced in 1986, the Oilseed Production Programme, R&D in Post Harvest Technology for Oilseeds and Oil-palm Development Programme are being implemented as Centrally Sponsored Schemes.

Besides, the National Oilseeds and Vegetable Oil Development Board (NOVODB) is supplementing the efforts of TMOP by opening new areas for non-traditional oilseeds and in non-traditional areas for promotion of additional oilseeds cultivation. It is also promoting tree-borne oilseeds.

Ninth Plan target of production of 30 MT of oilseeds is achievable if the achievement of the year 1998-99 is kept in view. The year 1999-2000, however, was a bad year during which the production is estimated to plummet from the previous year's figure of 25.21 MT to 21.18 MT.

COTTON

For accelerating the growth in production of cotton, Technology Mission on Cotton (TMC) has been introduced as a Centrally Sponsored Scheme during 1999-2000 in 12 States of Andhra Pradesh, Gujarat, Haryana, Karnataka, Madhya Pradesh, Maharashtra, Orissa, Punjab, Rajasthan, Tamil Nadu, Uttar Pradesh and West Bengal. The ongoing Intensive Cotton Development Programme (ICDP) has been merged with TMC. Although, the production trend during the first three years of the Ninth Plan are not very encouraging, the Ninth Plan target of 15.70 million bales is not very ambitious considering that the production in 1996-97 was 14.23 million bales.

JUTE & MESTA

The Special Jute Development Programme is being implemented in 8 major Jute/Mesta growing States of Andhra Pradesh, Assam, Bihar, Meghalaya, Orissa, Tripura, Uttar

Pradesh and West Bengal. From 2000-01, jute and mesta is being undertaken under Macro Management approach. Its production has successively declined during last three years. During the Ninth Plan no target of production of jute & mesta has been fixed.

SUGARCANE

The Centrally Sponsored Scheme on Sustainable Development of Sugarcane Based Cropping System (SUBACS) was introduced in 1995-96. During 1999-2000

Himachal Pradesh has also been added for the implementation of the scheme. Now, this scheme is being implemented in 21 States and one Union Territory. From 2000-01, SUBACS is being undertaken under Macro Management approach. Looking at the past trends, the Ninth Plan target of 336 MT is very ambitious.

HORTICULTURE

Varied agro-climatic conditions in the country provide immense opportunities for diversification of agriculture and for increasing gainful employment opportunities in rural and urban areas, and also for improving nutritional status of the masses. Agro-industrial base could be substantially widened with the horticulture development.

Horticulture sector, however, suffers from technological and infrastructure constraints such as small and marginal size of land holdings, pre-ponderance of old and senile trees, poor management, acute shortage of good quality seeds and planting material, prevalence of diseases and pests, inadequate post harvest handling/sorting/grading/packaging and storage facilities. Processing infrastructure and marketing network is far from satisfactory. Therefore, full potential is yet to be realized. Ninth Plan has accorded top priority to horticulture sector and it is being treated as a focus area for its all-round development.

The Ninth Plan envisages boost in productivity and improvement of the quality of the produce with objectives such as upgradation of production/farm technologies, development of strong base for supply of inputs, transfer of technology, human resource development and improvement in marketing infrastructure. Various programmes have been made operational to increase the productivity and quality of existing plantation and to increase availability of improved varieties of seeds and elite planting material.

Thrust is given on area expansion, technology transfer and post harvest handling/marketing. In order to improve the infrastructural support, a programme has been launched for setting up of 12 lakh tonnes of new cold storage capacity, rehabilitation/modernisation of 8 lakh tonnes of existing cold storage capacity and creation of 4.5 lakh tonnes of onion storage capacity.

Under this programme, 25 per cent subsidy, subject to a maximum of Rs.50 lakh for each unit (with more liberal subsidy amount up to 33-1/3 per cent subject to a maximum of Rs.60 lakh in North-East) is available. An outlay of Rs.175 crore has been provided for subsidy component for cold storage during Ninth Plan which is expected to bring in additional private/public/cooperative investment of Rs.477 crore, thus making total amount of investment upto Rs.652 crore.

The scheme was launched towards end of 1999-2000. An integrated development of horticulture on Mission Mode has been planned for all round development of North-East region. Ninth Plan target for production of fruits and vegetables is kept at 179 million. However, with the anticipated achievement of only 122 million tonnes in 1998-99, the achievement of Ninth Plan target seems to be a difficult task.

PLANTATION CROP

Southern and North-eastern regions of the country are endowed with high potential for plantation crops such as tea, coffee, rubber, etc. Commodity Boards are contributing their mite to the development efforts in enhancing the production and productivity of plantation crops by extending its coverage to new areas and increasing the productivity of small growers.

SOIL AND WATER CONSERVATION AND WATERSHED DEVELOPMENT

Various schemes such as Soil Conservation in Catchments of Flood Prone Rivers and in Catchments of River Valley Projects (FPR&RVP) and Watershed Development Programme for Shifting Cultivation Areas (WDPSCA) are being implemented to check siltation of water bodies and soil erosion. During 1998-99 as against a target of treating 5.90 lakh hectares, an area of 5.65 hectares was treated under these Programmes. During 1999-2000 a target of treating an area of 1.65 lakh hectares was fixed, which is likely to be achieved. During 2000-2001, these schemes are proposed to be covered under the Programme of Macro Management.

The development of rainfed agriculture is being addressed through National Watershed Development Programme for Rainfed Areas (NWDPRA). Watersheds are now proposed to be developed under Common Approach/Guidelines which have been framed/finalised. These guidelines aim at harmonious development of watersheds under various programmes of Ministry of Agriculture, Ministry of Rural Development and Ministry of Environment & Forest. During 1999-2000, a Watershed Development Fund (WDF) has also been created by NABARD with central assistance to cover 100 priority districts in a period of three years.

AGRICULTURAL INPUTS

Seeds

To augment seed supply, two new schemes namely, Pilot Scheme for Seed Crop Insurance and Scheme for Establishment and Maintenance of Seed Bank were introduced during 1999-2000. Incentives/assistance for production, storage, transport and distribution of quality and improved seeds under various crop production oriented schemes will be continued during 2000-01. The availability of certified/quality seeds has increased from 90.76 lakh quintals in 1997-98 to 104.38 lakh quintals in 1998-99. The production target fixed for the terminal year of Ninth Plan (2001-02) is 109.66 lakh quintals and achievable.

Fertilisers

The consumption of chemical fertiliser during 1999-2000 is estimated to reach 183.72 lakh tonnes of nutrients (NPK) as against 167.97 lakh tonnes during 1998-99, showing a significant increase. The Centrally Sponsored Scheme on Balanced and Integrated use of Fertilisers which aims at achieving the twin objectives of strengthening soil testing facilities and ensuring promotion of balanced fertiliser use will be continued during 2000-01. During the Ninth Plan period, the existing 519 Soil Testing Laboratories would be modernised and new laboratories would be established in areas where these facilities are weak and 36 new compost plants are proposed to be established.

Plant Protection

Credit Flow

- Setting up of specialized banks in each State.
- Issues of Credit Cards to farmers.
- Introduction of Rashtriya Bima Yojna.

Under the Integrated Pest Management (IPM) Programme, thrust on conservation of existing bio-control fauna and use of bio-pesticides, bio-control agents and products of plants origin will continue. The existing 26 Central Integrated Pest Management Centres located in 22 States/UT will continue their activities for organising field demonstrations and trainings on IPM technology to educate farmers and field functionaries. Demonstrations of IPM approach will also be continued under various crop production oriented schemes.

Agricultural Implements and Machinery

For the promotion of Agricultural Mechanisation a Centrally Sponsored Scheme is in operation since 1992-93. Under the scheme, during the first three years of the Ninth Plan, a total of 13406 tractors were distributed on subsidy. During 2000-01, 5200 tractors are proposed to be distributed. The training needs of machine operators, farmers and officers of State Governments, are being met through organisation of training programmes at

Farm Machinery Training & Testing Institutes located at Budhni in Madhya Pradesh, Hissar in Haryana, Garladinne in Andhra Pradesh and Bishwanath Charaili in Assam. During 1999-2000, a total number of 3638 trainees against the target of 3500 were imparted training. During 2000-01, 3500 persons are to be trained in operation and maintenance of farm machinery and equipment.

Agriculture Extension

Training infrastructure in the country for agriculture extension workers has been strengthened at the existing National Institute of Agricultural Extension Management at Hyderabad. During 1999-2000, the ongoing Centrally Sponsored Scheme "Women in Agriculture" was extended to five North-Eastern States with a view to provide extension services to the women farmers in these regions.

Agriculture Credit and Cooperatives

Agricultural credit is an important input for ensuring growth in agriculture. Agriculture credit is disbursed through a multi-agency network, consisting of Cooperatives, Commercial Banks and Regional Rural Banks (RRBs). The disbursements to Agriculture Sector was Rs.26411 crore in the terminal year of the Eighth Plan (1996-97). Although the actual disbursements of credit has been increasing in the first two years of the Ninth Plan, there has been shortfall against the projected requirement of credit recommended by the Ninth Plan Working Group on agricultural credit and cooperation. The credit flow from all agencies is targeted to reach a level of Rs.60,842 crore in 2001-2002 (the terminal year of Ninth Plan) as per the Working Group.

According to RBI Report on Trends & Progress in Banking (1998-99), the relative share of agriculture credit in net bank credit stood at 12.8 per cent in March, 1997 and 11.7 per cent in March, 1998 as well as in March, 1999. As against the target of 40 per cent for priority sector lending by banks, the sub target for agriculture has been fixed at 18 per cent. The declining share of agriculture in the net bank credit against 18 per cent target is a matter of concern. More credit needs to flow to agriculture for providing timely and adequate credit to farmers for increasing agriculture production and productivity.

Various measures have been taken to improve credit flow to agriculture sector concerning procedural simplification for credit delivery, delegation of more powers to bank managers, introduction of composite cash credit limit to farmers, introduction of one specialised agricultural bank in each state to cater to the needs of high-tech agriculture, introduction of cash credit facility, issue of Kisan Credit Cards to farmers to draw cash for their production needs, augmenting Rural Infrastructure Development Fund (RIDF), etc.

There is, however, problem of overdues that dampen the flow of credit besides affecting adversely the economic viability of the lending institutions especially, cooperatives and RRBs. A proposal for revamping of cooperative credit structure has been initiated by the Government during the Ninth Plan to revitalise the cooperative credit structure and enable the system to respond adequately and effectively to the emerging needs of the users and the market.

To strengthen equity base and improve financial performance of RRBs, the total capitalisation support given to RRBs is Rs.1094.21 crore till March, 2000.

Introduction of National Insurance Scheme (Rashtriya Bima Yojna) by replacing earlier Comprehensive Crop Insurance Scheme from rabi 1999-2000 has been a significant development in the Ninth Plan. Nine States and one UT have implemented the Scheme of Rashtriya Bima Yojna.

OUTLAYS AND EXPENDITURE

During 1999-2000 Department of Agriculture and Cooperation incurred an expenditure Rs.1440.63 crore on various schemes for the development of agriculture against an outlay (BE) of Rs.1941.00 crore. For 2000-01 an enhanced allocation (BE) of Rs.1950 crore has been provided to the department.

ANIMAL HUSBANDRY AND DAIRYING

Livestock Development

The major thrust in the Ninth Plan is concentrated on the improvement of production and productivity of livestock through genetic manipulation, production of quality feed and fodder, animal health care and prevention of important diseases. In pursuance of the strategy of doubling food production, the Department of Animal Husbandry and Dairying has reprioritised its plan priorities and identified 11 specific schemes for Special Action plan for achieving an accelerated growth of livestock products.

Livestock Development

- Genetic improvement.
- Disease control & prevention.
- National Project on Cattle & Buffalo Breeding introduced to provide breeding inputs at farmers' doorsteps.

Milk and Dairy Products

India has become the World's largest milk producing country and the milk output is estimated to achieve the level of 78.1 million tonnes during 1999-2000. However, it appears that with the present growth rate of milk production (about 4 per cent per year) it will be difficult to attain the Ninth Plan target of milk production set at 96.49 million.

Two centrally sponsored schemes namely (i) Extension of Frozen Semen Technology and Progeny Testing Program and (ii) National Bull Production Program which have boosted the dairy development efforts of the State Governments are now being merged into one program 'National project on Cattle and Buffalo Breeding with an emphasis on delivery of breeding inputs and services at farmer's doorsteps and improvement of indigenous cattle and buffalo breeds.

An Integrated Dairy Development Program in non-Operation Flood, Hilly and Backward areas was launched during Eighth Plan and has been extended during the year 1999-2000 with a total provision of Rs.45 crore. Since the starting of the scheme, 38 projects with a total outlay of Rs.189.84 crore have been sanctioned in 20 States.

Poultry Including Egg

Egg production during 1999-2000 is anticipated to be 31320 million compared to 800 million eggs two decade ago. The broiler production has also accelerated at an annual growth rate of 15 per cent and stands to about 450 million broilers per annum at present. The poultry sector has flourished with the active participation of organised sector, which controls about 70 per cent of the production, management and marketing. The rest 30 per cent of the unorganised sector whose contribution cannot be undervalued is now being focused upon by the Centre by promoting backyard poultry. Ninth plan target of egg production (35 billion no. egg) is likely to be achieved. A new Centrally Sponsored Scheme "Assistance to State Poultry/Duck Farm" is being implemented for the first time in the North Eastern States including Sikkim on a hundred per cent Central assistance to strengthen at least two duck/poultry farms in each State. The program will be extended to other States in the ensuing years.

Wool

Wool production of about 46.1 million kg is expected to be achieved during 1999-2000 as against 41.7 million kg during 1989-90. The Central Sheep Breeding Farm, Hissar is engaged in the production and dissemination of acclimatised stud-rams to various State Sheep Farms for crossbreeding and genetic upgradation. Presently importing of germ plasm for upgradation of indigenous breeds is proving difficult in the background of many leading countries getting affected by scrapie and BSE. Piggery development is of considerable significance, particularly in the North Eastern region of the country.

Improvement of Slaughter Houses

A large number of slaughter houses in the country have poor facilities for hygiene and sanitation. A centrally sponsored fisheries in hilly regions are being formulated by the Government for implementation during the Ninth Plan period.

Agriculture Research and Education

For carrying out research in identified frontline areas ICAR has built a network of National Agriculture Research System which have 46 Institutes including 4 deemed Universities, 4 National Bureau, 31 National Research Centres, 9 Project Directorates, 158 Regional Stations and 80 All India Coordinated Research Projects (AICRPs) besides 30 State Agriculture Universities (SAUs) and one Central Agricutlure University (CAU) for promotion of research in several frontier areas. The prominent institutions include National Gene Bank on Plant, Animal, Fish and Micro-organisms, National Research Centre on Biotechnology, DNA Finger Printing Technology, Integrated Pest Management, Weed control, Biological control and Phytotron Facility. ICAR also has collaborative programmes with several International institutes or their regional centres.

During the year, 40 improved varieties – 16 in cereals, 8 in pulses, 6 in oilseeds, 7 in fibre crops and 3 in forage have been released (1999-2000). Also, 2,3034.89 quintals of breeder seeds including cereals (1118.34 Q), oilseeds (7554.18 Q), pulses (3981.53 Q) and fibre crops (156.83 Q) have been produced. Integrated Pest Management (IPM) methods for management of pests have been refined in respect of rice, cotton, pulses and oilseeds. DNA Finger printing of varieties of aromatic rice (48), wheat (46), barley (15), Oliferous Brassica (42), sunflower (16), mungbean (32), cotton (70), tomato (30) and brinjal (16) have been undertaken. New Guava variety Lalit and new Papaya variety Surya have been released. Mango variety Tenneru has also been released. Three F1 hybreeds, one each in water melon, tomato and bottle gourd have been identified. Soil resource maps of 26 States in 1:2500,000 scale have been developed. Six row manual, 8 row self-propelled rice transplantor and 8 row pre germinated paddy seeder have been released for commercial exploitation. Solar dehydrators for fruits and vegetables, cylindrical dryers for soya based idli/dosa mix slurry have also been released. 8-frame honey extractors have also increasing the per capita availability and consumption of fish etc. The Ninth Plan also focuses on an integrated approach to sustainable development of fisheries and aquaculture.

Fisheries is a State subject and as such the primary responsibility for development rest with the State Governments. However, supplementing the efforts of the state governments, the central government has been implementing various central sector and Centrally Sponsored Schemes for the development of fisheries in collaboration with the States/UTs. The Ninth Plan fish production target is set at 70.40 lakh tonnes envisaging a growth rate of 5.64 per cent per annum. An allocation of Rs.800 crore has been earmarked for the fishery sector during the Ninth Plan period.

One of the strategies for development of inland fisheries has been propagation of scientific aquaculture in ponds and tanks through the Fish Farmers Development Agencies (FFDAs) under the Centrally Sponsored Scheme. A total of 422 FFDAs have been sanctioned for establishment under this programme covering all the potential districts in the country. The Agencies provide a package of technical, financial and extension support to fish farmers. Under another scheme, 39 Brackishwater Fish Farmers Development Agencies (BFDAs) have been sanctioned in all the coastal States and the UTs of Andaman and Nicobar Islands to develop brackishwater aquaculture in the country. In the marine sector, some of the major programmes are motorisation of traditional craft, reimbursement of central excise duty on HSD oil supplied to mechanised fishing vessels below 20 meters length etc.

In addition to 6 major fishing harbours, 45 minor fishing harbours and 153 fish landing centres, another 3 major fishing harbours, 10 minor fishing harbours and 30 fish landing centres have been envisaged during the Ninth Five Year plan. A number of welfare programmes for fishermen such as construction of houses, insurance scheme and saving-cum-relief are being implemented by the government.

Considering the inland fishery resources in the country, two new programmes (i) Integrated developmental of inland capture fishery resources: and (ii) Development of coldwater scheme "Assistance to States for Improvement/Modernisation of Abattoirs/Establishment of Carcass Utilisation Centres and Primary Flaying Units" was initiated to improve the conditions of the slaughter houses but the implementation of this schemes has not been satisfactory; projects sanctioned in different states in the Seventh and Eighth Plan are still to be completed.

Eradication Of Animal Diseases

National Project on Rinderpest Eradication (NPRE) is continuing in all the States and Union Territories since May 1992. Based on the documentation generated by NPRE, Govt. of India declared the country provisionally free from rinderpest w.e.f. 1.3.1998 which was accepted and notified by Office International des Epizooties (OIE). Under the scheme "Assistance to States for Control of Animal Diseases" grants-in-aid is provided to control various diseases including FMD. About 40 million vaccinations against FMD were carried out during 1999-2000 and 22 million vaccinations are expected to be carried out during 1999-2000.

FISHERIES

The fisheries sector plays an important role in the national economy and in the socio-economic development of the country. It also plays a significant role in supplementing family incomes and generating gainful employment in the rural sector, besides providing cheap and nutritional food to millions of people and provides employment to about 3.84 million fishermen. Moreover, an impressive segment of the population is engaged in ancillary activities associated with fisheries and aquaculture. This sector has been one of the major contributors of export earnings in recent times and is estimated to have attained a level of Rs.5096 crore in 1999-2000.

The main objectives of the fisheries development programmes of the government during the Ninth Five Year Plan are: optimising production and productivity, augmenting export of marine products, generating employment, improving the socio-economic conditions of the fisher folk/fish farmers, conservation of aquatic resources and genetic diversity, been released for commercial use. Backyard and rural poultry system have been standardised for farmers of remote and far-flunged areas. Grampriya and Vanaraja as layer strains and Krishibro as broiler strains have been developed.

New improved Diagnostic kits for diagnosis of brucellosis infectious bovine, rhino tracheitis (IBR), F&M D and Blue Tongue (BT) have also been developed. Embryo transfer technology (ETT) standardised at 10 centres and extended for production of elite germ plasm of Murrah and Surati buffalo, Tellichery goats, gaddi sheep and Rathi and Sahiwal cattle. Marine pearl culture has been commercialised and technology for breeding and export of ornamental fishery has been developed. ICAR have also demonstrated farm level production of 14 tonnes/ha of fish in the States of Punjab, Haryana and Andhra Pradesh. New Hatcheries to improve availability of fish seeds have been added. 53 KVKs have been added to an existing number of 261 KVKs in the country. This has been achieved through upgradation of Trainers' Training Centres (TTCs) and Zonal Research Centres (ZRCs) under NATP programme.

New Initiatives

National Agriculture Technology Project (NATP), which is an externally aided project is now fully functional. National Bureau of Agriculturally important Microbes have started implementation. National Research on Seed Spices is under implementation. A Regional Station of the Central Saline Soil Research Institute, Karnal has been set up at Lucknow. Agriculture University at Jammu is being set up. Network on Haemorrhagic Septicaemia has been established. Rural Agriculture Work Experience scheme is also now under implementation. Agriculture Technology Information Centres (ATICs) have also been set up at 40 places in SAUs and ICAR institutions.

WATER RESOURCES

Water is a precious natural resource and its planning, development and management should be governed by national perspectives. Water has been a key issue on the domestic and international agenda for the last 30 years starting with the 1 st International Conference on water in 1977. The development and management of Water resources of a region has to evolve together with that of land and biomass giving due weightage to the socio economic and environmental features.

The United Nations General Assembly at its 58 th session in December 2003 decided to proclaim 2005-2015 as the International Decade for Action "Water for Life" beginning with the World Water Day March 22, 2005. Coping with 'Water Scarcity' will be the guiding theme for World Water Day 2007 on 22 March. This years theme highlights the increasing significance of water scarcity world wide and the need for increased integration and co-operation to ensure sustainable, efficient and equitable management of scarce water resources, both at international and local levels. Estimation of water demand and its implications on water quality and quantity is extremely important. Agriculture has the dominant demand and it will continue to predominate for a long time.

Integrated management of water resource assumes greater importance and should be based on the treatment of water as an integral part of the eco-system and as a natural resource whose quality and quantity determines the nature of its utilisation. Water use, in turn, has its impact on water quality and therefore utilisation of water has to be so managed as not to contribute to the deterioration of water quality. Sustainable management of water resources with due respect to ecological, economic and ethical sustainability requires a holistic and integrated approach involving engineering, socio-economic and environmental aspects. Traditional system of water management through ponds and small tanks should be integrated with canal irrigation. There is good potential for water productivity gains in rainfed and irrigated areas. This will require a combination of agronomic, economic and social interventions including soil management and irrigation water management. In rainfed areas mitigation of dry spells with onfarm water harvesting or supplemented irrigation can potentially increase water productivity. Despite the fact that productivity in irrigated areas has increased as compared to that of rainfed areas, the increase is still below the world standards and developing countries like China. This is coupled with sub-optimal water management including low irrigation efficiencies. There is scope for considerable improvement in productivity and consequent reduction in the demand for water. Applying the right quantity at the right time and using the right cultivation and irrigation practices can achieve conservation of water on the field. Against the backdrop of such a situation of imminent scarcity and inter-sectoral competition on physical and financial resources, the water resources management has to undergo a paradigm shift. Integrated management of resources and their use assumes special significance in the context of the predictions regarding 'drought like situation' in 2007.

Water sector has undergone basic changes in recent years due to perceived scarcity. While focus in the past was mainly on investment in physical structures, recent developments are associated to a great extent with improved management, conservation and institutional changes. "Optimal sustainable development, maintenance of quality and efficient use of country's water resources to match the growing demands on the precious natural resource with active involvement of all stake holders in order to achieve accelerated, equitable economic development of the country" is the vision for integrated water resources development and management The primary task now is to find ways to make the fixed capital more productive. It is necessary to invest more on better water management, complete incomplete irrigation projects, investment in non-command areas through the watershed development approach.

Water Resources in the Country

As per the latest assessment, out of the total precipitation, including snow fall of around 4000 billion cubic metre in the country the availability from surface water and replenishable ground water is put at 1869 billion cubic metre. Because of topographical and other constraints about 60% of this ie,. 690

billion cubic metre from surface water and 432 billion cubic metre from ground water, can be put to beneficial use. The availability of water is highly uneven in both space and time. The per capita availability of water is declining progressively owing to increasing population.

The national average per capita availability in India was 5200 m m^3 in 1951. It has fallen to 2200 m m^3 in 1991 and further to 1820 m m3 in 2001 and with the projected population it may go down to 1340 and 1140 cubic meter by the year 2025 and 2050 respectively. The average availability is therefore likely to fall below the water stress level in the near future. The situation in certain parts of the country is likely to be critical and it is estimated that by the year 2050, 30% of the geographical area and 16% of population in the country will be under absolute water scarcity condition, with water availability of less than 500 cum. per year.

According to the international agencies, any basin having per capita availability less than 1700 cubic metre is categorised as water stressed and less than 1000 cubic metre as water scarce. According to these norms six river basins of the country have already fallen into water scarce category, and five more are likely to become water scarce in 2025 and by 2050. Only three or four basins would be water sufficient. Hence management of water becomes a challenge. As water could not be manufactured, conservation and management of water is the only way out for the growing demands.

The percapita storage in the country is about 207 m3 which is far below the storage achieved in many of the countries such as Russia (6103 m^3), Australia (4733 m^3), Brazil (3145 m^3), United States (1964 m^3), Turkey (1739 m^3), Spain (1410 m^3), Mexico (1245 m^3), China (1111 m^3) and South Africa (753 m^3). The country thus seems to be on the threshold of a grave water crisis in the none too distant future. In short, India is already on the verge of grave water crisis.

The fresh water availability of Kerala according to the available estimates is 77.35 billion cubic meters (BCM) including re-generated flow from ground water. Nearly 40 percent of available water resource is lost as run off. The utilisable resources as per the assessment is around 42 BCM whereas the requirement for water for various purposes like irrigation, domestic and saline water intrusion etc. is reckoned at 49.70 BCM. The total storage capacity created by the completed projects is 1478 million cubic meters and the projects under construction will contribute an additional storage of 332.75 million cubic metres. The ayacut (potential) envisaged in the completed projects is 2.398 lakh ha (net) and the area realised is 1.88 lakh ha. The envisaged ayacut of the ongoing projects in the tenth plan period is 1.17 lakh hectare (net). The potential realised in the completed projects is only 80 to 85 per cent of the potential envisaged on an average and the utilisation now is below 60 per cent.

Pricing of Water

The costs of providing irrigation water include a fixed cost of operation and maintenance and a variable cost, which depends on the quantity of water supplied. Irrigation water charges in most states are not even adequate to meet the O & M costs. In addition there is a capital cost of constructing a water project. The per hectare cost of creating irrigation potential in the major & medium irrigation sector has been increasing steadily from about Rs. 1500/- in the first plan to between Rs. 1,75,000 and Rs. 2,50,000. The establishment cost takes a large part of the meagre O & M allocation, leaving very little for works. In Kerala, the water rates now collected are based on the estimates of 1974. The rates are very low compared to the costs of maintenance of major irrigation projects.

Rain Water Harvesting

Kerala has two predominant rainy seasons caused by Southwest and Northeast Monsoon. On an average, the state receives 3000 mm of rains, of which 60 per cent is obtained during Southwest Monsoon, 25 per cent during the Northeast Monsoon and 15 per cent during summer months. The high variations in spatial and temporal rainfall add to the complexity of the problems associated with water management faced by the State. Though Kerala is the wettest state in the country and one of the wettest regions in the world, it may become a state of unquenchable thirst if adequate and urgent institutional and technological measures are not taken to address both the shortage and declining quality of water.

Hence rainwater harvesting, one of the various technologies of water harvesting assumes importance in our state. In order to promote rainwater harvesting, Government of India advised the State Governments to provide certain provision in building rules, pertaining to incorporation of rooftop rainwater harvesting arrangements in buildings.

The Government of Kerala has amended the Kerala Municipality Building Rules, 1999 in 2004 to incorporate provision for rooftop rainwater harvesting. The government also launched a state-wide awareness building and rain-water harvesting in public buildings, institutions and households.

A special 'Rainwater Harvesting Cell' has been formed for statewide co-ordination of the compaign activities. The physical progress of the programme was encouraging. KRWSA has constructed 1864 rain water harvesting structures, 1797 small rain water harvesting structures 465 structures with 10,000 litres capacity and 55 big structures, organised 7 state level workshops, conducted 11 exhibitions, 47 seminars, organised 4 national seminars/workshops.

Budgetary support was provided to Ground water department and Soil and Water Conservation department for implementing schemes for rainwater harvesting. Several non-governmental agencies are also constructing rainwater harvesting structures in the state. During the year under report, GWD has constructed 74 structures for rain water harvesting

Live Storage Capacities of Irrigation Reservoirs

There are 18 dams intended for irrigation. Out of this, 13 have storages and 5 are barrages. The live storage position of the reservoirs during the beginning and end of the monsoon period during 2005 and 2006 is given in Table.

Table : Live Storage Position in the Reservoirs

S.N.	Item	2005 (Mm^3)	2006 (Mm^3)
1.	Storage at the beginning of the Monsoon	357	566
2.	Storage at the end of the Monsoon	1194	1143
3.	Monsoon increase	837	577
4.	Average for 10 years		
	(i) at the beginning of the monsoon	299	344
	(ii) at the end of the monsoon	830	948
	(iii) increase in monsoon storage	531	598

In the beginning of the Monsoon (during the current year) the total storage was 566 Mm^3 and at the end of the monsoon the level of the storage was 1143 Mm^3. This is against the level of storage of 357 Mm^3 at the beginning of the Monsoon and 1194Mm^3 at the end of the monsoon period during the previous year. The current year's storage of 1143 Mm^3 is greater than the ten year average of 948 Mm^3 on the date. The total designed storage (at FRL) of the reservoirs is 1487Mm^3 whereas the total availability at the end of the Monsoon of 2006 is 1143 Mm^3 against 1194 Mm^3 at the end of the monsoon last year. The storage capacities of reservoirs are deteriorating due to silting in reservoirs. Sedimentation or silt removal need be done periodically for the proper upkeep of the reservoirs.

Safety of the existing dams is one of the items emphasized in the National Water Policy. Almost all of the 18 dams in the State were completed in the 1950's and are constructed of masonry/earth or a combination of both. Excessive seepage/ leakage, mal functioning of gates etc. caused distressed conditions as noticed by the State level Dam Safety Committee. Besides this, the storage capacity of the reservoir gets depleted due to excessive siltation. If these problems are not attended properly, it can cause downstream damages. Hence rehabilitation of the dams are essential. As per the Dam Safety Act-2000 every State having a significant number of dams shall constitute a body called 'Dam Safety Organisation (DSO). Accordingly in Kerala also constituted a 'Dam Safety Organisation' for Monitoring the post and pre-monsoon inspections of dams and maintenance and surveillance and safety activities of the dams, Hydrological review to check the adequacy of design flood, preparation of emergency action plan, prioritization of dam for rehabilitation purposes, interaction with the Dam Safety Organisation of the Central Water Commission, conducting structural analysis, and checking the safety of dams once in 10 years. During 2005-06, Dam Safety Origanisation along with Dam Safety Committee inspected the dams in Neyyar, Malampuzha, Chimmony, Vazhani, Kanjhirappuzha, Siruvani, Kallada and Peechi.

Investment in Irrigation

Irrigation development in Kerala is mainly centered on the development of surface water resources mainly on the development of major and medium irrigation projects. In each Plan, priority in allocation was given for the development of major and medium irrigation projects. Out of a cumulative expenditure of Rs. 3881.06 crores, Rs. 2740.13 crores (70%) is invested for major & medium irrigation. About 60 to 70 percent of the investment in each plan was made for this purpose.

Rice is the major crop benefited through irrigation infrastructure. Even in the case of this crop, the incremental yield, which the irrigation support could bring, is not significant. With the fast changes taking place in the farm front of Kerala with notable reduction in the area under rice cultivation, even the distribution systems already developed for gravity irrigation to service rice cultivation now require realignment. During the Tenth Plan period an outlay of Rs. 930 crore was set apart for the Irrigation sector which includes Rs. 600 crores for Major and Medium Irrigation, Rs. 205 crores for Minor Irrigation and Rs. 50 crores for Flood Control and Anti-sea Erosion works.

This is against the outlay of Rs. 1028.00 crores and an expenditure of Rs. 1078.73 crores during the Ninth Plan period. In the allocation of resources during Tenth Plan a small reduction was noted in the overall outlay of the sector. The percentage share of Plan outlay during Tenth Plan was 3.88% against that of 6.38% in the Ninth Plan. The reduction was mainly due to the transfer of Minor irrigation schemes to the local bodies and reduction in number of major projects. During the Plan period (2002-07) against the Plan outlay of Rs. 930 crores, an amount of Rs. 781.63 crores was budgeted and during the first four years expended Rs.702.8 crores. A major portion (73%) of the outlay on Water Resource Sector was budgeted for Major and Medium Irrigation Sector and the expenditure recorded for Major & Medium for the first four years was 76% of the total expenditure.

Over and above the State plan outlay a substantial amount has been invested for Minor irrigation and Flood Management from the schemes of Local Self Governments. During the first 3 years of the Plan period, an amount of Rs.97.44 crores have been invested by the LSGs for minor irrigation and flood management. Also assistance to the tune of Rs. 50 crores from 11 th FC Award and Rs. 175 crores from 12 th FC Award has been sanctioned for the coastal zone management. Moreover an amount of Rs.20.27 crores have been invested for centrally sponsored schemes during the first four years of the Tenth Plan. Public investment in irrigation has fallen significantly over successive Plan periods. This is largely due to resource constraints faced by governments both at the Centre and the States. At the All India level also, there is decline in the percentage of funding for irrigation.

The percentage of funding which was 23 percent in the 5 th Plan has declined to 20.85 per cent in the sixth plan and further to 15.9 per cent in the Eighth and Ninth Plans. This has resulted in cost over run and time over run of the projects. In Kerala, the percentage outlay for the sector which was 6.38% in the Ninth Plan has decreased to 3.88% in the Tenth Plan. This has adversely affected the completion of the major projects thereby increasing the spill over costs of the ongoing projects. However, resources are not the only problem. Potential irrigation projects are located in area which are either more difficult or environmentally more sensitive which makes it difficult to implement irrigation projects.

The Accelerated Irrigation Benefit Programme (AIBP) launched in 1996-97 for the expeditious completion of approved ongoing major and medium irrigation projects is a potentially important instrument for providing resources to state governments to complete ongoing irrigation schemes. Allocations under this programme have been massively increased.

Upto 2005-06, Government of India had sanctioned Rs.18157 crores to various states. The assistance sanctioned to Kerala was Rs.239.21 crores (1.32 %). Central assistance is given under the programme in the form of loan and is provided to those projects which have investment clearance by Planning Commission. The pattern of assistance was on a 50:50 basis up to 1999-2000 and later it was revised in the ratio of 2:1 (Central and State). The pattern of assistance was modified from 01/04/2004. In the modified pattern the central share will be 70% loan and 30% grant for general category states and 10% loan and 90% grant for special category states for projects under Fast Track Programme. The pattaern has again revised in 2006 and in the revised pattern the central government will provide 25% as grant and the loan component has to be raised by States.

Table : Physical Targets and Achievements under Irrigation during the Tenth Plan period (gross)

(000 ha)

Sl. No	Sector	Cumulative coverage up the end of 9th Plan	Tenth Plan Target	2002-06 Target 2002-07	Achievement 2002-06	Anticipated Achievement
1	Major & Medium	225	90	75	50	60
2	Minor	207	50	50	33	48
	Total	427	140	125	83	108.00

In Kerala, Kallada and Muvattupuzha Projects were assisted under the AIBP and the assistance received so far is Rs. 32.51 crores and Rs.206.70 crores respectively. The assistance was availed based on individual selected components of public works identified under each project.

The target set for the realisation of additional irrigation potential during Tenth Plan was 1.40 lakh hectares (gross) comprising of 0.90 lakh hectares under major irrigation and

0.50 lakh hectares under minor irrigation. The cumulative target for the first 4 years was 1.25 lakh hectares, which includes 0.75 lakh hectares under major and 0.50 lakh hectares under minor irrigation. The actual achievement for the first four years aggregates to 0.83 lakh hectares. Overall performance of the Major and Medium Irrigation sector was not encouraging during the Tenth Plan period. Additional irrigation facility could be created only in Muvattupuzha Irrigation Project.

Review of Major Projects

As far as the Major irrigation sector is concerned, under the new initiative of 'Modernizing Government Programmes', as part of implementing the policy on long pending infrastructure projects, four projects viz., Karapuzha, Muvattupuzha, Banasurasagar and Idamalyar were identified as long pending projects and action has been initiated for the speedy completion. In Karapuzha project about 90% of the work is over. Completion of distributories are pending. Though Partial commissioning of the project was expected in March 06, only impounding of water in the reservoir could be done in 2006.

In Banasurasagar project, construction of main canal is completed and in the case of branch canals only the survey and investigation is progressing. In Muvattupuzha project works relating to dam and main canal have been completed. Major portion of the branches and distributories are pending completion. In Idamalayar project, the progress of execution is very slow. Kallada project was completed. However, the reported irrigation potential realized was relatively low as compared to the potential created. The work of the Thrithala Bridge-cum-regulator is completed. The progress of execution of Chamravattom project has started recently.

The overall performance of the major and medium irrigation sector during 2005-06 was not encouraging. The cumulative area brought under irrigation through major and medium irrigation projects is 2.48 lakh hectares. (gross). The details of the progress of implementation of ongoing projects as on 3/2006 are given in Table below.

Table : Project-wise Details of Ongoing Projects

(Rs. lakhs)

Sl. No.	Name of Project	Year of Starting	Original estimate	Revised estimate	Year of revision	Cost escalation (%)	Expenditure upto March 2006	Target area to be irrigated (Ha)		Physical achievement as	
								Net	Gross	Net	Gross
1	2	3	4	5	6	7	8	9	10	11	12
1	Muvattupuzha	1974	2086	67800	2004	3150	60717	17737	34737	13629	27529
2	Idamalayar	1981	1785	30711	2004	1626	20676	14394	29036	-	-
3	Kuriyarkutty-Karappara	1987	1036	19700	2004	1801	3803	17488	34976	-	-
4	Karapuzha	1979	760	25300	1999	3228	23181	5221	8721	-	-
5	Banasurasagar	1979	800	4906	1999	525	1541	2800	4740	-	-
6	Chamravattom	1985	1327	12000	1999	804	1323	3106	9659	-	-
7	Thrithala	1998	1900	2660	1999	40	3914	1303	3997	-	-

Source: Department of Water Resources

Irrigation Status

Table : Net Area Irrigated (Source wise)

(in Ha.)

Sl. No.	Source	2002-03	2003-04	2004-05	2005-06
1	2	3	4	5	6
1	Government canals	101139	94859	101397	104669
2	Private canals	4272	5754	4729	4965
3	Tanks	66729	47856	43983	45062
4	Wells	117490	109360	108445	110000
5	Other sources	103541	123469	134802	135227
6	Total	393171	381298	393356	399923
7	Area irrigated more than once in a year		782892		918341
8	Gross irrigated area	447490	426765	455391	464765
9	Net area irrigated to net area Sown (%)	17.83	17.36	18	19
10	Gross irrigated area to gross cropped area (%)	14.77	14.35	15	15
11	Irrigated area under paddy to total irrigated area	41.16	40.00	40	38

Source: Directorate of Economics & Statistics

As per the assessment of the Directorate of Economics and Statistics the net irrigated area in the state as on 3/06, was 3.99 lakh ha. and the gross area irrigated is 4.65 lakh ha. Compared to the last year a slight increase of 1.50% is noted in the area irrigated in 2005-06.

The net area irrigated during 2005-06 has increased to 3.99 lakh ha. from 3.93 lakh ha. in the previous year. Only 19 per cent of the net cropped area is irrigated. The major source of irrigation is wells, which contribute 28 per cent followed by government canals 26 per cent., tanks 11.27 per cent and private canals 1.24 per cent. In the source wise irrigation, the contribution of private wells predominates.

Table : Gross Area Irrigated (Crop-wise)

(in ha.)

S.N.	Crops	2002-03	2003-04	2004-5	2005-06
1	2	5	6	7	8
1	Paddy	183703	169829	183601	174600
2	Tubers	1008	1020	2253	2958
3	Vegetables	9786	9657	14274	25075
4	Coconut	163550	159113	157768	158630
5	Arecanut	34205	32990	36858	35131
6	Nutmeg/clove	2948	2884	6285	6913
7	Other Spices and condiments	3212	3245	3403	3788
8	Banana	29209	28100	30265	33730
9	Betel leaves	990	947	891	850
10	Sugarcane	3426	3567	1630	2000
11	Others	15373	15413	18163	21070
	Total	447490	426765	455398	464745

Source: Directorate of Economics & Statistics

Among the crops, paddy continued to be the major crop supported by irrigation. It accounted for about 38 per cent followed by coconut (34%) arecanut (8%) banana (7%) and vegetables (5%). Though rice is the major crop supported by irrigation, it could only support 59 per cent of the total area under the crop. Similarly irrigation could be provided to 17 per cent of the total area under coconut, 35 per cent of the area under arecanut and 54 per cent of the area under banana. Compared to last year the area irrigated under crops like arecanut, betel leaves, etc. have been decreased.

GOI had launched a new scheme Bharat Nirman Yojana to create additional irrigation facilities in the next four years. Under this programme, action is proposed for the areas of irrigation, roads, rural housing, rural water supply, rural electrification and rural communication connectivity.

Irrigation is one of the six components for development of rural infrastructure under Bharat Nirman. Under irrigation, it is proposed to create additional 10 million hectares of irrigation capacity by 2009 through major and medium irrigation projects (4.2 Mha), minor irrigation (2.8 Mha), enhancing utilisation of completed projects (2.0 Mha) and ground water development (1.Mha).

Kerala is also eligible for assistance under the programme. GOK had proposed schemes worth Rs. 1873 crores comprising of major irrigation Rs. 1453 crores for creating an additional area of 0.80 lakh ha, and minor irrigation costing Rs. 134 crores for bringing an additional area of 0.31 lakh hectare and modernisation and restoration costing Rs. 286.23 crores to create an additional area of 1.84 lakh hectares.

Local Water Resources

Local water resource development and management would be an important element of the strategy of meeting the water needs of the future particularly in water-scarce regions. There is a need to lay emphasis on local water planning, water harvesting at micro level and integrated water shed development. Lakes are the largest fresh water storages and from time immemorial serve human beings in non-raining season for all water needs. Due to excessive withdrawal of water and pollution very sustainability of lakes has become questionable. Safe water supply and environmental sanitation are vital for protecting the environment. Unless the facilities for the treatment of domestic sewage and industrial effluents are increased manifold the increasing pollution due to urbanisation will further deteriorate the quality of waterbodies. National Lake Conservation Programme needs to be strengthened to arrest further degradation of lakes. Enlarged programmes of lake and wetland conservation need to be initiated and streamlined.

In order to promote the development of local water resources, particularly tank irrigation, Government of India has introduced a scheme 'restoration of water bodies' (renovation of tanks/ponds) with 75% central assistance under Command Area Development Programme. Restoration of Tanks in Palakkad and Pathanamthitta were forwarded to GOI and sanction has been accorded for taking up the work for the renovation of

Tanks in both the districts. An amount of Rs. 1.38 crores was sanctioned for Palakkad district and the implementation has started.

Minor Irrigation

Kerala has a wide network of rivers and rivulets and springs spread over the entire cropped area. Minor irrigation sector received considerable attention from Seventh Plan onwards and got a considerable boost during the Ninth Plan period consequent to the enhanced flow of funds from the grant in aid of the local bodies as well as on account of special support received from the external agencies like European Economic Community, Dutch Government and assistance under RIDF of NABARD. With the introduction of decentralised planning, all minor irrigation works (having cultivable command area up to 2000 ha.) were vested with the Panchayat Raj Institutions (PRIs).

But by the enactment of the new Act 'Kerala Irrigation and Water Management Act 2003' the definition of minor irigation has been changed and works benefiting an area less than 15 ha. only come under the category of minor irrigation and are vested with PRIs. All other works having cultivable command area greater than 15 ha. have been taken over by the Water Resources Department as medium irrigation. The major works implemented under surface water are minor irrigation Class – I, II and Lift irrigation schemes. Construction of check dams, Vented cross bars, weirs, tanks etc are the various works executed under minor irrigation Class-I & II.

The minor irrigation sector has always been a thrust area for NABARD not only in terms of providing increased refinance but also by introducing various developmental initiatives and financial incentives. Assistance to the tune of Rs. 109.17 crores has been sanctioned for implementing 733 schemes under the rural infrastructural fund of NABARD through its various tranche from I–X. The amount disbursed so far (31.10.2005) aggregates to Rs. 77.61 crores. Out of the 733 schemes sanctioned 595 schemes were completed and 51890 ha. of area has been reported to be brought under irrigation.

An amount of Rs. 101.92 crores have been expended for implementing minor irrigation schemes during the X Plan period. Besides this, an amount of Rs. 97.44 crores have been budgeted for implementing minor irrigation schemes by local governments during the first three years of the Tenth Plan. The additional area brought by implementing irrigation schemes aggregates to 35000 hectares including ground water schemes.

During the year under review (2005-06) the Department has invested Rs.12.77 crores for implementing surface water minor irrigation schemes. The additional area reported to be brought under irrigation during 2005-06 was 3611ha.

Ground Water Development

The dynamic ground water resource (recharged annually by rainfall) of the country is 432 BCM. As much as 80per cent of India's population manage to get their own domestic water supply and three fourth of the irrigated area in the country is through private sources – mostly through ground water. India is the largest user of ground water (200 BCM) followed by the United States (100 BCM) and China (90 BCM). However ground water resources are either over exploited or are in the critical zone in certain pockets --Tamil Nadu, Haryana, Punjab, Gujarat and Rajasthan. According to the Central Ground Water Board, out of 7928 blocks/taluks/watersheds, 673 are over exploited where the level of development is more than the quantum that can be replenishable and 425 are dark/critical. The provision of free or subsidised power to agriculture sector in many states is one of the factors responsible for indiscriminate use of groundwater.

The National Water Policy, 2002 has advocated that groundwater recharge projects should be developed and implemented for improving both the quality and availability of ground water resources. The policy also advocated exploitation of ground water resources so as not to exceed recharge possibilities. The Ministry of Water Resources has already prepared and submitted, a part of the second green revolution project of the Ministry of Agriculture, a scheme for ground water development in 5.2 m. ha.(loan-cum-subsidy cost of

Rs.15,310 crore) and another for artificial recharge of 3.9 BCM of water (at a cost of Rs.3,000 crore). Compared to 4,000 BCM rainfall/snowfall in the country and 1,869 BCM run off, recharge of this small quantity of groundwater will not adversely affect the existing hydrology of rivers and streams. The Ministry of Water Resources had also submitted a new state sector scheme costing Rs. 175 crore for artificial recharge in various parts of the country, which would serve as a demonstration exercise for various types of recharge structures.

The contribution of ground water in the total irrigation potential of the country has been estimated as 47 per cent. Although ground water is annually replenishable resource, its availability is non-uniform in space and time. Hence, precise estimation of ground water resource and irrigation potential is a pre-requisite for planning its development. The scientific assessment of the ground water resources of India has been made by the Central Ground Water Board in collaboration with concerned State Departments in 1997.

In Kerala, groundwater occurs under phreatic, semi-confined and confined conditions. The groundwater resources are largely concentrated in the sedimentary aquifers of the coastal regions. The groundwater resources are tapped mainly for drinking and irrigation purposes. The ground water potential of Kerala is very low as compared to that of many other States in the country. The state has a replenishable groundwater resource of 6841 million cubic meters. The net groundwater availability is 6229 million cubic meters. The gross groundwater draft is 2920 million cubic meters and the net groundwater available for future use is 3221 million cubic meters.

A district-wise analysis of ground water resources of Kerala shows that Palakkad has the higher potential for ground water recharge (12%) followed by Thrissur (11%), Ernakulam (9%), Kannur (8%), Kottayam (7%) and Alleppey (6.8%). Thiruvananthapuram has the lowest (4%) potential for ground water recharge. The stage of development of groundwater is the highest in Kasargod district (79%) and the lowest is in Wayanad (25%). The overall stage of development in the State is 47% which is greater than the national level.

Monitoring and preservation of groundwater is an important aspect, which requires serious attention. Factors like over exploitation of groundwater, the deep infiltration of surface water from irrigated fields using chemical fertilizers and pesticides, infiltration of saline soils, effluents from industries affect the quality of ground water.

The Central Ground Water Board monitors the ground water situation in Kerala state through a network of 615 observation wells and 241 piezometers. Water samples are collected in the pre monsoon period and maps showing ground water level, fluctuations are prepared to determine the long term water level trend, which helps delineating the areas of critical and overdeveloped nature. The State Ground Water Department is monitoring 440 piezometres and 303 observation dugwell stations across the state in different terrains under hydrology project. Monthly observed data for all the stations are analyzed and trend analysis reports were prepared. It is observed that 81 piezometres and 59 dug wells are showing falling trend when analyzed for pre monsoon and post monsoon seasons. This indicates that either overdraft or insufficient recharge is affecting these areas. These areas need special attention in the context of ground water recharge.

Artificial recharge and rainwater harvesting are the best-suited and cheapest methods to overcome this situation. A scheme for the construction of artifical recharge structures was introduced in the state with financial assistance from Government of India. Sub surface dams and dykes are the main structures built for the artificial recharge of ground water. The sub surface dams constructed at Odakkali in Ernakulam district, Alanallur, Bavaji nagar in Palakkad district, Sadanandapuram in Kollam district, Ayilam in Thiruvananthapuram district, Neezhur in Kottayam district showed a considerable rise of ground water levels in the upstream side of these sub surface dams and prevention of the decline of water table in the areas. Hydrogeologically suitable sites for sub-surface dams were located and works are in progress. For the rest of places detailed hydrogeological investigation are underway for the construction of suitable recharge structures. The sources of pollution have to be properly surveyed and identified. The Central Ground Water Board is carrying out artificial recharge studies in high water demand areas with critical stage of ground water development and the Board's Pollution Cell has undertaken studies to find out the ways and means to check the effect and spreading of pollution.

As per the latest groundwater estimation carried out by the Central Groundwater Board, Government of India and Groundwater Department, Government of Kerala based on Groundwater Estimation Committee norms, 15 blocks of the State fall under overexploited, critical and semi critical categories and 33 blocks show more than 70% development. Blocks were categorised based on the stage of development and long term trend of groundwater levels during pre and post Monsoon seasons.

The systematic approach to the management of ground water requires a sustainable legal framework. Government of India has also pointed out the necessity of legislation by the State Governments for the regulation of ground water exploitation. In this circumstance, in order to regulate the over exploitation of groundwater resources Government of Kerala have brought in a law The Kerala Ground Water (Control and Regulation) Act 2002 which envisages conservation of ground water and regulation and control of its use.

The Act has to be implemented by an authority named 'State Ground Water Authority' consisting of 13 members and the Secretary (WRD) as the Chairman and Director, GWD as the Secretary.

The State Ground Water Department is the nodal agency assigned with the responsibility of ground water development and utilisation. The main activities of GWD is to locate potential ground water resources for construction of ground water structures like open wells, bore-wells, tube wells and artificial structures like subsurface dykes and check dams. Technical guidance were given to local bodies for siting and construction of drilled wells and for the implementation of rainwater harvesting.

During the period under report (2005-06), an amount of Rs. 17.71 crores has been invested for minor irrigation out of which the share of ground water development was Rs. 4.93 crores ie. about 28% of the investment under minor irrigation.

During 2005-06 the Department has imparted technical assistance to identify sites for 3590 open wells, and constructed 999 drilled wells. The additional area reported to be brought under irrigation was 539 ha. Training was imparted to 45 personnel and analysed 3443 water samples, prepared 5 Ground water prospect maps from satellite imagery of Kerala under Rajiv Gandhi National Drinking Water Mission and developed new methodology for the detection of Fluoride content in drinking water, with the assistance of CCCM of BARC, Hyderabad. Under Rajiv Gandhi National Drinking Water Mission scheme, 36 bore wells were drilled in the non- covered/ partially covered habitats.

National Hydrology Project

The Phase I of the National Hydrology Project has been continued during the period under report and the second phase also has been initiated.

The Hydrology Project Phase-II is a follow on project of Hydrology project and to be implemented with the assistance of World Bank. The project objectives are:

(i) To extend and promote the sustained and effective use of the HIS by all implementing agencies concerned with water resources planning and management

(ii) Strengthening the capabilities of implementing agencies at state/central level in HIS data utilisation for efficient water resource planning and management.

(iii) Awareness building and outreaches services about HIS use.

The project would cover 9 ongoing states of HP-I namely Andhra Pradesh, Gujarat, Maharashtra, Karnataka, Kerala, Madhya Pradaesh, Chattisgargh, Orissa, Tamil Nadu and 4 new states Himachal Pradesh, Goa, Pondicherry and Punjab and the Central institutes CWC, MOWR, CGWB, CWPRS, NIH,, IMD, CPCB and Bhakra-Beas Management Board (BBMB).

Under HP-II it is proposed to enhance the current manual system of recording and reporting expenditures in the implementation by the Surface Water and Ground Water departments of two states by instituting a computerised Financial Management System.

The total cost of the project for the country as a whole is Rs. 631.83 million. The three project components namely institutional strengthening costs 36% vertical extension cost (44%) and horizontal extension costs (20%) of the total project cost. The project would be implemented over a period of six years from 2005-06 onwards.

The World Bank has approved the phase – II of the project in Kerala for a total cost of Rs.18.35 crores. The agreement for phase –II was executed in January 2006 and initiated implementation in April 2006.

Flood Management

India is prone to natural disasters. Due to its locational and geographical features, it is vulnerable to a number of natural hazards like cyclones, droughts, floods, earthquakes, fires, land slides & avalanches.

The reasons for the occurrence of the flood are not simple enough to comprehend in its true perspective. The short duration intense rainfall seems to create conditions leading to flood. The peculiar physiograpbic set up of Kerala with abrupt fall in slope from the Western Ghats to the midlands and the high rainfall pattern spread over two seasons and that too concentrated in a few days, are the major factors which make the state vulnerable to heavy floods of a recurring nature.

At the State level during the year under report, an amount of Rs 2.82 crores has been spent for protection of an area of 933 ha. of land from the ravages of flood. The cumulative area brought under flood control was 61242 ha. as on 3/2006.

Coastal Zone Management

Coastal erosion is affecting most of the coastal states. The situation in Kerala is also not different. Kerala has a long coastal stretch of 590 kms. and more than half of it is subjected to sea erosion. Unlike other parts in the country, Kerala seacoast is thickly populated and as a result the loss due to sea erosion is relatively very high.

Construction of sea walls continued to be the sole intervention for coastal zone protection. In the area of protection of seashore, modern technologies like geo textiles, polyethylene fabrics/sheets, nourishment of foreshore with biomaterials, etc. are emerging. During 2005-06 an amount of Rs.8.13 crores has been spent to construct 13.32 km. of new sea wall and for reformation works in 3.12 km. Out of the total coastal stretch of 590 kms, about 389.53 Kms has been protected by constructing new sea walls and reformed 116.66 Km. of old sea walls spending an amount of Rs. 286.18 crores upto 31.3.2006. The Eleventh Finance Commission has provided Rs.50.00 crores for anti sea erosion works for constructing 15.89 km of new seawall and reformation of 20.14 km. for the period 2000-05. Out of this, 12.70 km of new sea wall was constructed and reformed 28.63 km. of old sea walls as on 31.03.2005 spending Rs.38.00 crores.

Table : Financial and Physical Progress of Flood Management and Coastal Zone Management Programmes during 2005-06

(Rs. lakhs)

S.N.	Item	Financial Achievement	Physical Achievement	Cumulative Physical achievement as on 3/2006
1	Flood Management	282	933 ha.	61242 ha.
2	Anti-Sea Erosion Works			
	a) New sea-wall constructed	813	3.32 km.	389.53 km.
	b) Reformation of old & damaged sea-wall		3.12	116.66 km

Source: Water Resources Deportment

The Twelfth Finance Commission has awarded Rs.175 crores for the construction, maintenance and reformation of the sea walls. Kerala Coast is subject to severe erosion, which undermines the valuable coastal eco system and affects the lives of millions of people. Nearly 100 Kms. coastal zone, prone to severe sea erosion needs to be urgently protected on a long term basis.

The amount allotted is for construction and reformation of sea walls for the protection of the coastal area and for establishing permanent bench marks in the coastal area and conducting pilot studies using new techniques. The target envisaged for the utilization of Twelfth Finance Commission Award is to construct new sea walls to a length of 47.77 Kms, 21 groynes and reformation of 63.10 Km. during 2005-10.

Command Area Development

The Command Area Development Programme was launched with the main objective of bridging the gap between the irrigation potential created and utilised and improving agricultural production and productivity in the irrigation commands. The programme was restructured in 2003-04 and renamed as Command Area Development and Water Management Programme.

The restructured programme retains the components of the existing schemewhich have been found to be beneficial to the farmers, include a few new components considered necessary for correction of deficiencies in the irrigation system and delete those components which have lost their utility overtime.

Under the restructured Programme there is thrust on Participatory Irrigation Management (PIM) and, therefore, following features have been made mandatory for programme implementation.

(i) Central assistance to States has been linked to the enactment of PIM legislation. Till this is done, alternative arrangements have to be in place for formation and empowerment of Water Users' Associations (WUAs).

(ii) WUAs have to be in position before Project Components are taken up so that beneficiaries are involved in the implementing of Programme activities, since inception.

(iii) A minimum 10% beneficiary contribution has been made mandatory in the construction of field channels, reclamation of waterlogged areas and renovation of Minor Irrigation Tanks to ensure increased beneficiary participation and thereby improve the quality of works.

Central assistance for correction of system deficiencies upto distributaries of 150 Cusec capacity has been linked to formation of Distributories Committees and handing over of the distributories to such Committees for maintenance in future.

The main activities of Command Area Development Authority include construction of field channels, field drains, enforcement of warabandhi and reclamation of water logged areas. The Command Area Development (CAD) activities were carried out in the 16 completed irrigation projects, namely Malampuzha, Mangalam, Pothundy, Walayar, Cheerakuzhy, Vazhani, Peechi, Chalakudy, Neyyar, Gayathri, Pamba, Periyarvalley, Chithurpuzha, Kuttiyadi, Pazhassi and Kanhirapuzha with a total ayacut of 2.03 lakh ha.

Government of India had directed to restructure the CAD programme from the 3 rd year of the Tenth Plan onwards in the ongoing four projects namely Pamba, Periyarvalley, Kanhirapuzha and Pazhassi. Detailed project reports for these projects for the restructured CADWM activities were approved by Government of India. Finalisation of the detailed project reports of Kallada and Muvattupuzha projects are nearing completion. As part of reform initiative in the new CADWM programme new components like renovation of tanks and system correction are included. Assistance was provided for the restoration of 10 tanks in Palakkad and 13 tanks in Pathanamthitta districts under the scheme Restoration of Water bodies.

The progress during 2005-06 was not encouraging. The achievement recorded during 2005-06, include construction of field channels in 1614 ha~ drains to benefit 3275 ha. adaptive trials in 9 ha~ 117 training programmes, bench mark and evaluation studies in 1741 ha. The work on reclamation of water logged areas were done in 258 ha and one evaluation report was also published.

DRINKING WATER SUPPLY

Coverage

In Kerala 83.07 percent urban and 62.74 percent rural population have been covered by piped water supply as on 1-4-2006. The overall water supply coverage is 68.02 percent as against 67.52 percent as on 1-4-2005. The rural- urban coverage as on 1-4-2005 was 62.24 percent and 82.59 percent respectively.

During 2005-06, 85 water supply schemes taken up under various categories were commissioned. A total population of 9.01 lakhs have been benefited by these schemes. Out of this additional population covered is 1.60 lakhs and status level improvement is 7.41 lakhs. Of the additional population covered with protected water supply, 15705 (9.81%) are scheduled castes and 1825 (1.14%) are scheduled tribe population.

District-wise overall coverage of water supply varies from 91.16 percent in Ernakulam to 49.51 percent in Kozhikode. In rural coverage also Ernakulam stands top with 91.32 percent and Kozhikode is at the bottom with 35.42 percent. Urban coverage is highest in Kottayam district with 97.62 percent and lowest in Wayanad with 50.10 percent.

Habitation-wise Status of Water Supply Coverage

Habitations are mainly classified in to three namely Non-Covered (NC) Habitations, Partially Covered (PC) Habitations and Fully Covered (FC) Habitations. A fresh habitation survey has been conducted in 2003 based on 2001 census population and the number of rural habitations in Kerala increased to 12165 from 9776 in the previous survey in 1992.

The increases in the number of habitations were due to ward bifurcation as per 2001 census. In the new survey a number of Fully Covered habitations and some Partially Covered habitations have slipped back to Non Covered status due to various reasons such as bifurcation of wards, drying up of sources, sources becoming quality affected, population increase etc.

Habitation coverage status as on 1-4- 2006 (No. of habitations based on 2003 survey) and as on 1-4-2005 (No. of the habitations based on 1992 survey) is given in Table below.

Table : Habitation Coverage Status of Water Supply

Category of Habitations	2004-05	2005-06
1	2	3
Fully Covered	2365	3793
Partially Covered	7398	8152
Non Covered	13 (not reachable)	220
Total	9776	12165

Source: Kerala Water Authority

In 8372 habitations the supply of water is less than the stipulated norm of 40 lpcd.

Water Supply Schemes in Operation

Kerala Water Authority has 1940 water supply schemes in operation as on 1-4-06. It consists 65 urban and 1875 rural schemes. During 2005-06, 85 schemes have been commissioned. Out of this, 40 schemes are augmentation/improvement/ extension to the existing schemes and 45 are independent schemes.

Production and Distribution of Water

The total quantity of water produced by KWA during 2005-06 is 1635 million litres per day (mld) and the quantity supplied is 1259 mld. Hence the unaccounted for water (ufw) is 376 mld, which is 23% of the quantity produced. Production and distribution of water by KWA from 2001-02 onwards is given in Table-5.8

Table : Production and Distribution of water

Year	Production (in mld)	Supply (in mld)	Leakage (%)
2001-02	1511.96	1164.21	23
2002-03	1551.58	1194.72	23
2003-04	1583.60	1219.37	23
2004-05	1617.13	1245.78	22.96
2005-06	1635.00	1259.00	23

Source: Kerala Water Authority

The cost of production of water is Rs. 7.39 per KL. The summary of cost of production of water is given in Table-5.9

Table : Summary of cost of production of water

Particulars	**For the year 2005-06**	
1	2	3
	mly	mld
Quantity Produced	596,775	1635
Quantity Sold	459,535	1259
Direct Variable Cost	Total (Rs.in Crores)	Per KL (Rs)
Operators Salary	49.95	1.09
Power Charges	108.00	2.35
Chemicals	11.95	0.26
Total -Direct Variable Cost	169.90	3.70
Indirect overhead Cost	24.70	0.54
Repairs & Maintenance	78.11	1.70
Administrative Overheads	32.23	0.70
Interest (excluding GOK Loan)	34.57	0.75
Depreciation		
Total- Indirect overhead Cost	169.61	3.69
TOTAL	339.51	7.39

Source: Kerala Water Authority

Service Connections and Street Taps

KWA has 10.36 lakh service connections and 1.97 lakh street taps as on 1-4-2006. This is against 9.77 lakh service connections and 1.83 lakh street taps as on 1-4-2005. It shows that 0.59 lakh service connections and 0.14 lakh street taps were provided additionally during 2005- 06. Out of the total service connections, 9.58 lakh (92.5%) are domestic and 0.77 lakh (7.4%) are non domestic. Out of the total street taps, 1.56 lakh (78.77%) are in rural areas.

Table : Service Connections and Street Taps by KWA as on 1-4-2006

Sl. No	Category	Number
1	Service Connections	
	i) Domestic	958337
	ii) Non-Domestic	77090
	iii) Industrial	891
	Total	1036318
2.	Street Taps	
	i) Rural	155559
	ii) Urban	41915
	III. Total	197474

Source: Kerala Water Authority

Water Tariff and Revenue

The existing Water Tariff rates in Kerala was fixed in 1999 and it is given in Appendix.5.12. Total revenue collected from water charges during 2005-06 is Rs. 166.57 crore as against Rs. 115.23 crore during 2004-05. Out of the total revenue collected during 2005-06, Rs. 106.04 crore (63.66%) was from service connections and Rs. 60.53 crore (36.34%) was from street taps. Similarly out of the total income form water charges, Rs. 86.81 crore (52.12%) was from Urban Schemes and Rs. 59.82 crore (35.91%) from Rural Comprehensive Schemes and Rs. 19.94 crore (11.97%) from Rural Single Panchayat Schemes.

Arrears of Water Charge

As on 1-4-2006 dues from various category of consumers is Rs. 732.23 crore as against Rs. 746.85 crore during the previous year. Out of Rs. 732.23 crore Rs. 543.07 crore (74.17%) is from

Local Governments. Table below shows arrears due form various category of consumers.

Table : Arrears of Water Charges due from various category of consumers.

(Rs. crore)

Sl.No	Consumer Category	Amount	Percentage
1	Domestic	60.82	8.31
2	Non Domestic	103.64	14.15
3	Industrial	24.70	3.37
4	Panchayats	255.41	34.88
5	Municipality	153.95	21.03
6	Corporation	133.71	18.26
	Total	732.23	100

Source: Kerala Water Authority

Computerisation in Kerala Water Authority

Kerala Water Authority is implementing computerisation with the assistance of GOI. Twenty eight revenue units of KWA covering 60 percent of the total consumers at TVPM, Kollam, Kochi, Kozhikode Corporations and Alappuzha, Kottayam, Perumbavoor, North Paravoor, Thrippunithura, Aluva, Kalamassery, Palakkad and Kannur Municipalities were computerised and bi-monthly billing systems implemented.

Spot billing system is implemented in TVPM and it is proposed to extend in other parts of Kerala in a phased manner. A centralised Web enabled billing and collection system is under development and is decided to be implemented in Thiruvananthapuram, connecting all the 8 revenue centres under PH Division, Thiruvananthapuram and Govt.

Friends Centre. A master plan envisaging water supply schemes and sewerage schemes including project management has been approved and as per the master plan all the offices of KWA will be connected by a network. Action is being taken to implement the master plan with JBIC/GOI assistance.

Plan and Non-Plan Expenditure of KWA

Total expenditure of KWA during 2005-06 was Rs. 486.49 crore. Out of this Rs. 162.48 crore (33.4%) was under plan and Rs. 324.01 crore (66.6%) under non-plan. Under non-plan 37.27 percent is utilised for salary and establishment, 33.33% for power, 11.31 percent for operation and maintenance, 9.94 percent for payment of interest on loans and 5.90 percent for repayment of loans.

Table : Plan and Non-Plan Expenditure of Kerala Water Authority -2005-06

Sl.No.	Category	Expenditure (Rs. in crores)
	A. Plan	
1	State Plan	54.60
2	ARP Schemes	66.68
3	LIC/HUDCO Aided Schemes	26.35
4	Others(AUWSP- Central share, PMGY and JBIC	14.86
	Sub Total	162.49
	B. Non- Plan	
1	Salary & Establishment	120.76
2	Power Charges	108.00
3	Operation and Maintenance	36.65
4	Repayment of Loans	19.07
5	Interest on Loans	32.23
6	Others	7.30
	Sub Total	324.01
	Grand Total	486.50

Source: Kerala Water Authority

Ongoing Water Supply Schemes

Considering the need for extending the coverage of protected water supply in the state in addition to state funded and centrally sponsored schemes, various schemes are being implemented by KWA with loan assistance from funding agencies also. Altogether 579 water supply schemes consisting of 527 rural and 51 urban schemes are under execution.

Accelerated Rural Water Supply Programme

The works on 93 schemes sanctioned under Accelerated Rural Water Supply Programme are in progress-82 schemes with central fund and 11 schemes which have exceeded their estimated cost with state fund.

These schemes are designed with a per capita demand of 40 lpcd and centrally sponsored schemes are implemented with 100% assistance from GOI.

Accelerated Urban Water Supply Programme

The Accelerated Urban Water Supply Programme (AUWSP) for Census Towns having population below 20000 is sponsored by Ministry of Urban Development, Government of India. The main objective is to provide safe and adequate water supply facilities to the population of the Census Towns in the country within a fixed time.

The scheme will be funded on 50% grant basis by the central Government. The balance 50% will have to be provided by the state government including 5% beneficiary/local body contribution. Benefited community should be responsible for O&M of the assets created under the programme. So far 9 schemes were sanctioned under this programme and out of these one scheme has been completed. Works of other schemes are in progress.

Swajaldhara

Government of India launched community based, participatory, demand driven Water Supply Schemes viz, Swajaldhara for rural sector in the financial year 2002-03 by giving 90% of the project cost as Government aid and remaining 10% as beneficiary contribution.

As per the direction from Government of India, a District Implementing Agency, the District Water and Sanitation Mission (DWSM) in each district was constituted with District Collector as Chairman and Executive Engineer, Kerala Water Authority, District head quarters division as Member Secretary for implementing the schemes, in the district level.

Table : Year-wise details of Swajaldhara schemes

Year	No. of Schemes	Estimate Amount (Rs. in lakhs)
2002-03	117	627.28
2003-04	78	559.04
2004-05	67	533.43
2005-06	106	868.11
Total	368	2587.86

Source: Kerala Water Authority

Of the 368 schemes sanctioned from 2002-03 to 2005-06, 32 schemes sanctioned in 2002-03 were dropped. Out of the remaining 336 schemes taken up 163 schemes have been completed and works of the remaining are in progress. The allotment for 2006-07 is Rs. 914 lakh.

JBIC Assisted Kerala Water Supply Project

A package of five water supply schemes was approved for loan assistance by the Overseas Economic Co-operation Fund (OECF) of Japan (now the Japan Bank for International Co-operation) in 1996. The objectives of the project are to augment and rehabilitate water supply systems of two urban regions namely Thiruvanathapuram and Kozhikode and to construct water supply systems for three rural regions namely, Meenad, Cherthala and Pattuvam including their adjoining villages. The largest ever Water Supply Project in the state when completed will ensure drinking water to a population of about 43 lakh in the benefited area spread over five districts. The total estimated cost of the project is Rs. 1787.45 crore. Out of it external assistance is Rs. 1519.38 crore and state share is Rs. 268.07 crore.

As per the loan agreement, the project was proposed to be commenced in 1997 and completed by 2003. However the appointment of consultants for implementation of the project, a mandatory pre-requisite as per the loan agreement, had been inordinately delayed and the project could not take off as per the proposal.

The selection procedure for appointment of consultants started afresh in May 2002 and agreement has been executed with the selected consultants only on 4-8-03. The consultants commenced their work from 1/9/2003. As per the revised Terms of Reference the project implementation period had been reduced to four years from the original six years.

The works of the five water supply schemes under the project are covered in 23 contract packages of which 11 are under International Competitive Bidding (ICB) and 12 are Local Competitive Bidding (LCB).

Table : Scheme-wise and Category wise number of contract packages of JBIC Project

Sl. No	**Name of Scheme**	**Numer of ICB packages**	**Number of LCB packages**	**Total Number of packages**
1	WS Improvement to Thiruvananthapuram city Region	2	3	5
2	WSS to Meenad & Adjoining villages	2	2	4
3	WSS to Cherthala & Adjoining Villages	2	2	4
4	WS Improvement to Kozhikode city region	3	3	6
5	WSS to Pattuvam & Adjoining Villages	2	2	4
	Total	11	12	23

Source: Kerala Water Authority

Table : Details of work packages of JBIC Assisted Kerala Water Supply Project(KWSP)

Package No.	Category of Contract	No. and Description of contract
Package 1	ICB	One bid for each scheme comprising Intake,Raw Water Main and Water Treatment Plant
Package 2	ICB	This package covers Transmission Mains.One bid each for 4 schemes and 2 for Kozhikode scheme.Considering the long transmission system of Kozhikode scheme, this package is proposed in 2 bids
Package 3	LCB	One bid for each scheme; covers Distribution System
Package 4	LCB	One bid for each scheme ; covers Service Reservoirs
Package 5	LCB	One bid each for Thiruvananthapuram and Kozhikode schemes only and is for rehabilitation of existing schemes

Source: Kerala Water Authority

Fifteen out of the 23 contracts are already awarded. Five contracts in package 4 has been approved by the Empowered Committee and concurrence of the JBIC is awaited for awarding the works to the contractors.

Table : Status of Award of Contracts of KWSP

Name of Package	Name of Scheme	Date of Agreement
Package 1	Thiruvananthapuram	12/10/2006
	Meenad	13/10/2006
	Cherthala	13/10/2006
	Pattuvam	13/10/2006
	Thiruvananthapuram	31/3/2006
	Meenad	31/3/2006
	Cherthala	9/10/2006
Package II	Kozhikode 2A	31-03-2006
	Kozhikode 2B	31-03-2006
	Pattuvam	31-03-2006

Contd...

Name of Package	Name of Scheme	Date of Agreement
Package III	Thiruvananthapuram	3-10-2006
	Meenad	30-09-2006
	Chethala	9-10-2006
	Kozhikode	30-9-2006
	Pattuvam	30-9-2006

Source: Kerala Water Authority

Kerala Rural Water Supply and Environmental Sanitation Project (Jalanidhi)

The World Bank loan assisted Kerala Rural Water Supply and Sanitation Project (Jalanidhi) was conceived in mid 1999. Project Implementation Plan was prepared and project appraised in mid 2000.The agreement with the World Bank was signed on 4 th January 2001.The government has also created an autonomous institution 'Kerala Rural Water Supply and Sanitation Agency (KRWSA) to implement this project. The project is expected to cover three lakh households, benefiting a population of over 15 lakh in the selected Grama Panchayaths. The project has been designed as a demand responsive project, with a community driven development approach in implementation. The project integrates water supply with sanitation, health promotion, environment management and ground water recharge measures.

The overall development objective of the project is to improve the quality of rural water supply and environmental sanitation. The specific development objectives of the project are: (a)demonstrate the viability of cost recovery and institutional reforms by developing, testing and implementing the new decentralised service delivery model on a pilot basis (b) build the state's capacity in improved sector management inorder to scale up the new model state wide.

The Jalanidhi project was originally proposed to be implemented in about 80-100 Grama Panchayaths in four districts of Kerala (Thrissur,Palakkad, Malappuram and

Kozhikode),at an estimated cost of Rs.451.40 crore, over a period of six years from 2001.

During the Mid Term Review of the project in 2003, it was found that the project was achieving its target at a lower cost. Hence the estimates were revised and also decided to scale up the project to other districts. As per the revised plan, by the end of 2006, 92 Grama Panchayaths spread over Thrissur,Palakkad, Malappuram and Kozhikode and 18Grama Panchayaths spread over the remaining 9 districts, ie, 2 Grama Panchayats from each district, excluding Alappuzha were to be covered under this project. Besides 2 Grama Panchayats of Kollam district were selected to implement Tsunami rehabilitation water supply project. Thus Jalanidhi Project is covering 112 Grama Panchayaths. The revised estimate of Jalanidhi Project is Rs. 381.5 crores including Rs. 60 crore for scaling up the activities across the state and Rs. 60 crore for Tsunami rehabilitation project.

Table : Pattern of funding of Jalanidhi project

Stake Holder	**Percentage**	**Amount (Rs.in crores)**
World Bank	72	274.74
Government of Kerala	7	26.70
Grama Panchayaths	7	26.70
Beneficiary Groups	14	53.36
Total	100	381.50

Source: Kerala Rural Water Supply and Sanitation Agency (KRWSA)

There are 3960 active Beneficiary Groups in the 3674 water supply schemes taken up as on 30/9/2006. More than 12 lakh people are being benefited through these beneficiary groups. 54 percent of the total Jalanidhi membership is from BPL families and 16% from SC/ST households.

Activity-wise Present Status of Implementation Water Supply

As on 30-9-06, 2598 water supply schemes managed by 2702 beneficiary groups have been completed through Jalanidhi

Project. All these schemes are being operated and maintained by the beneficiary communities. Another 1076 schemes are at different stages of implementation. Fifteen river based large Water Supply Schemes have been taken up so far, of which 2 schemes are fully and one partially commissioned. 8 schemes are in the implementation phase and 4 schemes are in the planning phase.

Tsunami Rehabilitation Project

Out of the two projects proposed in Tsunami rehabilitation areas of Kollam and Alappuzha districts, only one scheme for Chavara and Panmana Panchayaths has been taken up. The estimated cost of the scheme is Rs. 28 crores. It is expected that the scheme could be completed by December 2007.

Sanitation

In order to ensure the quality of drinking water focus is given for the prevention of biological contamination by construction of sanitary latrines and conversion of unsanitary latrines to sanitary latrines. 63267 new sanitary latrines have been constructed so far against the target of 40000 and conversion of 23224 unsanitary latrines to sanitary latrines have been done against the target of 8000. A total of 83967 environment sanitation structures like compost pit, soak pit and vermi composting units have been already constructed against the target of 26667. The project also assigns equal weightage to build up community awareness on sanitation and hygiene and its relation to water.

Ground Water Recharge

This project is designed in keeping with the change in Government perspective on a holistic approach to water resource management. Thus source recharge measures have been in built in to the project design. GWR activities have been done in 758 BGs that are amenable for point recharge. Comprehensive GWR activities have been planned with the aim to implement GWR activities in the project panchayaths identified as 'difficult areas' which show a drop in ground water levels and face acute drought during peak summer.

Table : Physical Target and Achievement as on 1/4/2006

Sl. No	Name of the Component	Unit	Target	Achievement	Percentage of achievement
1	W.S.Ss commissioned	Nos	2083	2000	96%
2	Latrines (New)	Nos	33333	58731	176%
3	Latrines (Conversion of unsanitary Latrine)	Nos	6667	20948	314%
4	Environment Management Works (Soak pits + compost pits)	Nos	22222	72693	327%
5	Drainage	Kms	148	43.94	29.7%
6	Ground Water Recharge Schemes	Nos	468	563	120%
7	Rain Water Harvesting Structures-Small Scale units. Large DemoUnits, special proposals	Nos	782	704	90%

Source: Kerala Rural Water Supply and Sanitation Agency

Actual expenditure for the project as on 30-9-2006 including all stakeholders contribution is Rs. 277.43 crores.

Table : Year-wise Expenditure for Jalanidhi Project

Year	Expenditure (Rs. in crores)
2000-01	3.25
2001-02	9.15
2002-03	12.98
2003-04	57.99
2004-05	67.68
2005-06	78.55
2006-07 up to 30-9-2006	47.83
Total	277.43

Source: Kerala Rural Water Supply and Sanitation Agency

Beneficiary contribution collected as on 30-9-2006 for the project is Rs. 47.87 crores and contribution from Grama Panchayats is Rs. 25 crores. Budget provision for the project up to 2006-07 is Rs. 357.83 crores.

Table : Year -wise Budget Provision and Actual Release for Jalanidhi Project

Year	Budget Provision (Rs. in crores)	Actual release (Rs. in crores)
2000-01	8.50	8.50
2001-02	5.00	5.00
2002-03	40.00	40.00
2003-04	40.00	40.00
2004-05	90.00	76.50
2005-06	60.00	60.00
2006-07- up to 30-9-2006	114.33	nil
Total	357.83	230.00

Source: Kerala Rural Water Supply and Sanitation Agency

RAIN WATER HARVESTING CAMPAIGN

Government of Kerala launched a statewide campaign for promotion of Rain Water Harvesting (RWH) in June, 2004. Kerala Rural Water Supply and Sanitation Agency- KRWSA was appointed as the nodal agency for State-level co-ordination of the programme. In connection with this, the KRWSA formed a special RWH cell for statewide co-ordination of the campaign activities. Action has been initiated for establishing a separate unit named 'Rain Centre' with all demonstrative units of Rain Water Harvesting/Ground Water recharge including a meteorological station at the state capital. The campaign was initially for one year but was given extension up to June 2007.

Aims and Objectives

- To sensitize the stakeholders on the urgency and seriousness of the water scarcity
- To disseminate the existing good practice in rain water harvesting and locally adaptable sustainable

technologies in RWH by demonstrating these practices and adopting the same in public building/institutions of high seasonal demand.

- Awareness generation on the vitality of RWH and GWR and prepare ground for large-scale adoption of RWH/ GWR measures in the state.
- To equip the people/institutions/agencies with appropriate low cost technologies for rain water harvesting.
- To encourage individuals/communities/agencies in drought prone areas to take up RWH as a sustainable solution to their drinking water needs.

Table : Expenditure of the Rainwater Harvesting Campaign as on 31/10/2006

Sl.No	Items	Amount	Expenditure	Balance
A WB share				
1	IEC	1,00,00,000	48,48,781	51,51,219
2	Training	63,54,780	49,25,911	14,28,869
3	Rain Centre	13,34,000	11,11,023	2,22,977
	Total	1,76,88,780	1,08,85,715	68,03,065
B GOK share				
1	Demo 14 x 500000	70,00,000	63,00,000	7,00,000
2	Construction 490 x 120000	58,80,000	58,80,000	0
3	Capacity building	7,65,220	5,92,929	1,72,291
4	Rain Centre	6,66,000	5,46,762	1,19,238
	Total	1,43,11,220	1,33,19,691	9,91,529
	Grand Total	3,20,00,000	2,42,05,406	77,94,594

Source: KRWSA

8

Contribution to Agriculture and Allied Sector

Agriculture continues to be the most crucial sector of the Indian economy. With 26.8 percent contribution to the Gross Domestic Product (GDP) at current prices and providing employment to nearly 2/3rd of the work force, agriculture is so much at the center stage in the Indian economy that any situational change in this sector, positive or negative, has a multiplier effect on the entire economy. The largest industries of the country like sugar, jute, textiles, food processing, milk, etc. are dependent on agriculture for their raw materials. Besides, the agriculture sector and rural areas are the biggest markets for low priced and middle priced consumer goods, including durable use items.

Table - 1. Production & Growth Rates of some major commodities.

Commodity	Production (Million Tonnes)				Growth Rates(% per annum)					
	1949-50	1979-80	1989-90	1998-99	1979-80 to 1989-90			1989-90 to 1998-99		
					Area	Prod.	Yield	Area	Prod.	Yield
Rice	23.54	42.33	73.57	85.99	0.45	4.29	3.82	0.49	1.70	1.21
Wheat	6.39	31.83	49.85	70.78	0.57	4.24	3.65	1.64	3.64	1.96
Coarse Cereals	16.83	26.97	34.76	31.46	(-)1.19	0.74	1.84	(-) 2.36	(-) 0.48	1.63
Pulses	8.16	8.57	12.86	14.81	0.15	2.78	2.63	(-) 0.22	0.75	0.65
Foodgrains	54.92	109.70	171.04	203.04	(-)0.11	3.54	3.33	(-) 0.18	1.80	1.42
Oilseeds	5.23	8.74	16.92	25.21	2.45	5.75	2.93	1.27	3.06	1.93
Cotton	2.75	7.65	11.42	12.18	(-)1.32	2.19	3.56	2.71	2.22	(-) 0.47
Sugarcane	50.17	128.83	225.57	295.73	1.89	3.73	1.81	1.81	2.90	1.08
Milk	17.00*	30.40	51.40	74.70	----	5.39	---	---	4.78	---
Egg (Million nos.)	1832*	9523	20204	30150	----	7.81	---	---	5.13	---
Fish	0.75*	2.34	3.68	5.26	----	4.78	---	---	4.70	---

* Relates to 1950-51, Source: - Ministry of Agriculture

Foodgrains production recorded a growth rate of 2.5 percent per annum during 1949-50 to 1998-99 and reached 203.04 million tonnes (Table1).

Per capita availability of foodgrains went up from 395 grams in 1951 to 484 grams per day in 1998 (see graph). During 1949-50 to 1998-99, the oilseeds production increased at the rate of 2.85 percent per annum and went up from 5.23 million tonnes to 25.21 million tonnes. Cotton production increased from 2.75 million bales to 12.18 million bales yielding a growth rate of 2.56 percent per annum and for sugarcane, growth rate of 3.08 percent per annum was achieved resulting in increase in production from 50.17 million tonnes to 295.73 million tonnes.

The livestock sector also registered notable growth. Milk production increased from 17 million tonnes in 1950-51 to 74.70 million tonnes in 1998-99. Egg production increased from 1832 million nos. to 30150 million nos. The production of fish has increased by 4.2 percent per annum since 1950-51 having gone up from 7.52 lakh tonnes to 52.60 lakh tonnes in 1998-99.

Per capita daily availability of cereals and pulses in grams

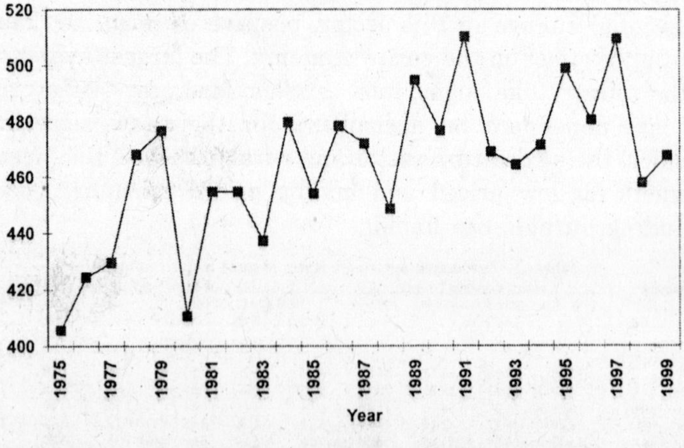

Growth Trends during Eighties and Nineties

During the nineties, (1989-90 to 1998-99) growth rate of production for both foodgrains and non-foodgrain crops taken together has declined to 2.35 percent per annum from 3.72 percent per annum achieved during the eighties (1979-80 to 1989-90). The decline in the rate of growth for foodgrains was sharper from 3.54 to 1.80 per cent per annum. Even for the milk and eggs sector, which had led the growth pattern in the

1980's, there was decline in the 90's, although not as severe as for foodgrains.

Table-2. Growth rates of foodgrains production in different States during Nineties (1990-98)

>2.5%	1.5-2.5%	<1.5%
Mizoram	Meghalaya	Goa
Rajasthan	Madhya	Pradesh Assam
Manipur	Uttar Pradesh	J & K
Nagaland	Punjab	Tripura
Haryana	Tamil	Nadu
Karnataka		A. P.
Bihar		H.P.
West Bengal		Maharashtra
Gujrat		Arunachal Pr
		Sikkim
		Orissa
		Kerala

Based on production estimates

Among the states, the Punjab, Haryana, Uttar Pradesh, Madhya Pradesh, Bihar and Orissa registered a decline in growth rate of foodgrains production during nineties. However, Gujarat, Rajasthan, Karnataka, and Goa have performed better. In the case of Tamil Nadu (0.78 percent), and Maharasthra (0.05 percent) the production growth remained very low whereas in Kerala and Orissa, it was negative. Slower growth in production in the poorer states of Uttar Pradesh, Madhya Pradesh, Orissa and Assam is a matter of concern, especially because these are ground water rich states, hence with a great deal of untapped potential.

How West Bengal did it

The rate of growth in crop productivity in West Bengal during 1977-95 was nearly 5%, due to land reforms and spurt in private shallow tube well irrigation. Security of tenure has altered the credit relations that had earlier trapped the peasants in debt cycles. With increasing access to institutional credit, farmer was able to put more land under HYV cultivation. He also invested in shallow tube wells, thanks to easy availability of groundwater. With assured irrigation, the cropping pattern during rabi also changed in favour of high value non-food crops, such as potato, oilseeds, etc.

Production growth rate of rice and wheat have declined because of lower growth in productivity, though there has been some expansion in area. The plateauing of yield of rice and wheat in high productivity areas under rice-wheat system and low yield levels in Central, Eastern and North Eastern parts of the country have affected the growth of production. Coarse cereals production recorded a negative growth rate mainly due to diversion of about 8 million ha to other more remunerative crops. Besides the decline in area, coarse cereals productivity has remained nearly stagnant. In case of pulses the growth in production has declined substantially because of sharp decline in the growth of productivity from 2.63 percent per annum to 0.65 percent per annum and also a negative growth (-0.22 percent) in area (Table-1).

Introduction of cross breeding programme and implementation of Operation Flood Scheme boosted milk production during eighties. During nineties, however, there was decline in the growth of production (Table-1). The rise in egg production has been mainly due to spurt in setting up modern poultry farms in the southern India, though the growth rate declined during nineties. However, the annual growth rate of fish production during nineties remained more or less, at the level achieved during eighties mainly because of increased growth in inland fish production.

Why the Slow Down in the 90's?

The policy approach to agriculture, particularly in the 1990s, has been more to secure increased production through subsidies in inputs such as power, water and fertilizer, rather than through building new capital assets in irrigation and power. This has reduced the pace and pattern of technological change in agriculture and effected TFP (total factor productivity) adversely. The equity, efficiency, and sustainability of the current approach thus becomes debatable. The subsidies also do not improve income distribution and the demand for labour. The boost in output from subsidy-stimulated use of fertilizers, pesticides and water may partly be coming at the expense of deterioration in the aquifers and soil – an environmentally unsustainable approach that may partly explain the rising costs and slowing growth and productivity in agriculture, notably in Punjab and Haryana. Moreover, the deteriorating state finances have meant that subsidies have, in effect:-

(a) crowded-out public agricultural investment in irrigation and roads and expenditure on technological upgrading,

(b) limited maintenance of canals and roads, and

(c) contributed to the low quality of rural power.

These problems are particularly severe in the poorer states. Although private investment in agriculture has grown, this is hardly a substitute for lower public investment and deteriorating quality of public services, in some cases involving macroeconomic inefficiencies (such as private investment in diesel generating sets).

At the same time, power capacity is underutilized because of poor distribution and maintenance, and excessive use of capital on the farms encouraged by subsidies. The fiscal problems of the central and state governments suggest that the subsidies cannot continue to grow, and the stock of rural productive assets and technological basis for growth will be limited by the past pattern of spending, unless low cost options are pursued, which have a higher capital-output ratio.

In addition, agriculture has seen much less reform than other sectors. Agriculture is still constrained by central and state regulations that limit movement and intra-state trade, public procurement, and canalization of trade. For example, simply allowing greater private trade in products would help reduce price fluctuations and improve the productivity of labour and land-use and stimulate agricultural exports.

Similarly, removal of small-scale reservation would help the growth of domestic agro-industry, which in some cases is now facing increased competition from larger size offshore producers as a result of lower tariff. According to a recent World Bank study cotton and textile policies effectively tax domestic cotton producers and oilseed producers by 15% and 30% respectively. To sum up, though there are region-specific causes to explain the decline in the growth rate in the nineties, but some of the possible reasons seem to be:

— Low public investment in irrigation and poor maintenance of rural infrastructure, specially canals and roads.

— Decline in investments in rural electrification, and in its availability. This has vastly affected production in eastern India, where huge groundwater potential remains untapped.

— Rising level of subsidies for power, water, fertilisers and food are eating into public sector investments in agriculture, besides inducing inefficient use of scarce resources, such as water. This further aggravates environmental problems leading to loss of soil fertility and groundwater, which intern reduces returns on capital. Farmers then demand further subsidies to maintain the same level of production.

— Inadequate credit support.

— Continuing imbalanced use of N, P, K fertilisers, (which was 8.5:3.1:1 in 1998-99 as against the desirable norm of 4:2:1) and increasing deficiency of micro nutrients.

— Stringent market controls on foodgrains that suppress their profitability. In the face of pressure from WTO, it is feared that if domestic market reforms are not carried out soon, it would create a situation that an opportunity to capture world markets would be converted into a threat to the future growth of Indian agriculture. The classic case is that of sugar where imports were opened at zero duty when controls on domestic markets remained.

— Growth in total factor productivity (TFP), which is a measure of technical change, seems to be decelerating, suggesting a decline in the force of technology.

— Demand constraints: slow growth of urban economy, restriction on exports, lack of land reforms, failure of poverty alleviation schemes, slow growth in rural wages.

— Controls on agro-processing industry

NINTH FIVE YEAR PLAN

Strategy

The Ninth Five Year Plan envisages a growth of 4.5 percent per annum in agriculture sector. For achieving the objective of 4.5 percent growth in agriculture sector, a Regionally Differentiated Strategy, based on Agro-Climatic Regional Planning, has been proposed to be implemented. Keeping in view the significance of agriculture sector in achieving a broad based growth of income levels and employment, especially in rural areas, a target of doubling food production and making India hunger-free in 10 years has been envisaged. Besides adequate availability of basic food products, the concept of food security has been broadened to include accessibility and availability of basic nutritional requirements. The strategy for food security aims at increasing overall employment and incomes by raising farm productivity, providing gainful supplementary employment through poverty alleviation schemes and distribution of foodgrains through public distribution system at subsidised rates to those living below the poverty line.

The objective of giving priority to the issue of access of the poor to foodgrains is important for two reasons. Firstly, despite the fact that the growth of foodgrains production in the period 1989-99 was lower than the increase in population during the same period, procurement has been going up, which is suggestive of a decline in people's consumption or the purchasing power of the poor. This may have happened because of the structural imbalances (rising capital intensity, lack of land reforms, failure of poverty alleviation programmes, growing disparity between towns and villages, etc.) created in the economy, as well as due to production problems in less endowed regions, which has led to a dangerous situation of huge surplus in FCI godowns coupled with widespread hunger. Therefore it is as important to correct these policy imbalances as to increase food production. Secondly, if consumption of the poor does not increase there would be serious demand constraints on agriculture, making the growth target of 4.5 percent per annum unachievable.

Thrust Areas

Keeping in view the above strategy, thrust areas for the Ninth Plan include;

— Conservation of land, water and biological resources.

— Development of Rainfed agriculture.

— Development of minor irrigation.

— Timely and adequate availability of inputs.

— Increasing flow of credit

— Enhancing Public sector investment

— Effective transfer of technology

— Support for marketing infrastructure & Export promotion and Enhanced support for research.

Financial Allocations

Table-3. Allocation of fund to Agriculture Sector for the Ninth Plan. (in Rs. Crores)

Period		DAC	DAH&D	DARE
Eighth Plan	Allocation	7000.00	1300.00*	1300.00
	Expenditure	5494.46	1125.00*	1257.71
Ninth Plan-	Allocation	9153.82	2345.64	3376.95
1997-98	Allocation	1416.00	319.15	331.17
	Expenditure	1196.85	201.07	323.30
1998-99	Allocation	1941.00	381.90	531.17
	Expenditure	1342.66	166.07	427.73
1999-2000	Allocation	1941.00	381.90	573.50
	Expenditure	1440.63	207.29	503.78

*Excluding fisheries sector- Rs.400 crore allocation and Rs.373.74 crore expenditure.

Source: Ministry of Agriculture/ Planning Commission

Department-wise allocations for the Ninth Plan and expenditure incurred during first three years of the Plan are given in Table-3. Besides, Ministry of Commerce has been allocated Rs. 705.03 crore for the developmental activities of plantation crops (tea, coffee, rubber & cashew) and promotion of export of spices.

Developmental Programmes

Besides the ongoing programmes, some new initiatives have been taken for achieving the Ninth Plan objectives which include;

— introduction of crop insurance scheme "Rashtrya Krishi Bima Yojana (RKBY)",

— establishment of Watershed Development Fund (WDF),

— launching of Technology Mission on Cotton (TMC),

— launching of Kisan Credit Cards,

— introduction of new Credit Linked Capital Subsidy Scheme for the development of cold storage and onion storage facilities

— implementation of World Bank aided National Agriculture Technology Project (NATP).

— formulation of On-farm Water Management Scheme for Eastern India.

— formulation of Project for Technology Mission on Horticulture Development for North Eastern States.

The RKVY has already been launched from Rabi 1999. The WDF have been established with the support of Rs.100 crore from NABARD and the DAC is to provide their share of Rs.100 crore during 2000-01.

The TMC have also been approved. The launching of Kissan Credit Cards have met with a good measure of success and needs to be replicated / expanded all over the country. The implementation of NATP has also commenced for the research and human resource development. However, the credit linked capital subsidy schemes is yet to become operational and the schemes on On-farm Water Management for Eastern India and Technology Mission on Horticulture for North Eastern States are yet to be finalized.

Performance Review

Foodgrains

As against the Eighth Plan (1996-97) achievement of 199.44 million tonnes, food grains production target for the terminal year of the Ninth Plan (2001-02) has been fixed at 234 million tonnes.

Production targets and achievements for foodgrains and other commercial crops for first three years of the Ninth Plan are given in Table-4. To achieve the targets, production will have to increased by 14 percent in the remaining two years, which seems to be an impossibility.

Table-4-Targets and Achievements of Foodgrains and Commercial Crops Production (million tonnes)

Name of the crop	9th Plan Target (2001-2002)	1997-98		1998-99		(1999-2000)	
		Tar.	Achi.	Tar.	Achi.	Target	Likely Ach.
Rice	99.00	83.00	82.54	86.00	86.00	86.00	88.25
Wheat	83.00	70.00	66.35	74.00	70.78	74.00	74.25
Coarse Cereals	35.50	34.00	30.40	34.50	31.46	34.50	30.35
Pulses	16.50	15.00	12.97	15.50	14.80	15.50	13.06
Total Foodgrain	234.00	202.00	192.26	210.00	203.04	210.00	205.91
Oilseeds	30.00	25.50	21.32	27.00	25.21	28.00	21.18
Sugarcane	336.00	280.00	279.54	300.00	295.73	305.00	309.31
Cotton *	15.70	14.80	10.85	14.80	12.18	15.00	11.99

*Million bales

Source: Ministry of Agriculture / Planning Commission

Pulses have been brought under Technology Mission since early nineties. However, there has not been any appreciable improvement either in area expansion or in productivity levels.

Lack of HYV seeds and cultivation on marginal lands, mostly in unirrigated areas, have mainly been responsible for low production of pulses. There appears no possibility of achieving a quantum jump in production unless a major breakthrough is made in development of high potential input-responsive and insect-pest and disease resistant varieties.

Oilseeds

Oilseeds production suffered a set back during 1997-98 but during 1998-99, record production of 25.21 million tonnes was achieved (Table-1). Oilseeds were brought under "Technology Mission on Oilseeds (TMO) " in 1986 and efforts made through the Mission have helped in area expansion and increasing productivity. Increased production of oilseeds helped to reduce the imports of edible oils drastically by early nineties.

However, reduction in import duty to 16.5 percent on edible oils in 1998 from the earlier peak level of 60 percent has resulted in heavy imports of more than 4 million tonnes of edible oils in 1998-99. Recent hike in import duty to 27.5 percent may have some favourable impact on production of oilseeds. As oilseeds and edible oils belong to the sensitive consumer basket, striking a balance between the interest of consumers and producers remains a delicate exercise.

Cotton

During 1997-98, cotton production declined substantially to 10.85 million bales from 14.23 million bales in 1996-97. However, during 1998-99, it increased to 12.18 million bales. Lack of pest resistant high yielding varieties is the main obstacle in raising productivity/production of cotton.

Emphasis is required to be given on enhancing the Seed Replacement Rate (SRR). To achieve this, the concept of Seed Village Programme (SVP) exclusively for cotton seed production in collaboration with Cotton Corporation of India (CCI) and other Institutions with buy back arrangement and distribution of certified seeds should be considered. The cotton crop alone consumes about 1/2 of total pesticides used in agriculture in the country.

Development of Integrated Pest Management (IPM) technology and its wider adoption should be a thrust area for minimizing the use of pesticides, lowering the cost of production and minimizing environmental hazard. Cotton trade is besieged with a plethora of restrictions which continue to hamper healthy/ competitive growth in its trade and in turn adversely affects the efforts for raising production and productivity. Therefore, all restrictions on movement, stocking, credit by financial institutions, monopoly buying, processing and exports have to be removed to allow the farmers to take advantage of free market.

Besides, in view of removal of Quantitative Restrictions under WTO, suitable tariff protection will have to be provided to Indian farmers. With the setting up of Cotton Technology Mission, the production may look up during the remaining years of the Plan.

Sugarcane

The Ninth Plan target of sugarcane production is 336 million tonnes. During 1998-99, production has increased to 295.73 million tonnes. The productivity levels of sugarcane in Northern States like Bihar, Madhya Pradesh, Haryana, Punjab, Assam and Uttar Pradesh are lower as compared to all-India average yield (72.58 tonnes/ha). Disease resistant short duration improved varieties need to be propagated in this region. Sugar industry, though delicensed, still continues with lot of regulations and controls, including the levy on sugar, release of free sale sugar quotas, distribution and pricing of molasses etc.

All these controls should be done away with as they have been hampering the process of modernization, diversification and waste and by-product utilization by the industry. The era of chronic shortages of sugar being over and the emergence of free trade regime under WTO make it more imperative than ever before that the industry is allowed to develop its own strength in terms of efficient production having competitive costs, quality and value addition, if it has to survive.

Sugar yield has gone up only by 1.3 percent in the last three decades, as area increase has brought 60 percent increase in sugar production. Not only are Indian yields 1/3 rd to ½ of those achieved in similar agro climatic conditions (Australia, Brazil, South Africa), sugarcane quality is also lower, with sucrose content of 11 percent, compared to an international standard of 13 percent. About 22 percent of sugar is lost in processing compared to an international benchmark of 17 percent and the best practice of 10.5 percent in Australia. These inefficiencies are due to government policies that encourage wasteful use of land and water, and regulatory obstacles in pricing, distribution, marketing and manufacturing.

India produces 20 percent more sugar than Brazil, but has four times as many mills on account of historical bias against setting up of large size sugar mills. However, this bias has since been rectified. Biases against the healthy growth of *Khandsari* units also need to be removed.

They will help in stabilizing the sugarcane-sugar equilibrium and generate employment in rural areas with relatively less capital. Major cause of instability in sugar production from year to year is the fixation of state Advised Prices which has no legal base and is fixed arbitrarily by the states, sometimes on whimsical grounds. This bad practice also needs to be stopped.

Excessive use of Water in Sugarcane

Sugarcane, occupying around 3% total cropped area in Maharashtra, gets about 60% of irrigation water. Subsidy on water discourages farmers to shift to drip irrigation, which will also prevent water logging and salinity.

HORTICULTURE

India is the second largest fruit and vegetable producing country in the world after China. Horticulture sector suffers from various technological and infrastructural constraints, preponderance of old and senile trees, poor management, acute shortage of seeds and planting material of improved quality and lack of post harvest handling, sorting, grading, packaging, storage and transportation etc. Besides, inadequate processing infrastructure and poor marketing network are other constraints for growth and expansion of horticulture.

The North-East region, which has tremendous potential for horticulture development, has severe constraints of connectivity. Organically produced, chemical free horticulture products are labour intensive. There is scope for organic farming, but potential remains under-utilized.

The Ninth Plan strategy for growth and expansion of horticulture sector is to improve productivity, reduce post-harvest losses and improve marketability and promote export. A number of schemes for development of fruits, vegetables, floriculture, root and tuber crops, spices, medicinal and aromatic plants etc. are under implementation.

There is vast scope for horticulture produce like mangoes of North, litchi and *makhana* of Bihar, fibreless ginger and mandarins of North-East and large cardamom of Sikkim etc. Considering the tremendous potential for development of horticulture in North-East region a mission mode approach has been envisaged to provide boost to the production of fruits and vegetables, medicinal and aromatic plants, floriculture, etc.

Table-5. Targets and production of horticulture products (in million tonnes)

Product	1996-97	9th Plan Target	1997-98	1998-99
Fruits	38.03		40.05	42.00
Vegetables	75.07	179.00	72.83	80.00
Sub-total	113.10*		112.88	122.00
Spices	2.50	3.36	NA	3.00
Cashew	0.43	0.70	0.36	0.35

*141.00Million Tonnes indicated in the 9 th Plan Document
Source: - Ministry of Agriculture.

For the Ninth Plan, combined production target of fruits and vegetables is 179 million tonnes. Production during 1997-

98 was 112.88 million tonnes, while in 1998-99 it was 122 million tonnes. Achieving Ninth Plan production targets for fruits and vegetables and cashew (Table-5) seems to be difficult. The financial outlays and expenditure during Ninth Plan for development of horticulture and plantation crops are given in Table-6.

Table-6-Financial allocation & Expenditure during Ninth Plan.

(Rs. In crores)

Sub-sector	9th Plan outlay	1997-98 (Exp.)	1998-99 (Exp.)	1999-2000 (Anti. xp.)
Horticulture (incl. Spices & cashew)	1200.00	182.42	221.01	130.68
Tea	130.00	27.52	15.05	17.27
Coffee	125.00	23.00	25.50	27.00
Rubber	373.19	44.46	63.20	81.72

* IEBR Source: Ministry of Commerce.

Plantations

The Ninth Plan (2001-02) production targets and achievements during the first two years of the Plan of tea, coffee and rubber are given in Table-7. To meet the requirements of rapidly rising domestic consumption and export of tea, coffee and rubber, the focus is on enhancing productivity and bringing more area under cultivation especially in North-East region and focus on block/group plantation. To overcome the situation of glut in production of natural rubber on account of recession in industrial sector concerted efforts would be required to promote the use of rubber wood in furniture and rubberisation of roads.

Table –7- Targets And Production(in lakh tonnes)

Product	1996-97	9thPlan target	1997-98	1998-99
Tea (in million kgs)	775	1000	838	850
Coffee	2.05	3.00	2.28	2.65
Rubber	5.49	7.17	5.84	6.05

Development of Degraded Land and Rainfed Areas

It is estimated that out of the total geographical area of about 328.73 million ha, 107.4 million ha are degraded land (DAC 1994). Out of this about 67.6 million ha are subjected to wind and water erosion. Water logged area is estimated to be about 3.20 million ha and 2.38 million ha are affected due to shifting cultivation in hilly regions of the country. Indiscriminate use of water in high productivity rice-wheat cropping system areas has resulted in depletion and up-surging ground water tables, water logging and salinity. Out of 142.82 million ha of net shown area, 89.82 million ha (63percent) is rainfed, where crop production suffers from low yields and year to year fluctuations. For the development of rainfed areas and degraded lands, Watershed Development and Soil and Water Conservation Programmes have been taken up by different Departments at the Centre and also by the State Governments. Besides, several externally aided projects are also under implementation. A Watershed Development Fund (WDF) has been created by NABARD with central assistance to cover 100 priority districts in a period of three years. It is projected that during the Ninth Plan about 16 million ha degraded /rainfed area will be treated/ developed under the various Watershed Development Projects.

It is estimated that upto the end of Eighth Plan about 16.5 million ha rainfed /degraded land has been treated/developed. However, these achievements do not get reflected in Net Sown Area, which has almost remained stagnant at around 142 million ha. This indicates that either the treated lands were already under cultivation or an equal area is getting degraded or diverted for non-agriculture purposes. The possibility of bogus reporting can also not be ruled out. This requires deeper investigation and analysis.

Several evaluation studies conducted on various projects implemented under NWDPRA, FPR and RVP indicate beneficial impacts such as increase in cropping intensity, change in cropping pattern, increase in crop productivity and increase in underground recharge as a result of conservation measures, reduction in soil and run-off losses with lesser siltation effect and reduction in sedimentation at watershed level. These projects have also generated employment and increased family incomes through diversified farming system such as livestock development, dryland horticulture and household production activities.

However, there is other side of the picture too. A survey of 70 villages of Maharashtra and A.P., covering several watershed programmes, revealed that increase in agricultural production did not last for more than two years. Structures were abandoned because of lack of maintenance and there was no mechanism for looking after common lands. Projects have failed to generate sustainability because of failure of Government agencies to involve the people.

For watershed projects to be sustainable, community managed systems are needed and they can succeed only with farmers contribution and their commitment of time and resources. This has been amply demonstrated in watershed programmes implemented by some voluntary organizations, in 25 villages of Pune. Equitable distribution of water amongst the families has also been one of the main factors in the success of Sukho-Majari (Haryana) and Relegan Sidhi (Maharashtra) Projects. The adoption of common guidelines prepared for implementation of six major watershed development programmes of Ministry of Agriculture and Ministry of Rural Development, which also envisage greater participation of people and creation of corpus fund for the maintenance of assets is likely to ensure active participation of beneficiaries and take care of the management of common property resources even after the project has been withdrawn.

About 63 per cent of the Net Sown Area of 142.82 million ha is still dependant on rainfall. In Eastern India, only 1/5 th of ground water resource is being utilized. Stimulating ground water development is crucial to kickstart the Green Revolution in this region and also address the problem of extensive water logging. Studies have revealed that pump subsidy schemes operated by the State Governments have fared poorly due to lengthy, irksome and complex procedures and heavy transaction costs which leave little real subsidy for the farmers.

For example, in West Bengal, the pump subsidy scheme has been co-opted by the State's minor irrigation administration and panchayat bodies and the process of accessing the scheme is so lengthy and cumbersome that small farmers without political support do not hope to benefit from it. Similarly, in Orissa a 50 percent subsidy is provided on the cost of diesel as well as electrified tubewells, but the process of accessing the subsidy is both cumbersome and full of corruption. The entire process of subsidy approval and supply of equipment, especially for the manual treadle pump, is controlled by a government Corporation, but farmers complained that the cost estimates made by the Corporation were more than twice they would incur if they went direct to the market. The result is that there is effectively very little real subsidy to claim.

Impact Evaluation Studies

The impact evaluation studies conducted by 10 Agro-Economic Research Centres on NWDPRA during the terminal year of the 8 th Plan indicated,

-increase in cropping intensity and change in existing cropping pattern.

-Increase in underground water recharge as a result of conservation measures.

-Reduction in soil and water run off losses with lesser siltation effect and

-Increase in family income through diversified farming and household production activities.

However, Uttar Pradesh transformed the diesel pump subsidy scheme by assigning the diesel pump dealer the role of central coordinating mechanism for the scheme. The absolute monopoly power itself is diffused through the competitive dealer dynamism resulting in a win-win situation for all. This experiment has many lessons for stimulating Eastern India's ground water economy. Essentially, East Indian States need to reform their pump subsidy scheme on similar lines to ameliorate the pump capital scarcity, which lies at the heart of the problem. It is also equally important to promote cost effective improved manual irrigation technologies for the sub-marginal farmers. Expansion of irrigation facilities through the development of minor irrigation would be more effective and economical as it ensures all time availability of water at low costs. Besides, the gestation period for the minor irrigation is just 1-2 years compared to 4-5 years for medium irrigation and 7-10 years for major irrigation projects. Capital required to create one hectare potential through major and medium mode is Rs.1,00,000 while through minor it is about Rs.20,000. Top priority needs to be accorded to massive development of minor irrigation in Eastern India to achieve quick increase in productivity and production in the region known for low productivity.

AGRICULTURAL INPUTS

Seeds

Although the availability of certified/quality seeds has increased from 90.76 lakh quintals in 1996-97 to 104.38 lakh quintals in 1998-99, the Seed Replacement Rate (SRR) has still remained much below the desired level and varies widely from crop to crop and state to state. Against the desired level of 20 percent SRR for self-pollinated crops, for paddy it is only about 8.8 percent and for wheat 9.2 percent. In other crops, especially pulses and oilseeds, where Seed Multiplication Ratio (SMR) is low, replacement rate is much below the desired level. The target fixed for the terminal year of Ninth Plan (2001-02) is 109.66 lakh quintals.

New Seed Development Policy (NSDP) adopted in 1988 has liberalized import of seeds and germplasm. Further, in 1991, 100 percent foreign ownership for seed sector units was also allowed. As a result, the number of private firms conducting R&D in the seed sector is on the increase. Private sector has contributed immensely in the development of hybrids. In some States like Andhra Pradesh and Karnataka, private bred hybrids cover sizeable area, despite higher prices compared to the public hybrids. The public sector seed producing agencies have added responsibility to produce high volume low value seeds to fulfill the National objective as private sector agencies generally concentrate on low volume high value seeds. There is need for setting up a National Seed Grid and Seed Bank by amalgamating, National Seed Corporation (NSC) and States Farms Corporation of India (SFCI), involving State Government farms, establishing seed villages and undertaking production of seeds upto foundation seed stage and facilitate development of certified / quality seeds production in private sector.

In pursuance of agreement on Trade Related Intellectual Property Rights (TRIPs), a bill to enact legislation to adopt *sui generis* system for granting plant variety protection has been introduced. The proposed legislation is expected to provide an effective system of protection to plant breeders' right, which will also facilitate growth of seed industry and safeguard farmers' and researchers' rights. Emergence of bio-technology as a means of evolving new varieties of seeds and the associated bio-safety concerns necessitate a careful review of policy framework for the seed-sector.

Table-8 Fertilizer Consumption (NP& K)

Year	'000' tonnes	NP&K Use Ratio
1980-81	5516	5.9 : 1.9 : 1.0
1990-91	12546	6.0 : 2.4 : 1.0
1996-97	14308	10.0 : 2.9 : 1.0
1997-98	16188	7.9 : 2.9 : 1.0
1998-99	16798	8.5 : 3.1 : 1.0

Source : Ministry of Agriculture.

Fertilizers

The rate of growth of fertilizer application has considerably slowed down in the 1990s, as compared to the previous decade. However, it is an encouraging development that during 1996-97 to 1998-99, while nitrogen(N) consumption has increased only by 10.7 percent, phosphorus (P) consumption has increased by 39.1 percent and that of potash (K) by 29.2 percent. This has slightly improved the NP&K use ratio (table-8). Fertilizer consumption per hectare has also increased from 77 kg/ha in 1996-97 to about 90 kg/ha in 1998-99.

There are, however, wide variations in fertilizer use in different regions, depending on irrigation facilities, adoption of crop production technologies and economic viability. In Punjab, Tamil Nadu, Haryana, Andhra Pradesh, which have high level of adoption of crop production technology, fertilizers consumption is comparatively high (142-179 kg/ha). In the North-Eastern States, where irrigation facilities are inadequate and agriculture is highly risky because of its proneness to floods and water stagnation, fertilizer consumption is very low. Besides, the marketing network is poor in the region. In states like Madhya Pradesh, Rajasthan and Himachal Pradesh also the fertilizers consumption has remained low because of larger dependence on monsoon and risk due to proneness to droughts.

Besides low per unit area consumption and imbalances in the NP&K use, deficiency of micro nutrients like zinc, iron, sulphur, etc. is increasing, especially in areas where intensive cultivation and multiple cropping are adopted. Over the last few decades, the carbon content in soil has also gone down, which is affecting soil health and productivity.

In addition to increased use of organic manures and biofertilizers, it is necessary to promote need based use of fertilizers on the basis of soil tests by adopting Integrated Nutrient Management (INM) approach. The use of organic manures needs to be promoted by recycling urban and rural waste in a scientific manner. Some success stories like Idar Composting, the Chakriya Vikash Pranali and the Bio-dynamic farming etc. need to be evaluated and replicated.

So far, 519 soil testing laboratories including 105 mobile laboratories have been set up in the country. It is proposed to establish 70 new soil testing laboratories and strengthen 200 existing laboratories for NPK, fertilizer and biofertilizer testing during Ninth Plan. It would, however, be desirable to establish composite facilities for testing soil, water, biofertilizers, pesticides, biopesticides to meet the needs of farmers on payment basis. These testing laboratories could also be encouraged in the private sector so as to have at least one such laboratory in each block.

PLANT PROTECTION

To minimize the losses/damage caused to various crops by pests and diseases, the thrust is on the adoption of Integrated Pest Management (IPM) approach with emphasis on bio-controls. Besides, being effective, the IPM approach poses no environmental health hazard and is economical in terms of cost as compared to chemical control. As a result of promotion of IPM concept, consumption of pesticides has declined. (Table-9). The programme can, however, achieve greater success if forecast about likely outbreak of pests and diseases is made regularly for the benefits of farmers and adequate availability of bio-control agents and other environment friendly devices is assured.

Table-9- Consumption of Pesticides (000' tonnes)

1990-91	75.03
1996-97	56.11
1997-98	52.24
1998-99	49.16

Source : Ministry of Agriculture.

Toxic residues of chemicals used in agriculture are affecting the environment, creating health problems and affecting adversely the export of agriculture commodities. Besides creating awareness and minimizing the use of chemicals, chemical residue testing facilities have to be strengthened and made available. Plant Quarantine and Fumigation Centres have been set up at international airports, seaports, and land frontiers to check entry of exotic pests and diseases. In the wake of liberalization of trade, it has become necessary to strengthen the quarantine facilities for testing and detection of pests and diseases in grains and plants and also for genetically modified materials, which may affect the bio-diversity if it gets introduced.

IPM in Cotton: A Success Story of Ashta (Maharashtra)

The IPM module for cotton crop developed by the NCIPM, which had been earlier tested on farmers' field, was validated on 200 hectares involving 124 cotton growers in village Ashta of Nanded district in Maharashtra. It comprised planting a row of maize with cowpea as interplants all around the field to enhance population of friendly insects (predators and parasites), planting of Setaria *in between 9-10 cotton rows to attract insect predatory birds, seed treatment with Imidacloprid at 7 g a.i/kg of cotton-seed, and release of parasitoids* Trichogramma chilonis *at 1,50,000 at egg-laying of* Helicoverpa, *and application of HaNPV at 250 LE/ha and 2-3 applications of home made NSKE (neem-seed, kernel extract) on the basis of ETL.*

The combined package of integrated crop production and IPM resulted in satisfactory control of different cotton pests to all the farmers in this village. This has reduced the use of chemical pesticides and the farmers could harvest an average yield of 1,000 kg/ha seed cotton during 1998 season. This was possible because of effective transmission of technology. The project was taken up jointly with the Marathwada Agricultural University, Parbhani. Agricultural Implements and Machinery

Assistance is provided to farmers for popularising improved farm implements for various field operations. Training programmes for machine operators, farmers and officers of State Governments are organised at Farm Machinery Training and Testing Institutes in MP, Haryana, Andhra Pradesh and Assam. Another training and testing institute would be set up in Tamil Nadu to strengthen training and testing facilities in the region. Studies by the Central Institute of Agricultural Engineering (CIAE) Bhopal have revealed that there has been substantial increase in productivity in Punjab and Haryana due to mechanization of farm operations. Changing profile of livestock sector also highlights the need for mechanization of dairy and milk processing operations. There is likely to be a shortage of animal power, which needs to be bridged by mechanization. There is urgent need for preparing a list of tools, implements and machinery used in agricultural operations throughout the world and modify these to suit India's needs and conditions. There is potential market for tools, implements and machinery developed in India for small farmers in the developing countries. Setting up of a "National Institute of Agriculture Engineering and Appropriate Technology" to take up these tasks should be considered by the Department of Agriculture and Cooperation. Research in animal drawn tools, implements and carriages has been lacking and needs to be stepped up.

AGRICULTURAL EXTENSION

The main thrust of the Ministry has been on achieving the set target of production by relying on the effectiveness of extension services. The main components of Agriculture extension system presently are (i) agriculture extension service with the State Governments, (ii) extension, education system of ICAR and SAUs and (iii) extension programmes of input industry in public and private sectors and NGOs. It has been noticed that in high technology adoption areas like Punjab and Haryana, farmer to farmer spread of technology is much faster. Thus, extension network has to take into consideration variations in degree of sophistication and attitude of farmers and other administrative and institutional structures of the region. The traditional Village Level Worker (VLW) based extension system will still be important in tribal and very backward areas, or in such places where irrigation is being introduced for the first time. Even in backward areas, where the potential of achieving higher production through extension exists, experience shows that VLWs and the extension staff are hardly devoting any time for this purpose and have not been found upto the mark. The reasons could be large area of operation, too much of office/file work, involvement in non-agricultural works and even non-residence in the area of work. Of late, the administrative environment, in which VLWs have functioned, has been undergoing change for worse.

The VLWs have responded to this environment in three ways. Firstly, they started falsifying and distorting reports. They soon discovered that they were encouraged to inflate the figures because each officer, be the BDO or the Collector, was being evaluated by his superior on the basis of these figures. Secondly, they started neglecting targets which they found were of a low priority. Thus, even if the Fisheries had a good potential for development in a village, the VLWs paid no attention to this programme because it was not considered to be important by their officers. Thirdly, they started using resources under their own control to stimulate the farmers' participation in unpopular programmes. Besides, the philosophy of extension is hardly consistent with the rigidity of superior-subordinate relations so characteristic of Indian administration as a result of which extension services have not been fully effective.

The original assumption behind the importance given to extension services that the Indian farmer is tradition bound, conservative and needs constant goading so as to effect a change in his behaviour needs to be challenged now. Although peasant societies till the nineteenth century all over the world have been cautious and somewhat hostile to outside interference, yet a number of studies on the responses of Indian farmer have shown that he is, on the whole, innovative, price conscious and receptive to modern ideas. If any generalization regarding peasant behaviour is to be made, it should be on the side of rationality and not otherwise.

In many schemes of the Ministry, there is an element of Transfer of Technology (TOT), which consists of crop demonstrations, farmer training, information support, trainers' training, etc. States currently employ over one lakh extension functionaries. In these schemes of about Rs.1000 crores annually, the share of TOT comes to about 15 to 20%. This does not provide for much flexibility to the states, and because of rigidity of the schemes, funds are fragmented and cannot be effectively utilized. As a result of lack of coordination between departments, absence of region-specific orientation, lack of role clarity for extension staff and inadequate investment in infrastructure for the development of agriculture and allied sectors, the overall growth rate in agriculture has slowed down.

However, the present Village Level worker (VLW) and Community Development Block based manual extension system, which has become outmoded, has got to be replaced with a more vibrant system using modern modes like print and electronic media. Research, education and extension agencies should interact with the farmers to know their needs and problems and come out with demand driven solutions. Printing and publishing of material on various crop production oriented activities and crop production technologies need to be taken up regularly for the benefit of the farmers. Task of listing success stories in extension, education and transfer of technology in public, private and NGO sectors and propagating their adoption at field level needs to be taken up.

The Danish model of extension through Folks' Schools, where workers educate farmers by making use of school and other public buildings during evenings and holidays, is worth studying and emulating. In today's administrative environment it is neither possible for a government servant to live in the villages nor is it realistic to expect him to provide knowledge to the farmers. If any service is needed at the village level, it must be entirely controlled by the user groups themselves, or transmitted to them through modern IT systems.

The role of non-government sector should also increase and an innovative approach in the field of TV broadcast including specific channel with an interactive mode will be useful. With far reaching changes in the communication technology and breakthrough in space technology, remote sensing, satellite broadcasting and the media spread revolution, extension workers will have to be totally re-oriented and re-trained to adapt themselves to these developments and make full use of emerging opportunities.

In future, extension services have to be responsive to changing agricultural scenario resulting from economic liberalization. Research and extension would need to focus on environmentally sustainable diversification and intensification of agriculture, location specific technologies tailored to suit local needs and greater efficiency in use of inputs. Besides, risk prone areas, such as dryland rainfed farming, would require much greater attention from extension workers.

AGRICULTURAL CREDIT AND CO-OPERATION

Disbursement of agricul-tural credit in the terminal year of the Eighth Plan and during the first three years of the Ninth Plan is given in Table-10. According to RBI report on Trends & Progress in Banking (1998-99), the relative share of agriculture credit in net bank credit stood at 12.8 percent in March, 1997 and 11.7 percent in March, 1998 as well as in March, 1999. As against the target of 40 percent for priority sector lending by banks, the sub target for agriculture has been fixed at 18 percent.

The declining share of agriculture in the net bank credit against 18 percent target under priority lending is a matter of concern. More credit needs to flow to agriculture for providing timely and adequate credit under simplified procedures to farmers for increasing agriculture production and productivity.

Table 10 : Flow Of Agricultural Credit (Rs. in crore)

Year	Short Term		Long term		Total
	Amount	Percent	Amount	Percent	
1996-97	16998	64.4	9413	35.6	26411
1997-98	20640	64.59	11316	35.41	31956
1998-99	23633	64.05	13264	35.95	36897
1999-2000	27239	65.38	14526	34.70	41765

A major bottleneck in the smooth flow of credit is the worsening recovery position of the cooperative credit institutions, which has gone down from an average of 90 percent to demand in 1995-96 to 80 percent to demand in 1998-99 (provisional). Persistence of chronic over-dues has caused poor re-cycling of funds from the borrowers to the financing agencies. The broad analysis of sectoral flows indicates that credit flows for minor irrigation and fishery sub-sectors have declined since 1996-97. There is potential for augmenting credit flow to agriculture through micro irrigation system in the form of sprinklers and drip irrigation networks in the irrigated areas especially in the low rainfall zones, hi-tech projects in floriculture, horticulture, mushrooms, dairy, poultry and cold storages. A Kisan Credit Card Scheme, aimed at providing adequate and timely support from the banking system to the farmers for the purchase of inputs in a flexible and cost effective manner, has been launched.

The need to suitably amend the Multi-State Cooperative Societies Act, 1984 to inject professionalism and autonomy in the functioning of these societies and free them from government control has long been felt. Choudhary Brahma Prakash Committee set up by the Planning Commission (1991) made recommendations for a Model Act, which were further examined by Ramniwas Mirdha Committee (1996). Amendment to Multi-State Cooperative Law by the Centre needs to be taken up urgently. A Model Cooperative Act was circulated to State Governments suggesting appropriate changes in their respective cooperative laws. So far only Andhra Pradesh, Bihar, Orissa, Kerala, Madhya Pradesh and J&K have amended State Cooperative Acts to make the functioning of cooperatives autonomous and transparent. All the states need to enact a Model Cooperative Law. In this context, it may be worthwhile to consider preferential assistance for development of cooperatives to compliant States.

Rising Capital Intensity in Agriculture

The much debated size-productivity relationship has so far looked at productivity from the viewpoint of land. Another scarce resource is capital, and it is equally important to keep in mind which class of farmers use capital more efficiently. Small farmers have better access to labour, as they use their own family labour, whereas large farmers have better access to capital and have to hire labour from the market. These differences result in small farmers using more labour to production than large farmers, and large farmers substituting machines and capital for labour.

Thus a small farmer may get an extra unit of output by using home produced mulch and organic manure and the large farmer may depend on chemical fertilizer bought from the markets. In fact, capital intensity per unit land is increasing for all category of farmers, but at a faster pace in green revolution areas and for large farmers. Thus, the weight of fertilizers, pesticides and diesel, which accounted for a mere 14.9 per cent of the total inputs in 1970-71 in the country, increased to 55.1 per cent in 1994-95. For a large farmer in commercialized regions, it could be as high as 70 per cent. But the proportion of output sold has increased at a much slower rate than the proportion of industrial inputs or of monetised inputs.

The implication of this is a resource squeeze in agriculture. Whereas the need for resources to purchase these inputs has been increasing faster, the marketable surplus has been increasing at a slower rate to absorb this, as growth in industrial employment has become very sluggish. It is not surprising that the repayment of loans is such a problem in Indian agriculture and has emerged as a major issue in farmers movements. Pressed by the increasing costs, big farmers demand higher output prices, thus setting the cycle of inflation. This is a serious problem, which has escaped the attention of both policy planners and academics. They both tend to view subsidies as a political problem. However, if 70% people continue to live in villages and dependent on home production, the cost of homegrown inputs to purchased inputs cannot be very different from 70:30, unless one considers exports as a major option in agriculture.

A better option would be to concentrate on eastern region and rainfed areas in respect of public investments, where returns to both capital and labour are high. The need is also better factor productivity in agriculture or of a new technology, which would be more labour intensive and would cut cash costs. The present high capital use is also sustained because of free power and water and other subsidies (unpaid loans, cheap fertilizers etc). One cannot simultaneously talk of reduction in subsidies and at the same time increase input use, especially in areas where they have reached a point of saturation.

Investments are higher than warranted on tractors, fertilizer use, and tubewells; while others are under capitalized. Small holdings do not need as much capital in substitution of labour. Numerous farmers committed suicides in Andhra Pradesh, Maharashtra, Karnataka and also in some parts of Punjab because of indebtedness owing to inappropriately large quantum of capital.

Agrarian Distress in Bidar: Market Forces, the State and Suicides

Farmers' suicides in Bidar are symptomatic of the larger and more pervasive ecological, economic and social crises in the region. The promotion of commercial agriculture based on hybrid seeds, fertilizers and pesticides in a semi-arid region results in loss of land-race seeds as local crops are displaced. There is loss of soil fertility and the crop becomes more susceptible to pests and diseases. Then, institutional credit is available only to large farmers forcing the small farmers to borrow at a high rate of interest. In times of outbreak of pest or diseases such a borrowing increases beyond their payment capacity. Some farmers had to pay for high-risk agriculture through taking their own lives.

Why is credit not available to small farmers through the official channels? Firstly, Bank credit to agriculture has been declining over the years. Between 1987 to 1992 credit to agriculture from the Banks as a percentage of total credit fell from 19.1 to 11.7%. Secondly, many farmers are defaulters and are thus not entitled to further credit. A NABARD report (1997-98) for Bidar shows that recovery of cooperative credit was 24% and for commercial banks between 27 to 30%. Low recovery rates render most farmers as credit-unworthy. High-risk technology and subordination of farmers to market forces without any safety net has high social costs resulting in suicides.

A R Vasavi:Economic and Political Weekly, Aug 7, 1999

CROP INSURANCE

Introduction of "National Agricultural Insurance Scheme" (Rashtriya Krishi Bima Yojana) from the Rabi season of 1999-2000 by replacing earlier Comprehensive Crop Insurance Scheme (CCIS) is a new experiment introduced in the Ninth Plan. India is the third country in the world and first ever amongst developing countries to have such a scheme.

Table 11: Gross Capital Formation in Agriculture

	Gross Domestic Capital Formation			Gross Capital Formation in Agriculture			Percentage		
Year	Total (Unadjusted)	Public Sector	Private Sector	Total	Public Sector	Private Sector	Col.5 as % of Col.2	Col.6 as % of Col.3	Col.7 as % of Col.4
(1)	(2)	(3)	(4)	(5)	(6)	(7)	(8)	(9)	(10)
At 1980-81 prices									
1970-71	16550	6984	9566	2758	789	1969	16.7	11.3	20.6
1971-72	17941	7650	10291	2924	851	2073	16.3	11.1	20.1
1972-73	17636	9053	8583	3180	1049	2131	18.0	11.6	24.8
1973-74	20007	8969	11038	3208	993	2215	16.0	11.1	20.1
1974-75	20729	8757	11972	2975	919	2056	14.4	10.5	17.2
1975-76	22908	11030	11878	3388	1041	2347	14.8	9.4	19.8
1976-77	22498	12326	10172	4258	1378	2880	18.9	11.2	28.3
1977-78	22415	10445	11970	4073	1534	2539	18.2	14.7	21.2
1978-79	28144	12512	15625	5246	1697	3549	18.6	13.6	22.7
1979-80	27334	13029	14305	5215	1772	3443	19.1	13.6	24.1
1980-81	25794	11767	14027	4636	1796	2840	18.0	15.3	20.2
1981-82	32437	15009	17428	4503	1781	2722	13.9	11.9	15.6
1982-83	32496	16261	16235	4590	1742	2848	14.1	10.7	17.5
1983-84	31920	15846	16074	4101	1711	2390	12.8	10.8	14.9

Contd....									
1984-85	33187	17718	15469	4549	1674	2875	13.7	9.4	18.6
1985-86	38654	18504	20150	4325	1520	2805	11.2	8.2	13.9
1986-87	38405	19911	18494	4011	1425	2586	10.4	7.2	14.0
1987-88	37679	17734	19945	4414	1458	2956	11.7	8.2	14.8
1988-89	44761	19296	25465	4346	1362	2984	9.7	7.1	11.7
1989-90	44263	20641	23622	4353	1156	3197	9.8	5.6	13.5
1990-91	49886	21592	28294	4594	1154	3440	9.2	5.3	12.2
1991-92	46718	20047	26671	4729	1002	3727	10.1	5.0	14.0
1992-93	52131	20583	31548	5372	1061	4311	10.3	5.2	13.7
1993-94	51330	21546	29784	5031	1153	3878	9.8	5.4	13.0
1994-95	71422	24945	46477	6256	1316	4940	8.8	5.3	10.6
1995-96	76820	22937	53883	6961	1268	5693	9.1	5.5	10.6
1996-97	74216	22992	51224	6999	1132	5867	9.4	4.9	11.5
At 1993-94 prices									
1993-94	198412	68853	129559	13523	4467	9056	6.8	6.5	7.0
1994-95	242113	81498	160615	15021	4971	10050	6.2	6.1	6.3
1995-96	269219	76755	192464	15876	4928	10948	5.9	6.4	5.7
1996-97	263883	72956	190927	16610	4689	11921	6.3	6.4	6.2
1997-98	298568	70743	227825	16344	4240	12104	5.5	5.6	8.9
1998-99@	297518	78640	218878	16457	3876	12581	5.5	4.9	5.7

Source: Central Statistics Organisation , @ - Quick Estimates.

Under the scheme, coverage has been enlarged to loanee and non-loanee farmers and to all foodgrain crops (cereals and pulses), oilseeds and horticulture/commercial crops, in respect of which past yield data are available for adequate number of years. The premium rates vary from 1.5 percent to 3.5 percent of the sum insured for foodgrain crops. Small and Marginal farmers will be entitled to a subsidy of 50 percent of the charges to be shared equally between Central Government and State Government. However, the premium subsidy is to be phased out over a period of five years. Out of Ninth Plan provision of Rs.730 crore, the expenditure in the last two years under CCIS had been Rs. 428.32 crore.

INVESTMENT IN AGRICULTURE

Public sector investment has played a crucial role in the development of infrastructure like irrigation, electricity, agricultural research, roads, markets and communications. However, the share of Gross Capital Formation in Agriculture (GCFA) in the total Gross Domestic Capital Formation (GDCF) has declined sharply to 9.4 per cent in 1996-97 from 19.1 per cent in 1979-80 (at 1980-81 prices). It has further come down to 5.5 per cent in 1998-99 (at 1993 prices) from 6.3 per cent in 1996-97 (Table-11) and 6.8 per cent in 1993-94. A more marked decline in capital formation has been in public sector which has come down from 15.3 per cent in 1980-81 to 4.9 per cent in 1996-97 at 1980-81 prices. Even at 1993-94 prices, the percentage of capital formation in public sector has come down from 6.5 per cent in 1993-94 to 4.9 per cent in 1998-99.

The share of public investment in agriculture has also declined to 23.6 percent in 1998-99 from 33 percent in 1993-94, whereas the share of private investment has risen from 67 percent to 76.4 percent during the same period (Table-11).

The decline in public investment is mainly due to diversion of resources in the form of subsidies for fertilizers, rural electricity, irrigation, credit and other agricultural inputs rather than on creation of assets.. Declining trend in public sector agricultural investment needs to be reversed by augmenting agricultural credit and also by increasing allocation to all the major States for agricultural growth. There is good potential for mobilizing private sector investment particularly for augmenting storage capacity. But, this is contingent upon removal of restrictions on trading, storage and movement as are in force in many states.

Public Capital investment in agriculture during 1974-75 to 1995-96 at 1980-81 prices in billion Rs.

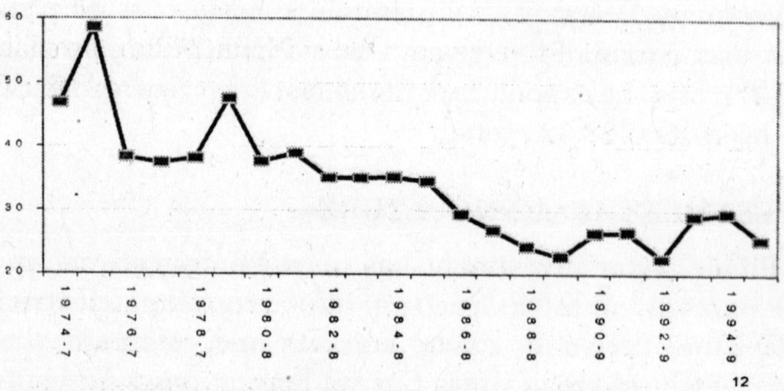

AGRICULTURE MARKETING

(I) Terms of Trade

The indices of terms of trade (base TE 1970-71) between agriculture and non-agricultural sectors showed an improvement in favour of agriculture during the period 1980-81 to 1990-91 as the index of prices received increased at the rate of 8.2 percent per annum while that of prices paid increased at 7.2 percent per annum. During this period the index of terms of trade improved from 82.9 to 90.0. Moreover, the index of prices paid by the Agriculture Sector for intermediate consumption (farm inputs) increased at the rate of 4.7 percent per annum indicating that the profitability of crop production increased even faster. During 1990-91 to 1994-95, the terms of trade improved further in favour of agriculture and the index increased to 91.7. However, the prices paid during this period by the farmers for agricultural inputs increased at the higher rate of 14 percent per annum, thus showing a fall in profitability in crop production, although overall terms of trade improved.

During 1994-95 to 1997-98, the terms of trade appear to have moved somewhat against agriculture with the index prices paid growing at higher rate (6.2%) as compared to the index prices received (5.9%). During this period, the index of terms of trade moved down from 91.7 to 88.5.

As per the new series (revised base of TE 1990-91) which has much larger coverage of items both for prices paid and prices received for the farm sector, the overall terms of trade have improved somewhat more than that reflected in the old series because while the index of prices received is similar in the two series, that of prices paid shows a slower increase in new series. If we have a look at the historical movement of relative prices, ever since 1960-61 the terms of trade for Agriculture has been hovering between 82% to 94%. This implies that agriculture sector has been loosing at the rate of about 12% p.a. and thus, large resources have got transferred from the farm sector to non-farm sector through the subtlety of price mechanism. The obvious consequence is a continuously widening gap between per capita income of farmers and other professionals, which used to be around 1:2 upto 1960-61 by now has become 1:6.

Index of terms of trade between agricultural and non-agricultural sectors (triennium ending 1971-72 = 100)

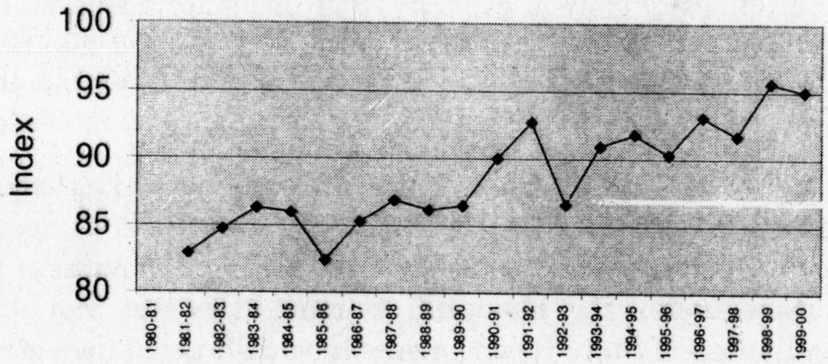

(II) Market Distortions

Farmers will produce more when there are sufficient incentives for them to do so. The experiment of Rayot Bazar of Andhra Pradesh and similar markets in Tamil Nadu where farmers directly sell their produce to consumers should be encouraged by setting up markets on the peripheries of all big cities at the trunk route connections in all States of India. In addition, we need to change several laws regarding the disposal of crop output, which are based on the mindset of the era of food shortages. The situation has changed now, but the effect of these laws, which have remained almost unchanged is that today, we procure more than we should, and then its disposal requires heavy subsidy to the consumers. If market distortions on food and other crops are eased, both farmers and consumers would benefit, and at the same time the burden of input and output subsidy would also be reduced.

STORAGE AND POST-HARVEST INFRASTRUCTURE

By the end of eighth Plan, the storage capacity in the public sector aggregated to 7.69 million tonnes of which 2.14 million tonnes was with Food Corporation of India (FCI), 1.08 million tonnes with State Warehousing Corporations (SWCs) and 0.72 million tonnes with Central Warehousing Corporation (CWC) and rest with other government agencies. FCI proposed to add storage capacity of 4.55 lakh tones during Ninth Plan, out of which 0.71 lakh tonnes is to be created in remote, hilly and other inaccessible areas. CWC had proposed an addition of 8.20 lakh tonnes of storage capacity. FCI has since added storage capacity of 1.54 lakh tonnes, while CWC created additional capacity of 3.18 lakh tonnes. SWCs added 2.65 lakh tonnes of storage capacity.

To bring in additional investment for strengthening storage, handling and transportation infrastructure, there is need to involve private sector. Present restrictions on movement and storage under the Essential Commodities Act and other regulations of State Governments have hampered the entry of private sector. For the expansion of storage facilities, it would be necessary to set up a chain of licensed godowns involving private investment in rural areas and credit facilities on the basis of receipts against stocks through banking sector. The ambit of future trading for agriculture commodities needs to be widened and the existing limitations such as those applicable for future trading in cotton and other commodities could be dispensed with. A National Policy on Handling, Storage and Transportation of Food is under consideration which will focus on greater involvement of private sector in strengthening storage and handling infrastructure.

The Cold Storage capacity, which in 1980 was 39.65 lakh tonnes, had almost doubled by 1990 at 76.77 lakh tonnes. During nineties, however, the pace of capacity creation slowed down and it was 103.53 lakh tonnes in December, 1998. Various measures such as licensing, rent control and requisitioning of cold storage space in some States have constrained capacity expansion in the past. Most of the States, except Bihar and West Bengal, have now done away with these regulations. The State Governments of Bihar and West Bengal should rescind the rent control orders on cold storage for promotion and expansion of the capacity in these states. Considering agro-climatic diversity and production pattern of horticulture throughout the country, the present cold storage capacity is inadequate.

The post-harvest losses of horticulture produce have been very high (37%) as the post-harvest technologies and infrastructure have not kept pace with production technology. A Credit Linked Capital Subsidy Scheme has been approved in 1999-2000, which aims at creation of additional 12 lakh tonnes of cold storage capacity and rehabilitation/modernization of 8 lakh tonnes of cold storage capacity particularly in U.P., Bihar and Orissa. It is also planned to create 4.5 lakh tonnes of onion storage capacity. The Scheme involves an investment of Rs.652 crore, of which Rs.175 crores is the subsidy component for entrepreneurs. A large number of cold storages are lying closed because of power and other problems. These need to be addressed so that the already created capacity is fully utilized.

AGRICULTURE EXPORTS

At the end of Eighth Plan (1996-97), share of agricultural exports in total exports was 20.4 percent. It declined to 18.5 per cent in 1998-99 (Table-12).

Table-12. Value Of Exports (in US$ millions)

Year	Value of Agricultural Exports	Value of Country's Total Exports	% Share of Agricultural Exports
1990-91	3521	18143	19.4
1996-97	6828	33470	20.4
1997-98	6375	33980	18.8
1998-99	6219	33659	18.5

Source: Economic Survey 1999-2000.

Under the Exim Policy, agricultural exports continue to be subjected to selective restrictions (Table-13). The export policy towards agricultural products is significantly influenced by considerations of domestic demand-supply balance. However, undue delay in release of quantitative ceilings for various agricultural products is certainly not conducive for sustained presence of India in world market for agricultural products. Similarly, untimely release of the ceiling does not help to enhance the unit value realization. The World Trade Organization commitments negotiated under the Agreement on Agriculture in GATT 1994, require developed countries to open up their markets faster than developing countries for agricultural exports by undertaking reductions in export subsidies, production subsidies and tariffs. However, the pace of implementation of these commitments has been very tardy and protracted negotiations have not yielded positive results in terms of market access for India and other developing countries. Moreover, developed countries have imposed non-tariff barriers which inhibit exports from India. This has resulted in poor demand for products like groundnut, oil meals, cashew, fresh fruits and vegetables etc.

The world trade in medicinal aromatic plants is currently valued at US$60 billion and India accounts for a negligible share valued at about US$100 million only, whereas China accounts for about 40 percent of world trade. This area needs to be fully exploited. The potential for export of organically produced natural agriculture products is yet to be fully realized. On the supply side, infrastructure support in areas such as inland transport and port facilities is far from satisfactory. As a result, a large volume of international trade is not being handled efficiently leading to trade disadvantages and loss of exports.

Table 13. Export restrictions on Agriculture Products

Product	Type of restrictions
Wheat	Quantitative Ceilings
Pulses	Licence (except in consumer packs upto 5 kg allowed freely)
Paddy	License
Onion	Canalysed through NAFED and/or State Government agencies. Often time frame prescribed for export and also realization of minimum export price (MEP)
Coarse Cereals	Quantitative ceiling/registration cum allocation certificate by APEDA
Sugar	Quantitative ceilings and registration with APEDA
Raw cotton	Quantitative ceilings, registration, Canalyzation and often subject to realization of minimum export price (MEP)
Niger seeds	Canalised through NAFED and TRIFED
Beef	Prohibited

Source: Ministry of Commerce.

In an increasingly globalised market arising out of trade liberalisation, *inter-alia,* through WTO Agreements impact on Indian agriculture needs to be analyzed in the context of both exports from India and imports into India. Apart from the agreement on Agriculture, another measure taken as part of India's commitments in WTO is the removal of Quantitative Restrictions, maintained for balance of payment purposes, including an agricultural products.

However, there is sufficient flexibility for India to protect its domestic producers as tariff bindings undertaken in the Uruguay round range between 100% to 300% as against much lower applied rates. Certain low tariff bindings undertaken before Uruguay Round have also been renegotiated upwards.

In the wake of Quantitative Restriction Removal and in order to provide a level playing field to domestic producers, the recent Exim Policy has stipulated that all imported goods shall be also subject to domestic laws, rules, orders, regulations, technical specifications as well as environmental and safety norms applicable to domestically produced goods (Para 4.12 of Exim Policy). However, an appropriate and suitably strengthened mechanism for enforcing the same needs to be put in place urgently.

Nature of Interventions by the Department of Agriculture & Cooperation

Introduction of High Yielding Varieties during mid-sixties and launching of crop-specific programmes during Seventh and Eighth Five Year Plans resulted in increase in production of foodgrains and achieving of self-sufficiency in foodgrains. However, the impact of these initiatives remained mainly confined to North and North Western regions of the country. There was limited impact of these programmes in many high potential areas, particularly in Eastern India. Second, in the initial phase there was thrust on development of infrastructure, but subsequently it petered out in favour of some populist subsidy oriented programmes. Third, some of the programmes implemented by more than one Department lacked direction and common guidelines. Each line department has its own hierarchy, with little interaction with each other.

Their services are supply driven with no effective feedback or mechanism for farmers to articulate their demands. As such, their impact was much below expectations. Foruth, the emphasis for too long remained confined to foodgrains production. Horticulture, dairy, fishery etc. and marketing and post-harvest infrastructure were not given due attention.

In many schemes of the Ministry there is an element of Transfer of Technology (TOT), which consists of crop demonstrations, farmer training, information support, trainers' training, etc. States currently employ over one lakh extension functionaries. In these schemes of about Rs.1000 crores annually the share of TOT comes to about 15 to 20%. This does not provide for much flexibility to the states, and because of rigidity of the schemes, funds are fragmented and cannot be effectively utilized. As a result of lack of coordination between departments, absence of region-specific orientation, lack of role clarity for extension staff and inadequate investment in infrastructure for the development of agriculture and allied sectors, the overall growth rate in agriculture has slowed down.

ANIMAL HUSBANDRY, DAIRYING AND FISHERIES

Animal Husbandry and Dairying

The livestock sector helps in providing essential proteins for human diet, besides providing self-employment opportunities to the rural people. Its contribution to the total agricultural output is 28 per cent. The Ninth Plan lays emphasis on improving the productivity of livestock through upgradation of the genetic potential of the livestock, developing adequate animal health care including control of diseases and creation of disease free zones, production of quality feed and fodder, revamping extension services, modernization of abattoirs, strengthening of dairy cooperative activities and rehabilitation of sick dairy cooperatives.

A Centrally Sponsored Scheme of Assistance to State Poultry/Duck Farms to encourage backyard poultry among small and marginal farmers has been taken up on pilot project basis. Another scheme on Cattle Insurance has been formulated with subsidized premium rate for the non-scheme animals of poor farmers. Two new schemes viz. 'New Primary Dairy Cooperatives' to establish 15000 new dairy cooperatives societies in Operation Flood districts and 'Assistance to Cooperatives' aimed at reorganizing of economically weak dairy milk unions/ federations have also been formulated.

The Ninth Plan target for milk and egg production and achievements during the first two years of the Plan are given in Table-14. With concerted efforts in improving genetic stock through crossbreeding, effective control of diseases and implementation of Operation Flood Programme, milk production has increased substantially. Similarly, poultry sub-sector has shown steady progress over the years.

Table 14 : Physical Progress during First Two Years of the Ninth Plan

Period	Milk (million tonnes)		Eggs (billion nos.)	
	Target	Ach.	Target	Ach.
Eighth Plan*	70.80	69.10	30.00	27.50
Ninth Plan (target)*	96.49	----	35.00	-----
1997-98	71.00	70.80	29.30	28.57
1998-99	74.80	74.70	30.12	30.14

*Terminal Year of Eighth Plan (1996-97)

Eradication of rinderpest (a dreadful disease) has been a significant achievement. Attempts are being made to control other important diseases like tuberculosis, brucellosis, etc. Creation of disease free zones in the states of Andhra Pradesh, Maharashtra (Zone I), Gujarat (Zone II), Haryana, Punjab, Delhi and Western U.P. are contemplated. Animal quarantine stations have been set up at New Delhi, Chennai, Mumbai and Calcutta to prevent the entry of exotic disease in the country. Import and export of livestock products are regulated through certification as per international standards.

Attention needs to be given to conservation, augmentation and improvement of native breeds of cattle the bufflow and all other domestic animals through selective breeding in view of their heat tolerance, disease resistance and production under nutritional scarcity. Implementation of schemes relating to improvement of meat processing facilities and modernization of abattoirs has not been satisfactory; projects sanctioned during the 7 th and 8 th Plans in Karnataka, Kerala, Tripura and Assam are still to be completed. Establishment of carcass utilization centers to make use of hides, bones and other body parts of dead animals and value addition thereon also needs to be considered.

Ninth Plan year-wise allocations and expenditure for the first three years are given in Table-15.

Table-15. Progress Of Plan Expenditure (Rs in crore)

Item	9th Plan Outlay	1997-98 BE	1997-98 Exp.	1998-99 BE	1998-99 Exp.	1999-2000 BE
Animal Husbandry	1076.12	160.02	94.84	170.40	51.48	160.08
Dairying	469.52	39.00	29.24	50.60	23.17	73.90
Total	1545.64	199.02	124.08	221.00	74.65	233.98

Source: Deptt. of AH & D

Attention is needed for cultivation of fodder crops and fodder trees to improve animal nutrition. The area under permanent pasture and grazing land has been estimated at 11.06 million ha. However, actual availability appears to be much less. An integrated approach for regeneration of the grazing lands needs to be evolved. A back up of technological innovations to evolve new varieties of grass/fodder would help to give a fillip to overcome fodder shortage.

The fodder available in the country includes normally agricultural crop residues, grass and grazing, green fodder raised on agricultural land, weeds from agricultural fields and field bunds and leaf-fodder from trees. The types of areas producing fodder are broadly the cultivated lands, the forests and the grazing areas (both under Government and private ownership). Green fodder is mostly obtained from cultivated areas; about 4.4% of the total cultivated area is devoted to fodder production.

Forests too contribute about 10-25% to the green fodder supply, besides providing dry grasses. The Committee on Fodder and Grasses estimated that in 1985 only about 57 per cent of dry fodder and 27 per cent of green fodder requirements were being met. Because of lack of fodder resources, cattle population has only marginally increased from 155 million in 1951 to 200 million in 1987. However the number of goats and sheep that can survive in harsher environment has increased by 100% and 26% respectively in the same period. This could be both-a consequence of land degradation as well as its cause. Including these two categories the total livestock population during 1951-87 has increased from 292 to 445 million, giving a growth rate of less than 1.2% annually. Had the productivity of grass lands and forests increased by more than 1.2%, the imbalance between the carrying capacity of present public and forest lands and livestock pressure would have been further narrowed.

Major Achievements in Livestock Sector

- *Country gained the position of single largest milk producer (74.7 million tonnes) & fifth largest egg producer (30.14 billion nos.) in the world.*
- *Dairy Cooperative network covering* ***376*** *districts of Operation Flood and Non-Operation Flood (hilly & backward) areas reached about* ***106.18*** *lakh people.*
- *Facilities for processing of* ***211*** *lakh litres of milk per day developed.*
- *Country achieved provisional freedom from rinderpest w.e.f.* ***31.3.1998.***

POLICY ISSUES

In the past, government owned public lands outside forest areas constituted an important source of grazing. In the absence of any policy for proper management, these areas decreased in extent and deteriorated. Decrease in their area and productivity resulted in under-nourishment of the livestock and also in the degradation of forests as a result of overgrazing. While the national forest policy deals with forest areas and the agriculture policy deals with agriculture areas under private ownership, Government owned wastelands are left uncared for. A clear policy for the conservation and development of these areas for grazing and fodder production is called for. Conflicting claims on these lands for expansion of agriculture or forestry will have to be resolved.

Under the present arrangement, fodder production is nobody's specific responsibility. The Agriculture Department is concerned with food production, while Animal Husbandry Department's interest mainly appears to be animal health and breeding. The mandate of the Forest Department is forest conservation and wood production (including fuel wood) although grazing and grass cutting is permitted. In the absence of clear responsibility for fodder production, the livestock has to survive mainly on the residues of agricultural crops and on grass and grazing available from forests and uncultivated wastelands. The agriculture policy should clearly provide that the responsibility of fodder for livestock should be of the owner if he owns land; Government wastelands should be used to produce fodder for livestock owned by the landless. Any fodder development programme should deal with all the land resources available such as cultivated lands, Government wastelands and forests. Fodder development on cultivated lands should deserve priority to make every farmer self-sufficient in fodder. A policy direction to use the Government wastelands according to land capability is necessary to stop encroachments of such lands for agriculture or for growing trees not otherwise suitable for such sites.

FISHERIES

The fisheries sector provides employment to about 3.84 million full or part time fishermen, with an equally impressive segment of the population engaged in ancillary activities associated with fisheries and aquaculture Potential of marine and inland resources has been estimated at 3.9 million tonnes and 4.5 million tonnes respectively. At present, total fish production is 5.26 million tonnes. Having almost reached a plateau in production from the coastal waters, the scope for increasing fish production from marine sources now lies in the deep sea. In the inland sector, however, there is considerable scope for increasing production and productivity by sustainable exploitation of the existing resources. The potential for fishery development in East and North Eastern states is immense and fish is an important constituent of diet of majority populace of the states in this region. Development of fisheries can go a long way in solving the problems of providing food as well as employment to region's predominant rural populace and water recharging.

Ninth Plan has focused on an integrated approach to sustainable development of fisheries and aquaculture and aims to optimize production and productivity, augment export of marine products, generate employment, improve socio-economic conditions of the fishermen and fish farmers, conserve aquatic resources and genetic diversity and increase per capita availability and consumption of fish. The major thrust is on expansion of aquaculture in freshwater and brackish water, development of reservoir fisheries, strengthening of infrastructure like fishery harbours and fish landing centres.

For the Ninth Plan period, Rs.800 crore have been earmarked for the fisheries sector. Against the outlays of Rs.119.15 crore for 1997-98 and Rs.159.90 crores for 1998-99, expenditures was only Rs.85.06 crore (71.4 %) and Rs.*91.42* crore (*57.2%*) respectively. Allocation for 1999-2000 is Rs. 145.92 crore.

The Ninth Plan fish production target of 7.04 million tonnes envisages a growth rate of 5.70 percent per annum. During the first two years of the Plan, fish production was 5.39 million tonnes (1997-98) and *5.26* million tonnes (1998-99) against the target of 5.65 million tonnes and 5.97 million tonnes respectively. Production target for 1999-2000 is 6.3 million tonnes. The riverine fisheries have been affected due to abstraction in various farms, sedimentation, effluxion and increasing pollution. The slow performance of brackish water aquaculture activities is due to the Supreme Court judgement prohibiting these activities within the Coastal Regulation Zone (CRZ). Legislation to regulate the brackish water aquaculture is yet to be enacted. Formulation of Deep Sea Fishing Policy is essential to exploit the fishery resources in the Exclusive Economic Zones (EEZ).

The giant, global fish and seafood market worth $ 8,000 million has encouraged mushroom growth of intensive and semi-intensive prawn farms along the elongated coastline as well as intensive and mechanized fish farming in the coastal waters. Boosted by the liberal Exim policy, shrimp farming developed feverishly and unpoliced in India. Of the 1.2 million ha of brackish water areas in India inclusive of ponds, lakes and lagoons spread along the coastline, about 80000 ha is under shrimp culture (80% under extensive methods and the rest under modified extensive and semi-intensive modes).

As aqua farming requires capital investment, the ownership of lands steadily gravitates to the cash-rich urban businessmen. Though there has been some investigation into the environmental impact of large shrimp farms, there is little, in terms of sound aquaculture policy taking care of above concerns in place to comprehensively deal with the loss of productive assets and threats to livelihood generated by aquaculture.

Some of the major constraints being faced in the development of the fishery sector are inadequate infrastructure for fish seed production and rearing space, lack of feed support to freshwater and brackish water aquaculture, lack of trained manpower and infrastructure for the same, inadequate infrastructures for fish gene banks, marketing linkages, lack of research input to control fish disease etc. Further, technologies for raising seed of minor carps, catfish and cold-water fish species area also required to fill the gaps.

Greater emphasis needs to be given by the research institutions for developing technology for breeding and seed production of commercially viable fresh water fish and package of practices for pen culture and cage fish farming. Advanced technologies for augmenting inland fish production through integrated fish farming, running water or flow-through systems are required to be promoted. Measures should also be taken to conserve coastal fishery resources and exploiting deep sea fishery resources in the EEZ of the country.

AGRICULTURE RESEARCH AND EDUCATION

Indian Council of Agriculture Research (ICAR) is the nodal agency at the national level for promotion of science and technology in the areas of agricultural research and education and demonstration of new technologies as frontline extension activities. ICAR has developed a National Grid comprising 46 Institutes including 4 Deemed Universities, 4 National Bureau, 9 Project Directorates, 31 national Research Centres, 158 Regional Stations and 80 All India Coordinated Research Project (AICRPs) in different parts of the country. The educational programmes are carried out by 30 State Agriculture Universities (SAUs) and one Central Agriculture University (CAU). National

Bureau of Animal Genetic Resources (NBAGR-Karnal), National Bureau of Fish Genetic Resources (NBFGR-Lucknow) have been further strengthened to enhance their work capacity in respect of collection, acquisition, quarantine, characterization, evaluation, maintenance, documentation, conservation and awareness generation.

The Ninth Plan outlay for ICAR has been stepped up to Rs.3377 crore, against Rs. 1300 crore for the Eighth Plan. Besides, a World Bank aided (US $ 239.7 million) National Agriculture Technology Project (NATP) in agro-eco system research, innovation in technology dissemination and organisation and management systems is under implementation since 1998.

All activities relating to transfer of technology (ToT) programmes of the Council have been integrated with Krishi Vigyan Kendras (KVKs) and their mandate enlarged to perform the function of on-farm testing/ research, long-term vocational training, in-service training of grass-root level functionaries and frontline demonstrations. During first two years of Ninth Plan 53 districts have been identified to strengthen the existing Zonal Research Stations (ZRS), to take up the additional functions of KVK raising the number of KVKs to 314.

Agricultural Research Institutes are multiplying at a fast rate and also growing in size. Research activity is initially taken up as All India Coordinated Research Project (AICRP), which later gets split into specialities, which after sometime gets converted into National Research Centre and thereafter as Project Directorate before its elevation to an Institute and if possible, to Deemed University. Separate National Centres and Directorates are opened for different crops/different aspects of crop/activity.

The above approach makes it difficult to take an integrated view of R&D work being carried under various projects viz. All India Coordinated Research Project, Centres, Directorates and Institutes of Excellence & their linkages with Agriculture and productivity improvement schemes of the Department of Agriculture and Cooperation and Department of Animal

Husbandry. Proliferation of institutes is pushing up the establishment cost significantly leaving very little for R&D work. This also places scientists in watertight compartments leading to sub-optimal utilization of manpower and equipment.

The results of research activities undertaken by ICAR are not commensurate with the huge infrastructure set up. While examining the ICAR proposal on Technology Mission on Horticulture in NE Region, the State Governments have adversely commented on the ability of ICAR to provide the desired inputs.

Similarly, while discussing Technology Mission on Cotton, ICAR wanted additional funds for undertaking work for the Technology Mission. It indicates that the research activities being undertaken by ICAR are not what are required by the end users and we have to make specific additional provisions for research activities that are relevant for the nation.

SUMMING UP-AGRICULTURAL REFORMS AND STRUCTURAL ISSUES

There are many structural and institutional issues which need to be addressed for stepping up agricultural growth. This is vital for promoting the welfare of masses, arresting the widening inequality and achieving the growth of the economy at a higher and sustainable level. A multi-dimensional reform agenda for agriculture should be drawn up for improving incentives to produce, rationalizing subsidies and promoting investments, besides, extending protective cover to the poor. A review of myriad controls in domestic market of agricultural produce is an urgent necessity.

Control on trading and processing of agricultural commodities block free movement of goods and impose stocking limits on private traders and processors. For example, rice and sugar processors are liable to levies and processing of major oilseeds is reserved for small-scale sector. Similar controls have been imposed under the Essential Commodity Act, which run counter to market and processing efficiency. Unless these are dispensed with, private sector investment would not be attracted.

Canal systems are in poor shape for lack of operations and maintenance outlay. These should be improved by involving users' groups in management and appropriate pricing of water to cover full operation and maintenance costs. Most of the States will have to rationalise power subsidy for improving the quality of power. Other institutional reforms relate to land laws and rural credit.

The lease market in land needs to be opened up to promote economically viable size of holdings. Rural credit structure needs revamping because of large number of unviable primary cooperatives. Most of the States have yet not amended State Cooperatives laws on the lines of Model Cooperative Act. These measures can put agriculture on higher growth trajectory as well as trigger growth in other sectors.

Capital intensity is increasing for all categories of farmers, but at a faster pace in Green Revolution areas and for large farmers. This is causing a resource squeeze in agriculture, as marketable surplus has been increasing at a slower rate to absorb incremental costs. As a result, though buffer stocks are increasing, there is co-existence of hunger because of poor purchasing power. The phenomenon of self-sufficiency is somewhat illusory as the demand is depressed. There is imperative need to adopt, labour intensive production technologies, particularly in rainfed areas to cut cash costs. Some of major reforms and structural issues are summed up below:-

(i) Removal of domestic market control on agricultural produce.

(ii) Rationalization of subsidies on inputs which adversely affect sustainable development and use of land and water resources.

(iii) Institutional reforms relating to rural credit.

(iv) Opening of lease market in land to promote economically viable size of farm holdings.

(v) To check tribal land alienation and protect the rights of women in land.

(vi) Intensification of development of rainfed areas and exploitation of ground water potential especially in Eastern Region.

(vii) Promotion of balanced use of fertilizers and strengthening of soil testing facilities

(viii) Augmenting the Seed Replacement Rate (SRR) through enhanced supply of certified / quality seeds.

(ix) Minimizing the use of pesticides, through popularization of IPM approach.

(x) Strengthening of post harvest handling processing, storage /cold storage and marketing facilities.

(xi) Strengthening of Dairy Cooperatives

(xii) Review of policy on deep sea fishing policy.

Future agricultural growth could be speeded by policy and institutional reform in the sector, namely (a) changed pattern of spending to building up of capital assets and a reduction in distortionary subsidies; (b) deregulation of the processing sector and termination of the use of credit subsidy as a transfer mechanism; and (c) empowerment of the poor by improving their access to land and common resources, increasing their control over services and infrastructure in rural areas, and improved safety nets.

The above-mentioned policy reforms would also help reduce poverty. For example, increased public spending on rural roads, agricultural technology improvement, and irrigation would all help reduce poverty. Growth in the rural non-farm sector would also benefit from improved infrastructure (roads, power, communications) and social services. More efficient and competitive markets can deliver better prices and greater market opportunities to farmers, without raising consumer prices, which would help farmers offset the impact of cuts in subsidies. Better markets together with futures markets and eased restrictions on commodity movements and private participation in international trade can help reduce price fluctuations.

9

Commodity Exchange and Agricultural Market

There is need to amend the Forward Contracts (Regulation) Act of 1952, since it was enacted under conditions of serious food shortages. Our commodity markets, both physical and futures, need review.

It will also be to the advantage of the farmers of India, if the Central and State Governments agree on an Indian Common Market, and remove all barriers relating to inter-state movement of farm commodities. This must be done after a consultation process amongst state governments, as interstate taxes are revenue-earning measures levied by states in the Indian federal system.

The Indian Common Market catering to a population of over a billion will serve as a buffer against violent price fluctuations arising from disturbances in the overseas markets.

COMPENSATING LOSS FROM PRICE FALL AND PRICE STABILISATION FUND

Another intervention is the creation of a price stabilisation fund or alternatively a mechanism for compensation of loss arising from price fall for these commodities. Although the Commission does not have full information, some initiative launched by the Government of India needs to be commended and the State Government should actively campaign and make its own contribution.

Export Promotion

Two sets of issues are arising as a consequence of the implementation of the WTO regime in this country. Those problems facing exporters and those arising from import of agricultural commodities, but both are be seen the separately.

Strengths and Weaknesses of Kerala in Exports

1. One of the major strengths of Kerala's agriculture is its long tradition of export, which has bequeathed a chain of institutions and networks for collection and transport, from the farm to the port through itinerary merchants, and retail traders at the villages, wholesale traders at the thaluk and district towns and commission agents and exporters at the ports. The orientation of the farmers to sale of commodities for export, access to market information, the external links established over generation are all assets, and survived the vicissitudes of time.

2. Though the system is resilient, it is inadequate to meet the challenges posed by the WTO regime especially international competition from emerging competitors (new players such as Viet Nam in black pepper and Guatemala in cardamom). Secondly the traditional methods of production. storage and processing are increasingly short of international quality requirements. Third weakness is that most of the products exported are without value addition. Fourth the system is not geared to capitalise on the opportunities offered through opening up new markets as sequel to the market access provisions of AoA. All these can be overcome through concerted and determined efforts.

3. Unlike many other competing countries which themselves are mostly developing nations like India, the state does not have a cost advantage in the products in which Kerala is competing, arising from low wages, because the wages prevailing in Kerala are relatively high. More and more low cost countries such as Vietnam

are entering as competitors in this field. Kerala may not be able to maintain its competitiveness through low wages, but only through higher productivity, which many of these newly emerging competitors have already achieved. Determined efforts are needed to achieve cost-effective productivity increases such as launching a massive systematic replanting with highly productive (which are indeed available) planting materials and adoption of management practices for the tree crops has already been elaborated earlier.

4. In order to maintain its advantage in the globalised environment, Kerala has to resort to product differentiation through labelling, creation of brand equity, etc. Kerala has enormous opportunity in the production of organic foods with eco-label, which has a ready market in developed countries. For realising this market, surveys are to be conducted in developed countries where Kerala's products are already in demand. Internationally recognized certification and labelling agencies may have to be created, to step up exports of environment friendly organic products. The certification criteria will have to be reviewed by setting up a special task force and periodically updated.
5. Though small at present, the developing countries, especially those in Africa offer opportunities for the traditional export commodities of Kerala. These opportunities are to be harnessed.

PREVENTING MISUSE OF IMPORT FOR RE-EXPORT

A major threat to the internal price and the primacy of Indian exports in the not so long run is the imports for re-export with value addition, apart from imports under the obligations under AoA. While in principle such imports are desirable, this provision is being abused in the case of coffee and tea, much to the detriment to the interests of the Indian producers and the country at large. It is reported that low quality materials (tea for instance) are imported from competing countries and re-exported with nominal value addition to our traditional markets by making use of the loophole in the law that does not stipulate any minimum addition of value should be provided to prevent the misuse/abuse of the provision of allowing imports of agricultural commodities for re-export in order to earn foreign exchange through value addition.

It should be ensured that value addition is significant, at least to the extent of import duty. Misuse at least in a few instances, has resulted in the loss of image of Indian products due to import and re-export of low quality products. Further, such re-exports cut into Indian share of the market, which has serious economic backlash especially in the case of surplus in products such as tea and coffee, which the Indian producers are struggling to dispose off. As such loss of markets in turn compels reduction in production and employment in the country. There is also need to specify the authorities, who are empowered to issue certificates of origin of materials.

The Commerce Ministry should study this issue carefully in consultation with the Commodity Boards. While importing at least the quality standards prescribed under the Food Adulteration Act should be insisted upon if there is no superior standards prescribed in the statute.

Data on Imports

Information and data on imports should be posted regularly in the websites of the Ministries of Foreign Trade and Commerce, so that proactive action can be taken to ensure a balance between demand and supply. Lack of access to reliable information and near absence of wider consultation in the various stages of GATT Round of negotiations have been primarily responsible for the poorly informed debate and emotional out bursts on the whole issue of India's entry into WTO and subsequent implementation of the AoA. The situation got retrieved to some extent around the Doha Ministerial Conference. This should be an object lesson of the imperative need for informed debate and taking people into confidence on so vital issue, such as the entry into WTO, the implications of which are pervasive.

Establishment of a Virtual University for Agricultural Trade

1. One consequence of trade liberalisation is that farming is becoming highly knowledge and information intensive. Enhancing trade competitiveness is a must. Hence, there is need for a continuous updating of the information available to farmers and planters on all issues relating to domestic and global trade. Information will have to be provided on quality related regulations such as sanitary and phytosanitary measures and *codex alimentarius* standards. Quality, trade and patent literacy will have to become widespread. Such a knowledge and information empowerment programme in farm trade should reach every farm family in Kerala and should include the excluded, in respect of information empowerment.

2. We suggest for this purpose the establishment of a Virtual University for Agricultural Trade as a 21 st century institution, drawing strength from the ongoing Information and Communication Technology revolution in Kerala. A computer-aided and Internet connected Virtual University can be established on a hub and spokes model.

   The hub can be located at an appropriate location like KAU, with the spokes being located in every district. The hub and spokes can be linked to Television Channels and Community Radio, so that relevant information reaches every farm household every morning.

3. The effectiveness of the Virtual University for Agricultural Trade will depend upon the quality and timeliness of the dynamic (i.e., time and location specific) and generic information provided to the stakeholders. The KAU has prepared a draft plan for the proposed Virtual University, which is, appended in Part II of this Report. It would be useful to convene a Brainstorming Workshop with the participation of data generators and providers (like ISRO, IMD, KAU, APEDA, NDDB, NHDB, Commodity Boards, Ministries of Agriculture,

Commerce and Foreign Trade of GOI, ICAR, CSIR etc.), data seekers (farm families, planters exporters, women's' groups, traders, etc), information managers (ICT specialists, media representatives, extension specialists, etc), policy makers (concerned secretaries to Government and Vice-Chairman, State Planning Commission) and representatives of UNDP and other potential funding agencies. A Business Plan may be finalised at this workshop. It will be appropriate to get the Virtual University for Agricultural Trade inaugurated by the Hon'ble Chief Minister on January 26, 2003, since sooner steps are taken for the knowledge and information empowerment of producers, traders, exporters and consumers, the speedier can be the founding of an effective Trade Security System to the state.

SANITARY AND PHYTOSANITARY MEASURES

Quality Literacy Movement

The GOI should participate actively in the process of determining a just and fair International Standards for Phytosanitary Measures. Otherwise, the standards may come in the way of our exports. In addition, the following steps are needed urgently.

- Strengthen post-harvest infrastructure.
- Improve the sanitary conditions under which food is processed and milch and meat animals are reared.
- Strengthen the capacity of State Government Institutions in relation to quarantine measures, sanitary and phytosanitary measures and *codex alimentarius* standards of food safety.
- Launch a Quality Literacy Movement, and train at least 2 men and 2 women members of every Gram Panchayat as Quality Managers.

Codex Alimentarius Standards

Factors relating to FAO *Codex Alimentarius* standards of food safety, that inhibit market access can be overcome only by strengthening post-harvest technology and sanitary and phytosanitary measures. Infrastructure for Sanitary and Phytosanitary Measures and *Codex Alimentarius* Standards needs urgent strengthening.

Prevention of Unconscious Introduction of Pests and Diseases and Invasive Alien Species

Numerous new pathogens, pests and weeds are coming into the country as a result of mass imports of pulses, oil seeds, poultry products and other agricultural commodities. The National Bureau of Plant Genetics Resources (NBPGR) of ICAR at New Delhi has sounded an alarm about the threat, which such invasive alien species pose to our agriculture. The poultry industry is also threatened with new diseases through imported poultry products, as had happened in the case of the prawn industry in Andhra Pradesh. There is need for urgent vigilance and action to prevent the unconscious introduction of such serious threats to our agriculture.

Disease-free Zones of Livestock for Export

Creation of disease-free zones for livestock production can improve the market access for livestock products. The programme of the Department of Animal Husbandry deserves to be supported. Support has to be extended for modernisation abattoirs and slaughterhouses.

IPR AND BIODIVERSITY

Indigenous Knowledge and Trade Related Intellectual Property Rights (TRIPS) and Biodiversity

Along with the concerns associated with WTA such as domestic support export subsidy, phytosanitary measures, the provision on Trade Related Intellectual Property Rights (TRIPs) reiterates the need for urgent measures to make gains from possible geographical indications of our commodities and from the rich biodiversity with the help of relevant domestic legislations. The ongoing negotiations in the TRIPs Council are expected to harmonise IPR with basic principles of CBD on access to biodiversity and indigenous people's knowledge, equity and benefit sharing. It is notable, in this context, that the Indian legislations, PPVFR Act and the Biological Diversity Bill have provision for equity and benefit sharing. Particular attention should be given to tribal wisdom and knowledge system and the IPR associated with this has to be recognised, protected and rewarded.

Protection of Plant Varieties and Farmers' Rights Act and the Biodiversity Act

1. The Biodiversity Board established in Kerala should undertake an intensive programme of Genetic Literacy, in order to acquaint primary conservers on their rights relating to recognition and reward from the provisions of the Plant Variety Protection and Farmers' Rights Act, as well as the provisions relating to prior informed consent and benefit sharing provided under the Biological Diversity Bill (passed by the Lok Sabha and Rajya Sabha). It would be useful to promote a cadre of "Barefoot Legal Advisors" to help to spread such Genetic Literacy among the tribal and rural families engaged in the conservation and enhancement of agro-biodiversity. This will help to avoid biopiracy and promote symbiotic biopartnerships.
2. Kerala is endowed with rich biodiversity and has rich medicinal plant resources. People in the state have inherited thousands years of knowledge in Ayurveda and traditions in herbal medicines. The new IPR regime offers opportunities as well as threats in profiting from the rich biodiversity and patenting biological products. What is urgently needed is documentation and research on finding the active principles. A sense of urgency is needed on the part of the government in mobilising state's scientific resources, liberal funding and vigorous effort in promoting patent literacy. Urgent steps should be launched to take advantage of the provisions to secure benefits from the National Gene Fund to be set up under the PPVFR Act. Vigilant measures are necessary to protect IPRs of the indigenous people.

3. Government of India is the signatory of International Treaty dealing with genetic resources, plant varieties, intellectual property rights, etc. It is imperative that the implications of these agreements with reference to agriculture policies and their impact on agriculture sector need to be understood by the State Governments, as the day to day administration of agriculture is under the domain of the state. Towards this end Government of India should establish a mechanism of consultation and interaction with States and put in place also familiarisation programmes for State agricultural officers on the legal and technical issues involved. The ICAR may also regularly update the State agricultural universities on these agreements and upgrade their capacity to advise the State Governments on these matters.

GEOGRAPHICAL INDICATIONS

Eligibility under Geographical Indications based on certain specific quality, reputation or other characteristics including appearance of the commodity or goods, which are due exclusively or essentially to the described three geographical elements namely geographical environment, biological factors and production factors. These specific qualities and characteristics are clearly definable or merely describable. For instance, it is generally perceived that the Malabar pepper, the Cochin ginger, Alleppey Finger turmeric and Tellicherry Extra Green Bold (TEGB) cardamom have high market reputation. This reputation in each of these produces could be attributed to certain tangible and intangible characteristics.

The tangible characteristics have to be elaborately defined with the help of data base, figures, photographs, etc. depending on whether the characteristics involve shape, size, colour and appearance, test weight, content and composition of chemical factors determining the intrinsic quality valued in the market parlour. The TRIPs regime and the national legislation on Geographical Indications empower the state in getting protection to these valuable, which are known for centuries with geographical appellations attributing to their origin in Kerala. Urgent measures are to be taken to identify geographical indication of products of Kerala to protect them under IPR. Apart from pepper and cardamom, Kerala can claim more commodities for securing their GI for trade leverage in accordance with Geographical Indications of Goods (Registration and Protection) Act of 1999.

REGIONAL AND DOMESTIC STRATEGIES

Understanding between India and Developing Nations of Asia

Competition from developing nations in South Asia and South East Asia and a few African nations are emerging in many crops on which Kerala's farm economy is depending. India's rubber has to compete with that of Thailand, Indonesia and Malaysia, coconut with Philippines and Sri Lanka, Tea with Sri Lanka, cardamom with Guatemala. black pepper with Viet Nam, etc. Competition is among developing nations in the neighbourhood to acquire the market share. The beneficiaries are the developed countries. Hence it is desirable and necessary to forge unity with these competing nations and develop understanding to the benefit of all.

Consultation with States

Agriculture is a State subject under Constitution of India. The brunt of the implications (adverse impact on the livelihood security, income erosion, etc.) of the decisions of the Central Government has to be borne by the state governments (not only the consequent political unrest but the financial/resource loss/ liability as well). Therefore, there should be adequate prior consultations (continuous) on such vital actions such as the accession to WTO and signing of the Agreement on Agriculture before decisions are taken. More over such consultations could be of considerable benefit to the Central government as the State governments are better aware and informed of the ground realities. Kerala's agricultural wealth is based on trade, since most of the farm commodities produced in the State are for trade within or outside the country. Kerala's experience with global trade is hence particularly relevant to the formulation of the national policy.

Compensatory Mechanisms for Protecting Livelihood Security

Even though the commodities that Kerala produces are the mainstay of the agricultural economy of the state; in the national context they are of not much significance to the economy of the country. Hence when decisions are taken on the import and export of commodities to fulfil bilateral or multilateral obligations, concerns of states, not only of Kerala, but some other states as well, are not generally seen adequately taken care of (in case of jute-West Bengal, soybean-Madhya Pradesh, for instance). Many a decisions of this kind taken in the national interest, (import of copra from Sri Lanka under SAARC, import of palm oil under a rail project deal with Indonesia, etc.) has had adverse impact on the economy especially on the livelihood security of the dependent population.

The suffering that has resulted from the signing the treaty is often due to lack of in-depth preparation apart from even consultation with states, which may be adversely affected by such diplomatic decisions. Therefore, when such decisions are taken prior consultations should be held with the concerned states. Concurrently a compensatory mechanism has to be built-in and bargained for to mitigate the hardships of the affected population groups. Considering the unique crops and circumstance under which they are grown, special protection for Kerala's agriculture need to be given in order to maintain the livelihood security of those who are severely affected by the implementation of provisions in WTA

Consultation among the Interested Groups of States

Kerala, Karnataka and Tamil Nadu on, coconut, tea and coffee; Kerala and Tamil Nadu on rubber etc. compete with each other in the national market. Many concerns are common, for instance, the control of mite infestation in coconut, procurement of copra, etc. Common approaches to common concerns are necessary. The meetings of the South Zone Council could be an ideal forum for such consultations.

Harmonising the Interests of Various Stakeholders

Farmers, manufacturers and the government are to forge a consensus to generate a win-win situation to all stakeholders. There should be a realisation that there is strong mutual dependence between the farmers and the manufacturers/ exporters. Farmers are to produce raw materials to sustain the industry. Manufacturers are to buy the commodities and thereby provide a demand for the produce. A sustainable market is as important to farmers as an assured source of raw material for the manufacturers/exporters.

If the commodity price is depressed beyond a limit farmers would be compelled to grow alternate crops and uncertainties would set in the supply of raw materials, which would put the industry in jeopardy. Farmers would lose the market demand if prices go abnormally high, as the manufacturers would find difficult to run the factory. The loss of market for rubber in the foam mattress industry to polypropylene foam and the loss of market for coconut oil in the soap industry to other vegetable oils are lessons to be learned. It should also be remembered that import of agricultural commodities also means import of unemployment and loss of income to the nation. Forging understanding between various interest groups before negotiating international treaties, such as the AoA and WTO is very critical in keeping up nation's interest ahead.

AREAS OF PRIORITY CONCERN IN RELATION TO RESEARCH AND INFRASTRUCTURE DEVELOPMENT

The potential high growth areas for Kerala, associated with agriculture and biodiversity, deserving special attention are the herbal medicine and ayurveda and tourism linked to health (ayurveda), spirituality (like Sabarimala, Guruvayoor, Malayattoor, Cheramaan Mosque at Kotungalloor) and nature (game sanctuaries, sea resorts etc.).

In addition, there is scope for promoting eco-tourism like "Holidays on the Farm" "Green Travel" in plantation and Kuttanad areas, where nature offers picturesque landscapes and biodiversity. This may provide urban youth opportunity for experiencing farm operations, farm life and fresh environment. Some of the steps needed to promote these are described below.

HERBAL MEDICINE AND AYURVEDA

Genetic Resources Conservation and ustainable Use

A priority step relates to the strengthening of *in situ* and *ex situ* conservation of medicinal plants and the establishment of Seed Banks for these plants, which are in demand for commercial use. Due to direct collection from their native habitats, many medicinal plants move to the Red Data Books of the Botanical Survey of India, indicating that they are threatened with extinction. The cultivation of plants in demand in the Ayurveda system of medicine by tribal and rural families on contract with appropriate pharmaceutical companies will help to foster organised sourcing of raw material. This will also help to strengthen the livelihoods of tribal and rural families and standardised raw material for medicinal use. The cultivation of medicinal plants for which there is a market, based on assured buy back arrangements, and could be an important component of Kerala Governments' programmes for tribal families.

Maintaining the Purity and Authenticity of Ayurveda

Steps will have to be taken to promote quality control and certification in the case of Ayurvedic medicines. Research will be needed for the validation of claims and for ensuring that the claims printed on marketing labels are rooted on scientific data. Medicinal rices like *Njavara* can be marketed abroad, if verifiable characteristics are discerned and listed on the label. If there is an effective certification agency, a suitable brand name can be given, as for example "Herbal Cures from God's own Country".

Growers' Associations

In order to give the power of scale to small growers of medicinal plants, Medicinal Plants Growers' Associations, each covering about 100 ha, could be formed on the model of self-help groups. Capacity building in the areas of cultivation and marketing will have to be organised. Such growers' associations can enter to a Memorandum of Understanding with companies with regard to sourcing of raw material for drugs. Herbal estates could also be promoted for bringing about an end-to-end approach in relation to medicinal plants and herbal medicine.

Herbal Sanctuaries

Areas rich in medicinal plants can be developed into Herbal Sanctuaries, so that this unique biological wealth can be safeguarded and conserved for posterity.

Herbal Biovalley

It would be desirable to develop the region extending from the Silent Valley Biosphere Reserve up to Wayanad as an Herbal Biovalley, on the model of the Silicon Valley for computer software. The Herbal Biovalley will provide the biological software essential for a dynamic medicinal plant industry. The infrastructure necessary for seed multiplication including tissue culture facilities, establishment of nurseries of elite material, validation and certification and producer-oriented marketing and other centralised facilities to facilitate efficient decentralised production, will have to be provided in the Herbal Biovalley. We suggest that GOK may constitute a Project Design Team consisting of experts from Kerala and representative of the Central Medicinal Plants Board, and Bioresources Board, as well as NABARD and APEDA to prepare a Business Plan for the world's first Herbal Biovalley. Kerala's goal should be the marketing of herbal medicine worth US $ 5 billion per year by 2010.

TOURISM

Kerala's unique advantages in tourism are well known. It is the only State in the country capable of launching a dynamic programme of home and global tourism, which caters to the needs of health, spirituality and eco-tourism. The infrastructure and service standards in all these areas need enforcement or strengthening. Specialist groups can be set up in these three areas of tourism to draw up detailed Business Plans. Again the aim should be to earn at least US $ 5 billion per year by 2010 from home and global tourism.

ORGANIC FARMING

The Union Minister for Agriculture, Shri Ajit Singh, recently announced the decision of the Government of India to set up a National Institute for Organic Agriculture, which will have the authority to undertake certification of organic products. Kerala is a national leader in the production and marketing of organic spices, tea, pineapple, banana, medicinal plants and other farm commodities. It also proposes to undertake the production of organic rubber specially for the manufacture of condoms for use in the fight against the dreadful HIV / AIDS menace.

Therefore, Kerala is an ideal location for the proposed National Institute for Organic Agriculture and the associated certification agency. About 200 hectares of land ideal for the location of this Institute are available with the Kerala Agriculture University at Thiruvazankunnu, Palakkad district. It is requested that the Hon.Chief Minister and the Hon. Agriculture Minister may write immediately to Shri, Ajit Singh, and Union Agriculture Minister, offering land and other facilities in Kerala for the proposed Institute. This will help to strengthen the organic farming movement in Kerala and help farmers to produce health foods and value-added farm products for internal and international consumption.

CLEAN ENERGY SOURCES

Drying the harvested crop presents great problems in plantation crops like coffee, pepper, etc, with the result mycotoxins develop due to high moisture content. Considering the acute shortage of energy especially in the plantation sector for preparing products, especially through drying enabling to improve quality to meet international standards, a large programme of renewable energy has to be mounted. We recommend that the Government of Kerala may prepare a project for financial support from the Climate Convention Fund, operated by the Global Environment Facility for introducing on a large scale solar energy devices in drying plantation crops like tea, coffee, pepper, etc. The Ministry of Non-Conventional Energy Sources (MNES) should launch a dynamic programme for setting up community drying centres using solar energy. This will help small producers to get the harvested crop dried properly

ENLARGING EXPORTS OF MARINE PRODUCTS

The following steps are urgently needed: • Enhance the quality of domestically consumed fish and launch a quality awareness campaign among fishers, traders and consumers.

- Undertake a multi-stakeholder study of the current subsidies prevailing in the fishery sector, so that support, which is non-actionable under the SCM agreement, can be provided for fostering sustainable resource rejuvenation and management programmes.
- Create an updated database that can help in taking well-informed decisions.
- Initiate aquarian reforms that will restrict the rights to own fishing vessels only to those who actually fish.
- Undertake measures for environmental protection and sustainable management.
- Retrain the Fisheries Department staff in eco-fisheries and low external input sustainable aquaculture.

THE ROLE OF THE MEDIA

The media has a special responsibility in reporting on the WTO and its impact, and in putting this information in the public domain. This is particularly so in a state where newspaper readership and media consumption are so widespread, and the media already so highly sensitised to the livelihood concerns. Unique to this Commission, which would normally be expected to represent government/private concerns, is its recognition of the media as a critical agency that is a part of the strategy to meet the challenges that WTO-regulated trade regime. Some of the measures which could make for a productive media-government engagement include:

- The setting up of a WTO Media Cell, which could perform/coordinate more than one task. It could handle regular media contacts plus perform the role of a clearing-house of information pertaining to the WTO and Kerala. The Virtual University and concerned departments and ministries could feed information to the cell, which could be made available to interested media through regular information briefs, and which can also be put on a web-site.
- For the general media, the Media Cell must put out briefs, hold regular briefings in different parts of the state, make officers and specialists available for comment and/or interviews. In a state with such innovative and evolved channels of communication, the Cell could use a variety of techniques to inform writers and journalists across a range of publications.
- Over the long term, the Media Cell could also help to build and train a core group of specialist WTO writers. This would help the development of strong and informed writing on WTO related issues and their global, national and regional dimensions.
- Documentation of publications on the WTO, including books, journals, newspaper reports, magazines, etc.

CROPS/COMMODITIES

Coconut

The Crisis and Dimension : The crisis is characterised by steep fall in price of coconut and drastic decline in production resulting from the coconut mite infestation. The fall in prices was from about Rs.500 per hundred nuts during 98-99 to less than Rs. 300 by the mid-2000, which largely continues to persist. The primary cause of this price crash started with steep decline in coconut oil prices, which dropped from the ruling prices between Rs. 5387 and Rs.5588 per quintal during 1997-99 to

Rs. 3251 in 2001. The decline in production (in quality rather than in number) was largely caused by the widespread infestation with Eriophyd mite during 1998. This loss in production coupled with loss in price created a crisis of unprecedented proportion to the coconut economy of the state and to the farmers largely depending on it for their livelihood. The human dimension of the crisis, directly affected the livelihood of nearly one million of the farm households, representing almost 20 per cent of total farm holdings of the state, and indirectly another two lakhs households, who solely dependent on the processing coir, a by-product of coconut, for their livelihood. While majority of the coconut farmers affected are small and marginal owning less than one half to one hectare of coconut gardens, the affected workers in the coir sector largely belonged to the BPL group.

The Oil Market Connectivity

Nearly 60 per cent of the coconut produced in the state is consumed at household level and the rest goes to oil extraction. Again a good percentage of the oil is consumed as the primary cooking oil. It is estimated that around 14-15 per cent of the oil produced in the country is used by the soap and toiletry industries. Yet, it appears, the shot on the prices of coconut oil is being called by this industry. Thus, the farm prices of coconut are depended on the supply-demand situation of vegetable oil in the country and edible oil prices. The cardinal elements of this supply-demand relationship are the domestic production of vegetable oil, quantity of annually imported oil and the market off take.

Over the years, production of coconut oil has been increasing while substitute oils have also been systematically making inroads into the national vegetable oil market. Here, the relative cost differences of different vegetable oils of various origin come into play and determine the periodic market preference. Continuous availability of alternate oil at low prices diverts long time users of coconut oil to such low cost oils. This virtually erodes the pre-eminence and indispensability of coconut oil in industrial sector, which was once considered to be depended on coconut oil. The case in point is the entry of palm oil and soya oil in the national market and the role of liberalised import of these oils to the disadvantage of domestically produced vegetable oils. In this competition, it is obvious that among the domestically produced oils, the one, which is the least dear in cost, shall bear the brunt, unless such high cost is linked with a unique quality indispensable to the industry. During the last decade, coconut production in the country registered 35 per cent increase and that of coconut oil by 60 per cent, from 2.81 to 4.49 lakh tons. This increase in Kerala was over 26 per cent for nuts, although the share of the state to national production declined from 47 per cent to 42 per cent.

This increase in production with increased availability of cheap alternate oils shifted the preference of industry away from coconut oil. In the absence of alternate demand creation, the slump was set in. While, there is a continuing national deficit in domestic vegetable oil production, the singular policy, which largely contributed to the price fall, is the import policy on edible oil and the committed low tariff line on soya oil. To what extent this price crash was encouraged by this policy is evident from the following import trend since 1995-96 (please note the coincidence with the establishment of WTO). While there is a justification for the import of vegetable oil to augment the domestic production, the level of import allowed seriously affected the domestic production sector, causing concern to the livelihood of thousands of farmers, who traditionally cultivate the oil-producing crops. Here again, while farmers growing annual oil seed crops have chance to move to alternate crops, the perennial oil seed crop farmers, like the coconut farmer, are forced into an economic trap.

During 1995-98, the average annual import of edible vegetable oil (predominantly palm oil and soya and sunflower oil to lesser extent) was about 1.2 million tonnes. This was increased to 2.4 m tonnes during 1998-99 and 3.05 m tonnes during 2000-01. During 2000-01, palm oil accounted for 72% of the imported edible/vegetable oil. This escalation in import by the Government of India and traders under the QR-less free trade regime, abetted with a low tariff rate, illustrates the high vulnerability of domestic agricultural production system, at variable degrees and the associated dangers to the livelihood of the depended population when the WTO regime becomes fully operational on domestic agriculture and agricultural commodity trade changes to the anticipated low or no tariff rate.

Strategy Proposed

The only immediate strategy to make coconut production to promote sustainable livelihood for the producers is appropriate intervention in the coconut oil market by regulating the import to maintain remunerative price to the domestic producers. The medium and long-term strategy should be management of production to bring down cost of production, where the government policies can play critical role.

RECOMMENDATIONS

Short Term Measures

Regulating Tariff Rates: Regulation of import under a trade regime without QR can be achieved only through periodic adjustment in tariff rates. Under the AoA commitment, tariff on edible oils could be increased upto 300 per cent. However, when the bound peak tariff rate of soyabean oil is at 45 per cent, there is little prudence in increasing the tariff rate on palm oil above 45 per cent. The current tariff rate on 'Edible grade crude palm oil and its fractions' is only 15 per cent. This has to be raised to a rate at or below 45 per cent, so that the tariff rise shall benefit the domestically produced vegetable oils rather than the soyabean oil being imported. This readjustment in tariff is the only immediate way out to solve the coconut farmers from their distress.

Long Term Measures

The long-term measures can have a two fold approach; first, increase the demand for coconut oil and second encourage by-product diversification to expand the demand for coconuts. Increase in demand may be possible by promotion as edible oil and popularising healthcare advantages in using coconut oil in the toiletry industry. There are several avenues to diversify the use of coconut as listed out subsequently.

Promotion of Coconut Oil as Edible Oil: National demand for edible vegetable oil is increasing at high rates with domestic production not able to cope with. The contribution of coconut is less than 4% of the oil seed production. Coconut oil is used as edible oil only in Kerala. It is not popular outside Kerala on palatability and health considerations. Palatability issue can be addressed through refinement, provided this process is cost effective. The dogma that coconut oil promotes cholesterol concentration is being challenged by modern research. On the contrary favourable properties, including bactericidal properties are being detected by research. Hence, there is scope to promote its use as edible oil through continuous campaign by the Coconut Development Board and the Kerala Government as part of development process. This has to be matched with appropriate measures to reduce the cost vis-à-vis that of other edible oils.

Diversification to Products with Massive use Potential: Diversification strategy rests on the contention that commercial market of coconut built largely around oil is the major cause for decline in price and remunerative income to producers. Hence, diversification means, uses other than for oil extraction. A number of coconut-based products, traditional and non-traditional include coir, toddy, desiccated coconut, coconut milk, coconut cream, coconut honey, Nata-de-coco, sweet toddy (neera), jaggery from neera, soft drink, coconut water concentrate, coconut jelly, vinegar from coconut water, activated charcoal from coconut shell and handicrafts. Although technologies for these uses are developed, their cost-effectiveness at commercial scale is not evaluated.

It is rational to examine these large varieties of uses and to identify commercially viable ones and to promote them. Here again, the rock bottom line price of raw material becomes critical for the commercial viability, as much as the potential size of market. All possible support, institutional, infrastructure, organisational, and financial may be extended to initiatives in ventures and enterprises on diversification, particularly by farmer groups. Creation of a single window system for promoting such ventures could act as a catalyst.

Promotion of Sweet Toddy as a Health Drink and Jaggery Making: Sweet toddy may command massive demand potential and it is a health drink. Production of jaggery appears promising on consideration that a coconut palm has capacity to produce about 50-75 kg of jaggery a year, which is equivalent to 10-15 tonnes/ha/year (200 trees). The limitation is the availability of manual labour for tapping, which is a skilled operation, and the existing legal restrictions. Like in Karnataka, Kerala should lift all restrictions on tapping coconut by farmers for promoting diversification to sweet toddy and jaggery products.

Promotion of Coconut Oil as Edible Oil: The safety and taste of tender coconut water as a nutritional soft drink are widely recognised. This demand is on the increase. The hitch is in packaging, transporting to urban markets and supplying as fresh from the tree. The Government may actively pursue the market potential from this use with the help of big players in the soft drink market, who have the resources and marketing expertise, especially in creating a marketing strategy without undue competition with other soft drinks. Innovations may be required to reduce the transportation cost and to maintain palm-fresh quality.

Coconut Oil as Lubricants in Two-stroke Engines: Recently claims have been made that auto-rickshaws are being run with an admixture of petrol and coconut oil, the latter as a substitute for lubricant oil, in two stroke engines. This lead is worth pursuing on commercial scale, if the claim is substantial on technical grounds. This, if proved successful, may create additional demand for oil from a lucrative sector, in and outside Kerala. It is recommended that the Agricultural Engineering faculty of the Kerala Agricultural University or other competent research group be requested to undertake validation of this claim in all aspects, including efficiency, wear and tear and cost-effectiveness. Adequate and specific support from the Government of Kerala or the Coconut Development Board is imperative for this research.

Massive Programme for Replanting and Rehabilitation (Integrated Coconut Development projects): This aspect has been discussed elsewhere under Kerala-specific recommendation in this report. Productivity of coconut gardens in Kerala is less than one half of Tamil Nadu and even below the national average, despite Kerala being endowed with high rainfall and other favourable conditions for coconut cultivation. The poor management, the debilitating root(wilt) disease, the more recent Eriophyd mite infestation and the extension of cultivation to agronomically less suitable areas, such as upper slopes and hill tops are the major reasons for the low productivity. One quarter to one third of the tree stand is over aged. A massive programme to systematically replace old and low yielding palms with pedigreed planting material during a period of 15-20 years is recommended. Such a programme should also aim to optimally utilise the land for maximisation of income per unit land with scientific inter-cropping and mixed farming. This can be linked with the integration of production, processing and marketing, as components of maximisation of income to the farmers.

Continuation of Minimum Support Price and Copra Procurement by NAFED: As long as unrestricted oil import is continued and market price of coconut oil is less than the production cost, the minimum support price and procurement through NAFED has to be continued. The procurement can be made more participative by a system comparable to the rice procurement, milling and marketing in Andhra Pradesh.

Price Stabilisation Fund: Recently the Government of India have announced a price stabilisation mechanism for the plantation crops. The possibility of extending the scheme to coconut cultivation has to be explored. There is high commonality among all plantation crops in their management by agronomic practices (all are perennial tree crops), and vulnerability to internal and external markets and consequent high fluctuation in price regimes. It is a misnomer to consider that all plantation crops are under large estates. Many small and marginal farmers grow these crops in regions where these crops are common in the State. The division of plantation crops including coconut for administrative purpose by the Government of India across its different Ministries also create discrepancies in policies governing this crop sector. There is need to correct all these maladies of the past in a regime of liberalisation and globalisation, with a view that the domestic agriculture, whatever be the sub sector, does not suffer and the livelihood of the farmer is not threatened. In this context policies like price stabilisation has to be applied with a dynamic and appropriately differential concept without discrimination.

BLACK PEPPER

Pepper in Kerala

Black pepper (hence forth just pepper only) is Kerala's advantage crop. Traditionally it is an export crop. Kerala accounts for 98 percent of the area and production of pepper in the country. Karnataka is the other state, which produces pepper. In 2000-01 pepper was cultivated on nearly 200,000 hectares of land, from which nearly 47500 tonnes of pepper was produced. Pepper is predominantly a small farmer crop and grown all over the state, especially in the foothills of the Western Ghat and the laterite midland belt. Idukki district with one third of the area, Wayanad with a quarter and Kannur with one tenth, are leading pepper-producing districts in the state. The productivity of pepper is highest in the Idukki and Wayanad districts with about 400 kg per hectare, which is two thirds higher than the state average yield 240 kg. The relatively higher yield in these two districts is attributed to larger holdings, and also to the cropping system evolved with pepper as the principal crop.

India is the largest producer of pepper in the world accounting for a little over one third (34%) and Indonesia is the close second with 28% (during 1989-98). Other major producers are Brazil, Malaysia and Viet Nam. India' productivity per hectare is the lowest among the competing nations (322 kg) while that of Malaysia is 7 times higher (2124 kg) and Vietnam three times (1085 kg). India with 32000 tonnes of average annual export (ranging from 19000-47000 tonnes during the last decade) continues to be a significant exporter of pepper.

During the 10 years between 1991 and 2000, exports exceeded 47000 tonnes in 1993 and 1999 and touched the low of 19000 tonnes in 1991 and 1992. Of course fluctuation in export of this kind, is true of other major pepper exporting nations in Asia, Indonesia and Malaysia. But in case of Brazil exports declined steadily from 50000 tonnes in 1991 to 20000 tonnes in 1999 while that of Vietnam steadily increased from 15000 tonnes in 1993 to 36000 tonnes in 2000.

Price Fall

Pepper experienced the largest fall in prices, both in proportion and magnitude, during the second half of the nineties along with other agricultural commodities grown in Kerala. During 1991 and 1993 pepper prices hovered around Rs. 50 per kg. Since then it moved upwards to touch Rs. 106 in 1995, jumped to Rs. 191 in 1997 and peaked the all time high of Rs. 251 in 1999. Since then price fell to Rs. 86 in 2001, further to Rs. 70 in the early months of 2000, and remaining at around Rs. 80 with fluctuations. The implications of the fall in pepper prices is far more pervasive though next only to coconut, as it is one of the most widespread crop grown in the farms of Kerala and is well integrated with several cropping systems.

The domestic price movement of pepper is in sympathy with the international prices, as predominantly pepper is an export-dependent crop. Two thirds to three quarters of the pepper produced in India is exported. The proportion is much higher, around 95% in Malaysia, Vietnam and Brazil and 75% in Indonesia. World prices of pepper doubled during 1996 to 1997 from US$ 1.14 to US$ 2.02 per lb. It steadily increased to US$ 2.53 in 1999 and since then started declining to US$ 2.32 and downward slide continued since then. The international price is supply dependent. Decline in production of pepper in Brazil and Indonesia is attributed mainly for the spurt in price experienced during 1997-1999.

Implications of AoA

Pepper like other spices has been brought under the purview of AoA of the WTO. From April 2001 quantitative restrictions on the import of pepper has been removed. The bound rate for pepper is 108%. The applied rate is placed at 70% (as on 01.03.2002). Import to the extent of 3 percent of the domestic consumption would have to be permitted under the provisions of the AoA and hence import of pepper cannot be averted. Even otherwise also, pepper could be imported as a raw material for re-exports after value addition as in the oleoresin manufacturing, which in fact is taking place. Vietnam is developing into a competing player in the world market with its dramatic productivity increases since early nineties. With its significant advantage in productivity Vietnam could be a strong competitor in the domestic market itself apart from threatening India's position in the external market.

Challenges, Opportunities and Strategies

Strengths and Weaknesses: Favourable climatic conditions especially the intense prolonged southeast monsoon (known as thiruvaathira njaattuvela) is the traditionally acknowledged as the strength of Kerala for sustaining pepper cultivation for centuries in Kerala. Pepper is traditionally cultivated as part of an integral part of the farming systems and cropping patterns prevailing in various parts of the state, primarily making use of various kinds trees as props and standards. Pepper cultivation is therefore is widespread and extensive. However, increasingly pepper is becoming specialised and a principal crop in the cropping systems of the districts of Wayanad and Idukki, especially in the settler areas. The integrated status is strength as well as a weakness of pepper cultivation in Kerala. It is strength because it is cost-effective and weakness as the management of pepper is least attended if not neglected.

Cost-effective Increase in Productivity

Despite very favourable natural resource endowments the productivity of pepper in Kerala is one of the lowest among the competing pepper producing countries. Increasing productivity is the major challenge. The extensive experience of testing the technology package of technology for increasing productivity under on farm conditions, has amply demonstrated that at least doubling productivity from the present level of around 240 kg per hectare is possible and very cost-effective.

The technology package is relatively inexpensive consisting of high yielding and disease tolerant varieties appropriate to the agroclimatic endowments from a large collection of materials evolved, simple agronomic management practices and biological control of diseases.

Rejuvenation and Replanting

It is reported that from two fifths to one half of the pepper vines in the pepper gardens of the state is in declining phase and needs urgent replanting, and rejuvenation.

Another major concern is the incidence and spread of the devastating quick-wilt (Phytophthora foot rot) disease in areas where pepper has emerged as the principal crop in the cropping system, especially in the districts of Wayanad and Idukki.

Expansion of Domestic Market

Pepper is traditionally an export-oriented crop. Fortunes of those who are dependant on this commodity have always been therefore, tied to the vicissitudes of the international market for pepper. Over the years a strong domestic market is emerging. Since the early nineties domestic market has expressed an annual grown of 9-10 percent in demand for pepper. As it happened in the case of cardamom, expansion of domestic market will act as a cushion to absorb the shocks from international price fluctuations.

Quality Improvement

The increasing quality consciousness and consequent rigorous insistence on phytosanitary stipulations especially pesticide residue, being a product ultimately destined to consumed directly as food, is a major threat to expanding the export markets for Indian pepper. Major consumers of the Indian pepper are the developed countries such as the USA (21%), Singapore (16%) Germany (8%) The Netherlands (5%)

France (5%) Japan (3%), all countries practicing stringent food standards.

Strategy

Instability in pepper prices and the uncertainties arising from the increased threat of competition both in the external and internal markets, in the latter from imports as a consequence of India's entry into AoA, are the major constraints in converting the advantage Kerala has in pepper production for improving the livelihood security of the farmers for whom pepper is an integral part of the farming system. It is the instability in price that primarily dissuading pepper farmers from undertaking long term investment in rejuvenation and replacing old low productive plants with superior and productive clones, which is an imperative measure in building competitiveness for Kerala's pepper.

In the short run it may not be possible to protect pepper farmers from the fluctuations in price as this commodity is heavily dependent on external markets. As in case of any commodity for export, the market is centralisesd (in transactions and to some extent in the physical possession of the commodity) and controlled by a limited number of players.

Further, being historically an export crop, the marketing system is well established. Hence market intervention by the state has its own limitations, as its institutions are not adequately equipped to intervene in the market strategically, more so in the terminal market.

However it is possible to face the challenges of competition both in the domestic market from imports and in the external market, by improving cost competitiveness by increasing productivity through cost-effective technologies and practices. A two-pronged strategy is proposed. First taking advantage of pepper as part of the existing farming system, improve the productivity of the existing plants through rejuvenation. Second, in areas where pepper is the principal crop and the cropping system is centred around pepper, rehabilitate pepper gardens, which have been devastated by the quick-wilt of disease through replanting. In the long run, stability in pepper prices could be brought about significantly by increasing pepper consumption in the domestic market as it happened in the case of cardamom.

The expansion of the Indian economy and consequent increase in income provide the opportunity for promoting pepper consumption within the country. World over increasingly processed extracts such as oleoresins are replacing unprocessed spices. Kerala is a pioneer in the country in oleoresin extraction from pepper. Such value addition can help increase the consumption, and income from pepper several fold. Quality improvement of Indian pepper and adherence to phytosanitary stipulations would not only help promote Indian pepper but even necessary to stay on in the international market.

Cost-effective production or value addition through processing need not always result in benefits to the farmers in the existing marketing system with its monopsonic tendencies (limited number of players) because the interests of both are not necessarily co-terminus. Farmers' organisations could be encouraged and supported to enter decisively in the internal market by acquiring a strategic share of the internal market.

Recommendations

1. The initiatives and programmes proposed under the Pepper Technology Mission, which has taken a comprehensive look at the sustainable development of pepper in the state, be accelerated and put in operation immediately.
2. A systematic and targeted campaign with focus on revitalising and rejuvenating the existing low productive and over-aged pepper wines in the homesteads using a package of practices consisting of replanting with appropriate high yielding disease tolerant wines, fully making use of the trees and other live standards for increasing the pepper stand in the farms, agronomic management practices including regulation of shade of existing trees used as support, organic manure application and biocontrol of diseases. This initiative

needs more than financial investment, a dynamic extension system and access to sufficient quality planting materials. The resources currently made available under local self-government institutions for agricultural development can be effectively mobilised in support of this programme.

3. Similarly a targeted and systematic log-term investment programme be launched for rehabilitating and replanting the disease affected pepper gardens in areas where pepper based cropping systems are practiced especially in the Wayanad and Idukki districts, mobilising resources from NABARD and such other long time financing institutions.

4. Support, especially institutional credit and incentives, be given to groups (especially women groups) and individuals in order to establish a net work of nurseries including tissue culture propagated ones, from where reliable quality planting materials could be accessed by the farmers to meet, rejuvenation and replanting needs of pepper gardens. The institutions under the Kerala Agricultural University and Indian Institute of Spices should be able to provide the necessary back up especially in supplying high quality parent materials for propagation.

5. The Kerala Agricultural University may develop a package of practices suited to different agroecological zones for rehabilitating pepper wines and pepper gardens taking a holistic view of the resource system that sustains pepper in such systems.

6. Programmes be initiated to promote consumption of pepper in the domestic market in order to help minimise instabilities in the price regime. Promotional efforts especially with focus on medicinal qualities can help expand the domestic market.

7. Farmers organisations be encouraged and supported for initiating value added ventures to enable them to secure a higher share of income from such ventures.

8. A campaign for quality improvement with appropriate institutional support to reward the quality production, at farm level be launched. The farmers and their groups engaged in quality pepper production should be encouraged and rewarded.
9. Opportunities for organic pepper production be explored. Projects are to be formulated on area basis. The experience of NGOs such as the Peemade Development Society could be profitably used.
10. The Malabar Pepper is attributed to be unique to Kerala. Immediate steps be taken to get the special qualities and characteristics identified and defined under geographic indicators to protect them under the new IPR regime.

CASHEWNUT

Cashewnut in Kerala's economy

Both in the cultivation of cashew and processing of cashewnut, Kerala is the pioneer in the country. Over decades the State has developed advantage in the processing industry in the form of skills in processing and knowledge on the external market for cashewnut exports, all are indeed invaluable assets. The processing industry provides livelihood security for over one-lakh workers (though only 32000 are registered workers for welfare) mainly in the southern districts especially in the Kollam district.

Country's net (less of import of raw cashew nuts) foreign exchange earning from processed cashewnut (including the shell liquid a by product of processing) ranged between Rs. 600 crores in 1996-97 to nearly Rs. 1400 crores in 1999-2000. Value addition is almost 100 percent. One major constraint in fully utilising the potential assets is the shortage of raw cashewnut for processing. Substantial quantities of raw nut are imported annually to meet the needs of the processing industry. During 1999-00 and 2000-01, annual import of raw cashewnut into the country averaged 2.5 lakh tonnes valued at Rs. 1000 crores The corresponding figures for Kerala are about 1.5 lakh tonnes valued at over Rs. 500 crores. Area put under cashew in the state is declining steadily from 1.2 lakh ha in 1990-91 to 0.9 ha in 2000-01. Concurrently production also declined from 1.03 to 0.62 lakh tonnes and productivity as well from 890 kg to 720 kg. However area under cashew has been increasing in the country from 5.32 to 6.86 lakh ha, production from 2.95 to 5.20 lakh tonnes and productivity 554 kg to 758 per hectare.

Thus Kerala had to give away its lead enjoyed in the production of cashewnut. Since 1998-99 productivity of cashew in Kerala registered is lower than the national level. Most of the cashew holdings in Kerala are of small size. Cashew cultivation in Kerala is predominant in the northern districts. Kannur has the largest area of nearly 30%, followed by Kasaragod 24% and Malappuram 11%.

Contribution of production is also from that part in the same order: Kannur 44%, Kasaragod 19% and Malappuram 8%. Kannur district has the highest productivity: 883 kg against the state average of 601 kg (1997-98).

Price Movement

Cashew is only the crop other than cardamom, which has not been subjected to the general fall in the price of farm commodities in Kerala. In fact the price of cashewnut has been rising steadily from Rs. 11.55 per kg in 1990 and more than trebled to Rs.36.39 in 2000. The imported price of raw cashewnut ruled higher ranging from 26.83 in 96-97 to 40.93 in 1998-99. As the price of processed cashewnut (kernel) price is declining in the international market, it is likely the raw material prices would follow suit and domestic prices of raw cashewnut might decline. The kernel price declined from Rs. 265 a kilogram in 1999-00 to Rs. 230 in 2000-01, to Rs. 207 in April-July 2001 and further to Rs. 189 in April-July 2002.

WTO Implications

Even though a raw material used for processing, cashewnut has been brought under the purview of AoA of the WTO. From

April 2001 quantitative restrictions on the import of cashewnut has been removed. The bound rate for cashew 108%. The applied rate is put at 70% (as on 01.03.2002). Import is inevitable since internal production (about 48000 tonnes) is less than one third of the Kerala's import (one fifth for the country) to meet the needs of the processing industry, which is a significant foreign exchange earner and source of employment. But imports of raw cashewnut need not necessarily adversely affect the domestic price as locally produced raw nut has a premium on account of its size and boldness.

During the post Doha period, import of raw nuts into Kerala increased three times the local production. Still the domestic price has been on the increase till 2001 (Rs. 36 per kg), although since then the decline has set in. That slump in price is more attributable to the decline in kernel prices in the international market rather than to imports of raw nuts.

Challenges, Opportunities and Strategy

Time for a Big Push in Chew Development: The basic challenge facing cashew cultivation in the state is that of meeting the raw material needs of the processing industry. Notwithstanding the steady increase in the price of raw cashewnut (price increased three times since 1990) there is an all-round decline in cashew cultivation: in area, production and of late in productivity. Research institutions under the Kerala Agricultural University and the Indian Council of Agricultural Research have realised significant developments in technology, in terms of high yielding varieties (suited to a variety of agroclimatic conditions), agronomic management (especially the high density planting), and plant propagation. With profitable technology on the shelf and a price regime incentive enough to profitable returns, the economic environment is ripe enough for a big push in cashew production but for lack of long-term investment and focussed programme.

Strategic Instrument for Regional Development

Cashew development in the context of Kerala has to be seen not just fulfilling the needs of the processing industry but as a strategic major instrument to trigger of agricultural development in the northern districts of Kasaragod, Kannur and Malappuram, which are relatively poorly endowed with natural resources. Even though these districts receive high rainfall (about 4000 mm) it is concentrated in 3-4 months leaving 6-7 months of prolonged dry period. The topography in these districts is undulating with alternating massive hills and narrow valleys. Landscape is that of extensive flat laterite formation with a thin over burden of gravely soil, which is inherently of low moisture holding capacity. In such harsh environment cashew is the most suitable crop to productively utilise the poor land resource endowment. That is why cashew cultivation is seen concentrated in these districts. Better-endowed lands within these districts are put under crops such as coconut, which require more congenial agronomic environment.

A cashew-based agricultural development programme would make a substantial dent into the agricultural economy of these districts.

Quality Improvement and Environmental Concerns: Quality improvement, especially adherence to SPS (sanitary phytosanitary) measures assumes great significance for the very survival of the processing industry as cashew kernel, the output of the processing industry, is directly consumed as food. Presence of pesticidal residue is of grave and sensitive concern. It is not only that the final product should be free from any harmful chemical residue or other materials, but also that the process through which the product is produced should be environment-friendly. Environmental concerns in the production process are under close scrutiny in the developed countries, which are the principal markets for Indian cashew kernels. Some times such controversies could also be used against the product as non-tariff barriers. It is in this context that the disturbing reports and the controversies that had arisen on the application of insecticides on cashew for pest control in the Kasaragod district has to be viewed and avoided, apart from the human dimension concerns. In fact, it is very vital for the sustenance of the cashew industry itself that such controversies are resolved convincingly and proactive steps are taken to forestall their recurrences. Determined efforts are called for to convince that cashewnut in the state is produced through environment-friendly processes. Good agricultural practices could be promoted through certification..

Environment Hygiene and Health Hazards of Women Workers: Another concern that could affect cashew kernel export is the preservation of hygienic conditions, and attending to the health hazards to workers, a vast majority of whom are women. Hazards are associated with some aspects of cashewnut processing, such as breaking fried nuts and peeling, which are skill, demanding but vulnerable too. Again, poor hygiene conditions and the health hazards could be used against cashew exports in the future.

The commendable tradition of labour welfare measures provided to the labour in the cashew industry should be seen as a positive measure for the long term sustainability of the cashew industry in the international cashew kernel market, and not as the burden inflicted on the processing industry.

Among others, labour-friendly production practices could be used as a means for promoting Indian cashew, as products produced under labour-unfriendly processes are being discouraged by consumers in the sophisticated markets of the developed countries to which cashew kernel is targeted.

Strategy

A two-pronged strategy is proposed for increasing the production cashew in the state. First rejuvenate the existing cashew trees in the state and wherever necessary replace them with new high yielding varieties. Second in the cashew concentrated areas in the initiate a cashew centred area development programme encompassing the total development of the land resource endowment. In these areas the existing cashew trees are replanted with high yielding cashew varieties and cashew cultivation is extended wherever suitable land is available.

RECOMMENDATIONS

1. Time bound targeted programme for the rejuvenation of old cashew trees, with high yield varieties appropriate to the agroclimatic zone, be launched all over the state. For the cashew growing farms in the districts of Southern and Central Kerala early maturity should be a criterion as the dry period is short, and early incidence of pre monsoon showers result in poor quality nuts. Resources needed for the programme could be mobilised from the development plans of the local bodies and women's groups such as the Kudumbashree could be mobilised.

2. Systematic, time bound targeted cashew based area development programme for the rehabilitation and replanting of existing cashew garden and extension area to suitable lands in the Kannur, Kasaragod and Malappuram districts be formulated and implemented. This project could be taken as a developmental initiative for these districts with the inclusion of other crops also, rather than a project for cashew production promotion alone. High density planting, high yielding varieties, soil and moisture conservation, intercropping for the premature period, environment friendly pest control should become the integral technology package. Replanting could be done in such way as the existing trees be removed only after new plantings start bearing so that loss of income from removal of yielding trees can be minimised. Farmers be provided with technology support, access to planting materials and long term credit. Resources for investment could be pooled from NABARD, Commercial and Cooperative banks, development funds of the State and central governments (Cashew Development Council of the Ministry of Agriculture, GOI). If merged with area development then the resources available for Wasteland Development and Watershed Management could also be pooled.

3. The possibility of creating a cess fund for cashew development on the lines of in rubber cess, imposed on the raw material used (domestic and imported) may be

explored. The cashew development is also meant as a support for the industry, which gains from value additions. The meagre support from government budgets is far inadequate to meet the developmental needs of cashew.

4. A network of nurseries for producing and making available high yielding planting material in support of the replanting effort be launched concurrently. Women's group such as the Kudumbashree could be involved by providing then with adequate training as was demonstrated successfully by the Kerala Agricultural University at its cashew research facility at Vellanikkara. The University should be able to provide the necessary back up including training and quality planting material for multiplication.

5. Not only out of the anxiety to sustain the cashewnut processing industry and its international market, but recognising the need for removing convincingly the environmental concerns associated with cashewnut production (for that matter production of any agricultural commodity), it is suggested that the Kerala Government may take steps to institute a permanent set-up such as the initiative of the Royal Society of London in commissioning a study on the side-effects of GM (genetically modified foods) which helped dispel public apprehensions. By doing so issues are resolved at the very beginning itself before swelling into a national controversy. For this initiative, the support of ICAR or other such institutions could be mobilised.

6. A programme be initiated to cover cashew cultivation through environment friendly pest and disease control measures, in order to demonstrate and assure the consumers that the products produced are safe. Support specifically for this could be sought from the industry that ultimately benefits the most.

7. Studies be undertaken on the nature and magnitude of the health hazards of women workers engaged in the

cashew industry, in order to design appropriate remedial measures so that health related concerns should not lead to a barrier (non-trade) in promoting Indian cashew kernel in the sensitive international market.

PLANTATION CROPS

Holistic Comprehensive Policy Framework for the Sustainable Development of Plantation Crops

Plantation crops defined under Sec.2 (44) of the Kerala Land Reforms Act, 1963 (tea, coffee, rubber, cardamom, cocoa, or cinnamon) historically evolved under unique socio-political, economic and ecological conditions. Of these, the development and management of the first four are governed by Central Acts and agencies appointed (Commodity Boards) appointed under them. Over the past one-century of evolution and more so after independence, various interventions to meet the objectives of the development of these crops prevailing during those times have been attempted. Several legislative measures including the Kerala Land Reforms Act, Land Utilisation Act, and the latest (June 2000) in the series the Vesting and Management of Ecologically Fragile Lands although not directly enacted for the development of this sub-sector of Agriculture have serious implications to the development of these crops. Similarly the various taxation measures both by the Centre with respect to income tax and excise duty and the State Government with agricultural income tax, sales/purchase tax, land tax etc. including the various taxes imposed by the local bodies are levied on this sector. Labour laws both under industrial and other domains, are applied for the welfare of the workers involved.

The very roles expected to be played in the economy by the crops in this sub-sector have changed. Also considerable economic, social and demographic changes have occurred in the area in which these crops are grown. Finally with the WTO regime coming into being the economic environment has drastically changed. All these have led to the present economic and social crisis gripping this vital sector affecting the economy of the state. The Commission is of the view that a holistic perception on the development of this sector should be evolved and operationalised for its sustainable development and it is time that the State took the initiative in evolving a comprehensive policy direction embracing all aspects including production and productivity, investment support, land use and land reform, ecology and environment, trade and marketing, labour and management, legal institutions, taxation, centre, state and local body responsibilities and commitments. The Commission recognises the imperative need for an initiative of this kind, but leaves it to the government as to the manner in which such a holistic comprehensive policy could be evolved and implemented.

Review of the Mandates of the Commodity Boards

The various Commodity Boards came into being over five decades ago under the sanction of various Central legislations enacted by the Parliament. Various mandates were vested with the Boards on the basis of the then prevailing national and international situations, and demands of the national economy on these commodities such as meeting the internal demand and or earning foreign exchange etc. The socioeconomic conditions in the country have changed since then. Structural changes in production have also occurred. The share of the organised estate sector declined in production while that of the small growers has increased substantially.

Production has moved out of the traditional areas and expanded to newer areas. Similarly the international economic and political environment altered drastically with the collapse of the socialist world, globalisation of the national economies and the installation of the WTO regime in the international trade. The mandates of the different Boards varied from crop/ commodity to crop/ commodity. In the case of Rubber Board development and research were the focus and very little on marketing. So too the then Cardamom Board and now Spices Board. In case of Coffee Board marketing and price control were the centrepiece of the activity. Tea Board laid emphasis on marketing and promotion of Indian tea abroad but not significantly on research and development. It is understandable when tea was the largest single foreign exchange earner, emphasis was given on export promotion. Now the situation has changed. Value addition and processing have assumed great significance in all commodities. With international competition cost-effective production rather than just increasing production under a safe and secure domestic market has become imperative even for survival. International trade, production shortage, expansion to other areas are converging the interests of the governments with the livelihood security of the farmers / growers engaged in production.

The state government institutions engaged in R & D have gained considerable strength. Further state governments are increasingly compelled to take responsibilities for the fall out actions and initiatives under the WTO regime while accrual of resource originating from these commodities still continue with the Central Government. Against this emerging scenario, the Commission is of the opinion that the time has come to have a second look on mandates of the Commodity Boards so that they can be geared to face the challenges of the future and the nation can be proactive rather than reactive.

RUBBER

Rubber in the Economy

Kerala accounts for 84% (4.75 lakh ha in 2001-02) of the area under rubber 92% (5.80 lakh tonnes) of the natural rubber production in the country. The crop occupies almost one fifth of the total cultivated area in the state. Apart from ensuring livelihood security to 9.13 lakh holdings, 2.82 lakh workers involved in production in the state, and 3.7 lakh workers employed in the industrial sector based on rubber in the country. This crop brings in Rs. 250 crores revenue to the State Exchequer by way of purchase tax and agricultural income tax (one of the very few crops that attracts agricultural income tax) and over Rs.80 crores (in 2001-02 Rs. 81.10 crores) to the national exchequer by way of excise duty on rubber (cess). The rubber plantation crop sector therefore has tremendous socio-economic implications to the economy of the Kerala state. Rubber is overwhelmingly a small growers' crop as 98% of the holdings are of 2 hectares and less, cultivating 88% of the area with average size of 0.5 hectare, which contributes 88% of the production, while the estates sector (above 20 hectares and numbering 316) accounted for 2% of the area and 12% of the production in 2000-01.

Commendable Performance of the NR Sector

In spite of the predominance of small farmers, the productivity of NR attained in Kerala with 1612 kg per hectare of tapped area in 2000-01 (1222 kg by including immature area also) is the highest among the major NR producers of the world against 1456 kg of Thailand, 679 kg of Indonesia and 881 kg of Malaysia. During the past two decades rubber production in the state, more than quadrupled from 1.40 lakh tonnes in 1980-81 to 5.80 lakh tonnes in 2000-01, planted area nearly doubled from 2.54 to 4.74 lakh hectares and tapped area from 1.80 to 3.60 lakh hectares. This commendable performance has been made possible thanks to the diligent and enterprising group of growers and planters who were found ever eager in adoption of technology and embracing innovations, a vibrant rubber industry consuming the entire NR produced, imaginative policies of the government implemented through the Rubber Board that provided sound research and development support, efficient network of extension and most important of all, a remunerative and fairly stable price regime through balancing supply and demand by timely market interventions including procurement and regulating imports.

Price Fall

Following the liberalisation policies adopted by the Government of India, which triggered a spurt in industrial growth, the domestic price of NR rose steeply to reach the all time high of Rs. 5,000 plus and Rs.6, 000 plus per quintal (Kottayam price of RSS4 sheet, the grade mainly used by the automotive tyre manufacturers) during 1995 and 1996. Since November 1996 price started declining. In 1997-98 the price averaged to Rs. 3580 and fell further to Rs. 2994 during 98-

99. Although increased marginally during 99-00 but again further declined to Rs. 3036 during 00-01. The recovery is apparently slow, as a host of factors have affected the fluctuations in NR price, which are not domestic alone, but international too.

Reasons for the Fall in Price of NR

Accumulated Surplus Due to Imports: The price fall is attributed to excess supply during the years 97-98 to 2000-01. The stock of NR as at the end of March 2001 was 183,900 tonnes, almost one third of the total production (630,405 tonnes in 2000-01). After providing for 105,000 tonnes required as stock reserve for two months' consumption needs in the country, the accumulated surplus at the end of March 2001 was around 79,000 tonnes. Even though production of NR matched with consumption needs of the industry, massive imports were permitted during the second half of the nineties under a variety of import schemes. (As much as nearly 1.5 lakh tonnes during the period from 1995-56 to 2000-01 when the country had surpluses though marginal).

Bibliography

Ahmad, E.: *Financing Decentralized Expenditures: An International Comparison of Grants*, Edward Elgar, UK, 1997.

Auerbach, Alan J.: *Fiscal Policy, Lessons from Economic Research*, The MIT Press, Cambridge Massachusetts, London, 1997.

Banerjee, G. and Banerjee, S.: *Borrowing from Financial Institutions*, UDH Publishing House, Delhi.

Basch, Antonian: *Financing Economic Development*, New York . 1964.

Borio, C.: *"The Implementation of Monetary Policy in Industrial Countries: A Survey"*, BIS Economic Papers, BIS, Basel, 1997.

Chand, Ramesh (2003) *"Impact of Trade Liberalization and Related Reforms on India's Agricultural Sector, Rural Food Security, Income and Poverty."* Mimeo. Paper prepared for the GDN meeting Delhi, 2004.

Chant, John F.: *The Market for Financial Services: Deposit-Taking Institutions*, The Fraser Institute, Vancouver, 1988.

Chapman, John M. and Frederick W. Jones: *Finance Companies: How and Where they Obtain their Funds*, Graduate School of Business, Cotumbis University, New York 1959.

Ciocca, Pierluigi: *Money and the Economy, The Central Bankers Views*, MacMillan Press, London 1987.

Coler, Mark and Ellis Ratner: *Financial Services Insiders' View of the Future*, New York Institute of Finance, New York 1988.

Cooper, S. Kerry and Donald, R. Fraser: *Banking Deregulation and the New Competition in Financial Services*, Ballinger Publishing Company, Cambridge 1984.

Dagli, V. : *Financial Institutions of India*, Vora and Company, Bombay 1972.

Edminster, R.O.: *Financial Institutions, Markets and Management*, McGraw Hill, New York 1986.

Fenstermaker, J.V.: *Readings in Financial Markets and Institutions*, Appleton, New York 1969.

Friars, Eileen M. and Gogel, Robert N.: *The Financial Services Handbook, Executive-Insights and Solutions*, John Wiley and Sons, New York, 1987.

Goodhart, Charles: *The Evolution of Central Banks*, The MIT Press, Cambridge, 1988.

Hayami, Yujiro: *"From the Washington Consensus to the Post-Washington Consensus: Retrospect and Prospect,"* 2003.

Huat, Tan Chwee: *Financial Institutions in Singapore*, Singapore University Press, 1981.

Jha, N.K.: *Bank Finance and Green Revolution in India*, Amar Prakashan, Delhi, 1985.

Kindleberger, Charles P.: *A Financial History of Western Europe*, George Allen & Unwin Ltd., London 1984.

Posterba, James N.: *"Public Policies and Household Savings"*, A National Bureau of Economic Research Project Report, The University of Chicago Press, 1994.

Rao, M.G. and R.J. Chelliah: *Survey of Research in Indian Fiscal Federalism*, National Institute of Public Finance and Policy, New Delhi, 1991.

Rao, M.G.: *Fiscal Imbalances in Indian Federalism*, National Institute of Public Finance and Policy, New Delhi, 1987.

Ritter, L.S., Silber, W.L.: *Principles of Money, Banking and Financial Markets*,Basic Books, New York, 1977.

Shome, Parthasarathi: *Fiscal Issues in South-East Asia*, Oxford University Press, New York, 1986.

Index

□□□